American Ghosts

Also by David Plante

American Ghosts

David Plante

BEACON 150

BEACON PRESS *Boston*

BEACON PRESS
25 Beacon Street
Boston, Massachusetts 02108-2892
www.beacon.org

Beacon Press books are published under the auspices of the
Unitarian Universalist Association of Congregations.

07 06 05   8 7 6 5 4 3 2 1

This book is printed on acid-free paper that meets the uncoated paper
ANSI / NISO specifications for permanence as revised in 1992.

Text design by Isaac Tobin
Composition by Wilsted & Taylor Publishing Services

Library of Congress Cataloging-in-Publication Data
Plante, David.
  American ghosts / David Plante.—1st ed.
    p. cm.
  ISBN 0-8070-7264-8 (hardcover : alk. paper)
  1. Plante, David—Childhood and youth. 2. Novelists, American—20th
century—Biography. 3. Catholic youth—United States—Biography.
4. Gay youth—United States—Biography. I. Title.

PS3566.L257A824 2004
813'.54—dc22   2004008570

To Philip Roth

If all of space is open to me, at what place do I put down my chair to look around?

I

ON OUR WAY TO AND FROM PAROCHIAL SCHOOL, MY younger brother and I walked through a wooded lot between our house and our nearest neighbor. In the spring the thin branches of the trees were leafed in bright green and in the autumn in bright red, and through these branches appeared a big granite boulder that I always paused to look at, and I imagined, from a time long, long past when there were no houses and everywhere was forest, an Indian standing on that boulder and looking back at me. All I knew of my ancestry was that the first to have come to the continent of North America from France would have often seen Indians in the woods.

A summer night, when the window of my bedroom was wide open and the shadows of trees were cast on the screen, I, in bed with my younger brother, Lenard, who slept deeply, remained wide awake, staring at that window. The fresh nighttime air seething through the screen smelled of wild roses that grew between our narrow yard and the small lot of woods, and also some other smell, perhaps skunk cabbage or skunk, which I thought of as *bête puante*. Moonlight fell on the trees out there, and I was terrified that, among the rusted automobile fenders and tires dumped in those woods, the ghost of the Indian was hiding and would come up to my window and look in. My terror became so great that I beat my fists against the headboard until my knuckles were bloody.

I woke Lenard, who lay still and silent. My mother, followed by my father, came rushing into the room, which was dim in the moonlight through the window. My mother grasped my wrists to stop me from hitting the headboard, then she pulled me out of bed and to the window, where she made me look out into the moonlit woods, repeating over and over, gently, "There's nothing there, nothing, nothing." For me everything was out there, and this everything would at any moment make itself present to me as a face in the darkness. My mother said to my father, who was standing back, "Tell him nothing is out there," but my father, from whom I expected no more or no less, said nothing. Upset for me, my mother insisted, "Tell him."

Instead, my father said, "I'll sleep with the boy."

I wanted my mother, her soft body loosely contained by her white, wrinkled nightgown, in bed with me, to reassure me that there was in fact nothing to frighten me in the outside woods, that there was nothing in all the outside world to frighten me. And I wanted, too, my father, wearing the tee shirt and boxer shorts he wore during the day, to be in bed with me, as if his presence allowed me a deeper reassurance than any my mother could have given me: that however terrifying it was, the possibility of that face appearing in the darkness released in me the greatest sense of everything that was most important to me.

I was seven years old, the age of reason. At times I loved my mother and hated my father; but these times could suddenly be reversed, and I would hate my mother and love my father.

(This reversal of feelings towards my parents was like the reversals in a dream I often had into my maturity, a nightmare in which at one moment I could not get out of our house because the door was locked and some presence in the house was menacing me, and in the next moment, or even simultaneously, I could not lock the loose, wobbly outside door against a menace from without.)

"He's got to get over being frightened of the dark," my mother said to my father, still holding my wrists. "For his own sake, he's got to."

"Yes, yes," my father said.

She drew me to her to hug me closely, so I felt all her body under her nightgown. "It's for your own good," she said. "You know that."

Trembling, I said, "I know."

Now pulling away from me as I held on to her, she said, "I should tell you that you've got to get back into bed with your brother and go to sleep. But I'll let you decide if you want your father or me to sleep with you. Chose one of us, and Lenard will come sleep with the other."

In a high voice, hardly in control, I said, *"Je veux Daddy."*

She took me into the bathroom to wash my hands and wrap gauze around my knuckles, then, back in the bedroom, she told Lenard to get up, and, in his boy's underwear, he went with her to our parents' bedroom.

I got into bed, my father beside me, and he covered us both. I heard his breathing. He said nothing. He fell asleep.

This was in 1947, in Providence, Rhode Island.

2

IN THE SIXTH GRADE, WHEN I WAS TWELVE YEARS OLD, our classroom teacher was Mère Sainte Flore. Lenard, now ten, was in the fourth grade. We walked to school together but were separated in the asphalted yard between the church and the school, when Mère Supérieure opened the large black doors to the school and rang the bell. The grades formed ranks with their respective classroom teachers. Mère Sainte Flore stood at the head of our rank and with us listened to Mère Supérieure warn everyone that the girls had to wear blue ribbons and the boys had to wear ties. I wore my tie with a golden tie clip that had a plastic ruby in it. I didn't understand disobedience, and, listening to Mother Superior tell us, in French, that it was forbidden to come to school without the blue ribbon or a tie, I touched my tie clip and felt, a little, that she was warning me not to do something I would never, ever do.

Mother Superior stood on the granite steps of the school, and as she spoke she held the hand bell among the heavy folds of her long black skirt. She spoke in French and English to make sure everyone understood, as there were a few Italians who came to school in the French parish, and it was mostly the Italians who didn't wear the blue bow or tie and who didn't seem to care that they disobeyed.

The sleeves of Mother Superior's habit were wide, and when she raised her hands to ring the bell they slipped far up her arm. Under the sleeves were what looked like the tightly fitted black sleeves of an undershirt, and I saw that the tight inner sleeves ended at her white elbows. She lowered the bell, and her outer sleeves fell to cover her hands. She went into the school first.

As our class filed into the school, Mère Sainte Flore stood back and watched us; then, surprising me, she walked beside me, her arms swinging. She turned to me, her pale face enclosed within a tight, white ruff, and she said, "David," and for a second neither of us moved. Her dark eyes were lined by darker lashes. "David," she said again, and I rushed to catch up to the student ahead of me in the line.

The seventh-grade classroom was towards the end of the school corridor, its green and brown linoleum tiles highly waxed, and along it large brown doors with transoms. Just beyond the classroom, at the end of the corridor, was a small door, and this led to the convent where the Mothers lived. The door was now open, and I, passing it at a distance, glimpsed a flight of worn wooden stairs that turned as it descended. Someone from inside shut the door.

In our classroom, in our school, in our parish, in our French fortress surrounded by Yankee territory, we all sang, led by Mère Sainte Flore:

Ô, Canada, terre de nos aieux,
Ton front est ceint des fleurons glorieux—

We lived in what we called LePetit Canada, where we preserved the beliefs of Le Grand Canada. Le Grand Canada, from which we were so isolated by the surrounding territories that we had lost any contact with it, was an unreal country to me, a country where, according to Mère Sainte Flore, miracles occurred that could never occur in the United States of Yankee America. In Canada was the Church of Sainte Anne de Beaupré, built high up on the side of a mountain, with a view of rivers through forests of pine trees. People went there for miraculous cures. They climbed hundreds of steps on their knees, and they prayed at the church's

main altar. Sores were healed, cancers disappeared, mal-
formed arms were restored, and crutches were flung down
and left behind, later hung on the walls by the priests. Many
Indians from all over Canada, who had a special belief in
miracles, made pilgrimages in their canoes along the rivers,
rough with rapids, to get to the church.

I sat towards the center of the class, watching Mère Sainte
Flore, who, as much as she wanted to talk about Canada in
French, had, in this lesson, to teach us the geography of the
United States, and this she must do in English. From time to
time she pointed with a stick to a map of the United States
—frayed at the edges—that was rolled down over the
blackboard.

Her veil, of a fine, light, black cloth that hung in folds
down her back, was held by pins with black, round, shiny
heads to a starched white bonnet, which extended all around
her face in the ruff, and the bonnet was revealed when—
maybe because it had slipped—she put her hands under
her veil at the back of her head to adjust it. Then she let her
hands drop, and her veil and all her long, loose habit would,
with a shake of her head and body, fall into place, the rosary
attached to her belt and hanging against her thigh rattling
lightly among the black folds. It was odd that though her
head was so trussed up with the stiff bonnet, which was
sealed tightly under her chin with a snap, her neck was bare.
Her white neck, to the inward curve at the base of her throat,
was visible, as her habit didn't have a collar.

She set the end of the pointer on the floor and held it upright like the pole of a flag or standard, and, as if she had had
enough of identifying the States of the Union, she contin-

ued in French to tell us the truth of the geography of North America. Really, North America, the entire continent, belonged to the French.

To us, French meant French Canadian, for we were, in our parish, from France by way of French Canada, but at a time when Canada was called La Nouvelle France. Not one of us would have been able to make an ancestral connection beyond Canada to La Vieille France. Yet we called ourselves French in the way Italians in our school called themselves Italians, or in the way the parishioners of the Irish parish called themselves Irish or those of the Polish parish called themselves Polish. Unlike these others, however, who were able to make connections with their old countries that went no further back than their immigrant grandparents, we French knew—were told by Mère Sainte Flore—that, with our ancestry reaching back to so long ago it was beyond memory, we were the first Europeans to discover North America. She told us about how Cartier planted the cross and French standard on North American soil in 1534, and how Champlain founded the city of Quebec in 1608. And Champlain was the first to claim Maine, which was named in honor of Henriette de France, duchesse du Maine, and also Massachusetts, both parts of La Nouvelle France but later taken over by the English and called New England. The state of New York, too, was once French, with its French capital at New Rochelle, and Manhattan was called Nouvelle-Avesnes before it was taken by the Dutch and called New Amsterdam. The state now called Pennsylvania was French, and the southern states and all of the Midwest was French, for French forts were established all along the Mississippi

River, which was discovered by the Frenchman Jacques Marquette. We were told of his explorations, and those of Louis Jolliet and his claim to have discovered the Mississippi River, and of René-Robert Cavalier, Sieur de la Salle, who discovered the Ohio River. The French missionaries were the first to enter into the camps of Indian tribes never before seen by Europeans; and these missionaries learned the Indian languages and baptized the Indians Catholics. And there was the whole of Louisiana, which, Mère Saint Flore lamented, was sold to the United States for fifteen cents an acre.

The class, even the Italians in it, became silent with attention, for Mère Sainte Flore seemed to begin to sing, her eyes for a moment closed, when she went on to talk about the long, long past French continent. We had lost that French continent, but even if we did not know its history, it remained an invisible presence to us, in the same way that what is invisible is more of a presence to us than what is visible. We may try to see the invisible, and may, at moments, see it in a slouch hat with a plume or a lace fan, in a stone arrowhead, or in a beaver pelt, but it cannot be made visible, as much as we try.

The invisible was like that lost French colony, founded on the continent long before any other European colony was founded, which Mère Sainte Flore liked to remind us of. The French colonists constructed a palisade and dug a moat around it, and houses of wood and earth, with roofs of straw, were built inside. It was called Charlesfort, after the then king of France, Charles IX, who was twelve years old. The colony disappeared—no one knew how or why—and the only evidence that it had once existed in the New World was the word of the only survivor, a boy named Ruffi, who ran away, took refuge among the Indians, and later told a Spanish expedition about the French fort, but he couldn't say why or how it had disappeared, and he couldn't say where it had been. To this day, no one knew.[1]

At moments, I had a strange feeling that Mère Sainte Flore kept looking at me, and I wondered if I had done something wrong. I touched the plastic ruby on my tie clip.

At the end of the morning classes, the school bell was rung in the corridor, and the classes, one after another, filed out into the school yard, where, again, Mother Superior warned us all to tell our parents that it was forbidden to come to school without the blue ribbon or a tie. Then the classes marched down the hill, past the brick church, to the crossroads where there was a drugstore and a hairdresser and a grocery store, and from there the classes dispersed into the parish in different directions, and my brother and I met to walk home together. But he went ahead when I stopped at the wide window of the drugstore, which reflected, behind me, the Mothers walking back up the hill to the school. Their long black skirts swung, and their veils billowed a little with the movement of their heads as they talked to one another. One of them fell behind the others and walked slowly. I knew

---

1. When, recently, the site of this fort was found by archaeologists on the coast of South Carolina, I was at first disappointed that the invisible had been made visible, that the ahistorical had been made historical. But that the colony of Charlesfort had consisted of Huguenots seeking refuge from persecution in France became of vital interest to me for the altogether historical reason that Huguenots in France were centered mainly in La Rochelle.

this was Mère Sainte Flore. I waited until she had walked off the edge of the glass.

It was autumn, and on our walk home, Lenard and I passed fires of fallen maple leaves burning at the curbsides of the narrow, almost trafficless streets, the smoke rising up into the branches of the large maple trees lining the sidewalks, the branches still dropping red leaves.

Home was a white clapboard bungalow up the hill from the factory where my father worked. My mother ironed while Lenard and I ate our sandwiches and drank glasses of milk at the kitchen table.

My mother was a soft, slightly plump woman in a house-dress and apron. She spoke to us in English.

She asked me, "What is your class going to do for the school play this year?"

"I don't know."

"Mère Sainte Flore hasn't told your class yet? I met Mrs. Vanasse in the grocery store this morning, and she told me that her Louis said his eighth grade is already rehearsing for its play."

"What's the play?"

"A French minuet. The girls will wear gowns and the boys powdered wigs, like a ball in Paris. It sounds beautiful."

"No," I said, "Mère Sainte Flore hasn't said anything about our class play."

Lenard was not interested in plays.

Having eaten our sandwiches and drunk our glasses of milk, we remained at the table and watched my mother, leaning her weight on it, pass the iron up and down a pair of my father's gray work pants.

Lenard said quietly, "Don't iron."

Smiling at him, my mother said, "You want me to stop ironing?"

He said, "Stop ironing and sit and talk with us."

My mother, smiling more, tipped the electric flat iron on its end and unplugged it from the socket, then sat at the table with us.

"What do you want to talk about?" she asked Lenard.

But he didn't have anything he wanted to talk about.

I asked my mother, "Have you ever been into the convent where the Mothers live?"

"I haven't. Why do you want to know?"

I shrugged a shoulder.

My mother said, "I know that in the convent the lower panes of all the windows are painted."

"Why?"

"The Mothers aren't allowed to look out of windows."

"What else do you know?"

"I don't know anything else."

I asked, "Do you know when we came from France?"

"You mean, our ancestors?"

"Our ancestors," I repeated, as if that word had occurred to me for the first time in a way I had never considered it before, and it roused in me both a pull to know about my ancestors and a sadness in the pull, perhaps because I felt that there was no way to make ancestors, who were invisible, visible. And yet, in their invisibility, they were all around me, in the same way that the smoke from those fires of autumn leaves had, almost in dancing figures, circled around me as I'd walked through it.

"I don't know where my ancestors come from in France," my mother said, "but I know where they come from in Canada—L'Acadie. The English took over L'Acadie and called it Nova Scotia. Those English burned down the French churches and packed the French into boats without oars and shoved the boats out into the ocean. The boats drifted down to the United States. There is a poem about this by Longfellow, a famous poet, and it is named 'Evangeline.'"

"What's it about?"

"Evangeline is separated from the man she loves in Acadie by the English, who shove them off into different boats. But they are reunited in the United States. It's a beautiful poem." My mother, who did not take herself seriously, liked to make jokes about my taking myself seriously. She laughed in a way that made me aware she was joking, and that the joke was against my so serious credulity. She said, "Evangeline is an ancestor of mine, you know, and that means she's an ancestor of yours."

But, though I didn't understand why not, I was not interested in my mother's ancestry, even if it did include Evangeline.

I asked, "And what about Dad?"

"Ask him," my mother answered.

"Do you know?"

"Ask him."

She knew that I had asked him, and all he'd said was, "*J'n'sais pas.*" He didn't want to talk about his ancestry.

Lenard had fallen asleep in his chair. Not to wake him, my mother put a finger to her lips, then continued to iron.

Back in the classroom in the afternoon, I stared at Mère

Sainte Flore's sleeve rising and falling on her arm, sometimes down to her naked elbow, when she wrote in chalk on the blackboard.

At the end of the class, the Italian girl, Maria, raised her hand, and when Mère Sainte Flore nodded at her she stood by her desk and inquired in English, "What is our play going to be? We heard that in the eighth grade they're already practicing for their play." Maria wore not a blue ribbon but a golden chain and medal.

I expected Mère Sainte Flore to tell Maria that she'd talk about the play another time, but Mère Sainte Flore put the piece of chalk on the ledge below the blackboard, brushed her fingers against one another to get the dust off, and said, "I've been thinking that our play should be about that French boy, Ruffi, who was the only person left from the colony of Charlesfort."

There was a shifting movement among the students.

"I'll tell you more when I know what the parts are."

Just as the bell in the corridor rang to announce the end of the school day and the students were opening their desktops to put away their notepads and books, Mère Sainte Flore called, "David," and I went still. She said to me, "I want you to go to the music room and wait for me there until I come back from bringing the class down to the crossroads."

Apprehensive about why I was being kept after school because students were kept after school only when they did something wrong, I stayed at my desk as the class was taken out by Mère Sainte Flore. I didn't want to go to the music room. Alone in the classroom, I went to the cupboard behind Mère Sainte Flore's desk and, though I knew this really wasn't permitted without her permission, I opened it. There was the bottle of ink, and there, too, was an open shoe box of raw cotton balls, the black seeds caught in the fibers, the dry stems cracked. There was a lump of rock crystal, a large seashell, and a small, crumbling sheaf of wheat. Hearing footsteps in the corridor, I quickly shut the cupboard door. Mère Sainte Flore would be back and would ask me why I hadn't gone to the music room.

Along the empty corridor, all the doors to the classrooms were shut.

As I opened the heavy door to the music room, I thought no one was there. The round table on an oriental rug in the middle was covered with a green chenille cloth and piles of old scores, and beyond the table was the upright piano with a glass vase of dry red maple leaves on it. And as I opened the door more, I saw, drawn on a blackboard with colored chalks and in elaborately illuminated letters, the imperative: *La langue est le gardien de la foi.* I opened the door more and saw Mère Sainte Flore at the back of the room, looking out a window.

She wasn't aware that I had come into the room. I remained at the door. Turning to me, she frowned a little, as if she wasn't sure who I was, then, smiling, she went to sit on a wooden chair. I approached and stood before her.

Mère Sainte Flore put her hands in her sleeves and leaned back. I watched the crucifix on her bosom rise and fall with her breathing. She said, "For a long while, I've wondered about you."

I nodded.

She stared at me for a long moment, then she told me,

abruptly, to go. Not knowing why she had asked to see me in the music room, or, more, what she had been wondering about me, I left, stumbling on the threshold.

I went back to the classroom, where I had left my school bag. For a while, I sat at my desk in the empty room. Leaving the classroom, I saw Mère Sainte Flore at the door to the convent at the end of the corridor. She held the door open, but she didn't enter. I drew back, and, scared that she might turn around and see me, I stayed just by the doorjamb to watch her. She closed the door halfway and again stood still; then she opened the door, went in, and closed the door behind her.

Though he didn't ask if I was all right, Lenard was waiting for me by the drugstore to walk back home with me.

After school, we played with friends in the neighborhood just outside our parish where people from different parishes lived. They were Italians, Irish, and Polish. Our project was to dig a foxhole in the woods of a lot. Our mother called Lenard and me in for supper when, at five o'clock, our father came back from the factory, which was owned by a Yankee.

That night, in bed next to Lenard, I, after my prayers, couldn't sleep for wondering why Mère Sainte Flore had wanted to see me and why she had sent me away.

The next morning at school, the Italian girl Maria asked Mère Sainte Flore if she had thought about the parts for the play.

Mère Sainte Flore said to Maria, "You want a big part."

Maria, standing by her desk, laughed.

"All right, you'll get a big part. You'll be the Spanish queen."

I thought Mère Sainte Flore looked at me for a moment, then away. She began to assign the different parts: the Spanish king, the Spanish soldiers, the missionary, and, for the girls to play, forest fairies. She seemed to be holding back on assigning the part of the boy Ruffi. There was the Indian chief, and there were the Indians. Mère Sainte Flore told me I would be one of the Indians. The part of Ruffi was given to a boy who had had an operation on his brain and whose head was shaved.

At lunchtime, my mother darned socks while Lenard and I ate our sandwiches and drank our glasses of milk, and, as usual, Lenard wanted us all to stay together, though he didn't say anything.

My mother asked me, "Did Mère Sainte Flore tell you what your play is going to be?"

"Yes."

"Well, what is it going to be?"

"About a French boy who escapes from a fort and becomes an Indian."

"And what will you play?"

"An Indian."

The night of the play, I, at my desk in the classroom with the other students, waited to be told what to do. Looking at the dark through the classroom windows was strange, and so was the electric light. No one moved when Mère Sainte Flore came in carrying a stack of flat boxes, followed by other nuns, who also carried boxes. These were the costumes, for which we, the students who were to play Indians, had already been measured. Swinging her veil to get it out of the way as she moved, Mère Sainte Flore called out the names of the students who would go with the different nuns and get into their costumes. I was the last student she called, and I joined the other boys, each carrying a box. Mère Sainte Flore led us down the corridor to the door to the convent, which she opened. She went ahead of us.

Among the other boys descending the wooden stairs, which curved so that it wasn't possible to see the bottom of them, I, as if suddenly unsure of how to walk down, held my box close to my chest with one hand and touched the wall with the other. At the bottom of the stairs was a narrow passageway, lit by an overhanging bulb in a globe; along each side were rows of windows, the bottom panes painted gray. Our shadows passed under our feet and out before us.

We followed Mère Sainte Flore through another doorway and along a corridor with painted windows on one side and closed doors on the other, and halfway down the corridor Mother opened a door. Inside the room, she stopped, and we stopped behind her. The room was dim, and as if people were sleeping in it and she didn't want to wake them, she whispered, *"Ecoutez,"* and we listened, but she didn't say more.

White curtains hung out into the room, and between the curtains, which were a little parted, I saw a bed with a black crucifix leaning back on the smooth white spread where it covered the pillows. The air in the room was as still as those hanging curtains.

"Put your boxes on the floor," Mère Sainte Flore whispered after a while, and we placed our boxes down. "Now open your boxes." We all opened our boxes. The costumes, a brown jacket and green trousers, both with a stiff fringe along the seams of the arms and legs, were folded inside.

Lying on the costumes were headdresses of colored turkey feathers. "Take off your clothes and put them in the top part of the box," Mère Sainte Flore said, and she left us and went behind a white curtain.

Among all the other boys silently undressing, I, trembling, unzipped my trousers and tried to take them off, but I couldn't get the legs down over my shoes. I had to pull my trousers up to take off my shoes. The floor felt cold under my stocking feet. With my trousers off, the air felt cold about my bare legs, but also warm. As I was unbuttoning my shirt, I saw Mère Sainte Flore push the curtain aside and come towards me, and I couldn't unbutton a button.

Leaning over me, she said in a low, pitying voice, "Let me do it for you."

My jaw set, I looked up at her and let my hands fall to my sides. She unbuttoned my shirt and took it off, and I felt all over my chest and back that cold air and at the same time warm air. She folded my clothes and put them in the open top of the box, then took out the green trousers of my costume and, holding them open, gently told me to step into them. The jacket she also held so I could thrust my arms into the sleeves. The cloth of the costume was thin. Mère Sainte Flore buttoned the brown buttons. She also placed the feather headdress on my head. With the tips of her cool fingers she touched me on the nape of my neck. "David," she said softly. My body began to shake.

I saw behind her another Mother, darker and bigger than Mère Sainte Flore, and behind this Mother another Mother, still darker and bigger, and behind this Mother yet another, the always darker and bigger Mothers going back and back into a vast darkness.

3

WE HAD SUNDAY DINNER AT NOON, AND, IN THE
winter afternoon, the house was closed up so tightly it seemed
to me I wouldn't be able to leave if I tried to. Through the
frosted windows the light was grainy and dull, and everything in the living room, where my parents and my younger
brother and I were, became flat.

My mother said she was tired of the wallpaper in the living room. Couldn't they change the wallpaper in the living
room? Couldn't they have wallpaper with a little more color,
something different?

But he'd changed the wallpaper just a year before, my father said.

She knew that. But she'd like something with a little
more color, something different. Every day was the same in
the house, and she never got out of the house. She understood he was tired and, after a week's work at the factory,
didn't want to go out, but stay in. But she was in all week
long, and day after day was the same in the house, and sometimes she wished for something different.

My father closed his eyes.

My mother stood and walked about the living room, from
wall to wall.

My father got up, went into their bedroom, just off the living room, and shut the door, to lie on their bed. My mother
continued to walk about the living room, more and more
quickly, her face harder, her nostrils tighter. She hit the jamb
to the door of their bedroom with her hand. If she opened
the door, turned the handle, and threw the door open, there

would be a fight, she would shout at him as he lay motionless and silent on the bed, and I, trembling a little, waited for her to put her hand on the crystal handle. She turned away from the door and went through the living room and out.

My younger brother, Lenard, simply sat still where he was and, as my father would have done, stared out into space.

I found our mother in the pantry, standing at the window and looking out.

"I think I'll go for a walk," I said.

"Do," she said, "go out."

"Come with me."

"Your father will wonder where I am when he comes out of our room. You go."

I walked to my aunt Cora's. In the afternoon, her home was chilly, the fire in the coal stove low.

She told me that the great pleasure of her childhood was oranges at Christmas. *"On n'avait des oranges ainques à Noël."* Because she had had no toys, my father, though younger than she, had made her a small doll's house, and because she had left it hanging about—*une traînerie,* which no French household could tolerate—her mother had burned it, and the last Cora saw of it was when the black hot plate of the coal range closed down on its burning roof.

My aunt Cora, unlike my father, was incapable of withdrawing into silence, and while she was telling me, again, how her mother burned her doll's house, the church bell clanged for Sunday Vespers, and only then, as the bell rang—rang as I imagined a bell rung by the wind in a deserted, snow-bound fortress far, far away—did my aunt go silent.

Seeing my aunt made me feel a little sick to my stomach, as though I were allowing myself something I shouldn't allow and should have had the moral strength to deny myself. Though I thought of her, as my mother did, as a joke and an embarrassment, I also thought of her as allowing in me embarrassing feelings I couldn't express to others, perhaps especially to my mother, except by joking about them. And my aunt Cora would talk about what my father never would.

Though my father did not talk about his mother's mother—said he couldn't remember, if I asked him, anything about her—my aunt Cora did.

From my aunt Cora, I knew that my great-grandmother, a Blackfoot, smoked a corncob pipe and smeared her body with bear fat in the winter to keep warm. She met Adolphe, my great-grandfather, called *le Grand Coq*, in a lumber camp in northern Michigan. Her mother's name was Kirou, and she called herself Cliche Kirou. She was baptized Rosalie, which was the name of her husband's mother, so her full name was Rosalie Cliche Kirou. She moved with Adolphe to his village, Saint-Barthélemy, Province of Quebec, Canada, and helped him with his work as fur trader with the Indians. Most of the Indians would come into the house without knocking, and if Adolphe was not there or was eating, they would place the bundle of pelts on the floor and sit on a bench behind the wood stove and wait. Some Indians did knock before they came in and, thinking this was what always had to be done to open a door, also knocked before they went out. My great-grandfather, who recognized certain Indians by their footsteps, went to sit with the one who was waiting behind the stove, and there they smoked, forehead to forehead.

Cliche Kirou stood just behind Adolphe when he discussed the pelts with the Indians. When she was about to give birth, her mother, my great-great-grandmother, came from wherever she lived in the forest to deliver her daughter's baby and bind it to a board with lengths of cloth, then she went away into the forest again. My great-grandmother carried her children—my grandmother among them—as papooses on her back.

Rosalie Cliche Kirou was the farthest back in our ancestry my aunt Cora could go.

For my aunt as for me, the native religion of Rosalie Cliche Kirou was unimaginable. The lives of our Indian ancestors, before they were seen by Europeans, were invisible to us, as if it was only our European ancestors' having seen them that allowed us to see them. There was no way I could see Cliche Kirou in herself. I could only see her as a dark presence behind my grandmother, who was a dark presence behind my father.

My grandmother as I remembered her was a gaunt woman, her cheekbones high and sharp edged, and her jaw square. She appeared to have permanent bruising about her eyes, as from the bony edges of the eye sockets of her skull. Her eyes were small and set close to her large nose. She wore her white hair in a long braid rolled up with hairpins at the nape of her neck.

She lived on the top floor of the tenement, and my father said she had once carried a washing machine up the stairs by herself, grasping the two front legs and lifting the whole thing, wringer and all, and simply climbing. I asked my aunt, Was that story Indian?

She prepared medicines from weeds she collected. Was that Indian?

She couldn't write, was unlettered, and when making out a shopping list for her daughter Cora drew carrots, potatoes with the eyes, and a chicken, with marks after them to indicate how many pounds were to be bought. And was that Indian?

When my aunt Cora told me that my grandmother had given to my father, not to her, the eldest daughter, clothes—including purple silk stockings and white undergarments—which she had instructed him to give to the undertaker on her death so she would be buried in them, I asked:

"Was that Indian?"

My aunt Cora said, *"J'n'sais pas."*

The bits of information that my aunt Cora gave me about Rosalie Cliche Kirou—that she made moccasins and peed in them to soften the leather—made her not brighter but darker to me, and she was especially dark because my aunt Cora was not able to tell me what the religion was of Cliche Kirou, was not able to tell me who the God of Cliche Kirou was, though I was sure she had a religion, had a God.

She was invisible to me, but in her unimaginable difference she pulled at me so strongly I felt that if I gave in to her pull, I would be lost. She frightened me, and she especially frightened me when, at moments, I felt she might appear to me.

My father frightened me. One evening at the supper table, looking at me, he suddenly rolled his eyes up into his head so his irises disappeared and I saw only the gleaming whites, which made me shout, and my father rolled his irises back down again and looked at me, but I continued to shout, and my mother told my father not to do that again.

I asked my aunt Cora, "Why is it that my father doesn't know anything about his French history?"

She said, "He knows."

Surprised by the revelation, I exclaimed, "He knows?"

"I tell you, he knows." She breathed in deeply, then settled her large shoulders. "Our mother gave him a list of ancestors, all the way back to France. She gave it to him at the same time she gave him the prayer for curing burns. And he'd no more tell you about the list than he would about the prayer."

"What prayer?"

"She should have given it to me. She should have given the list to me. I was her daughter. She gave it to her son instead."

Pressing her, I asked again, "What prayer?"

"I don't know it. He knows it. I remember one time he used it, just once, when we were going past a smithy and heard a shout from inside and went inside and saw the smithy's son had a bad burn on his arm. Your father wrapped the boy's arm in a rag and plunged it into cold water, and I saw his lips move and I knew he was saying the prayer, and when he took the boy's arm out, he wiped the burn away with the rag. I saw it."

"Why doesn't he tell me about the prayer?"

"Maybe he's ashamed to."

"Why doesn't he tell me about the list?"

"He's ashamed of that, too."

After I left my aunt Cora's, I didn't want to go home. I wanted to go somewhere different, or, perhaps, back somewhere I felt I should have been able to go back to. I went down the hill from the parish to the flats and the river and past the closed brick factory where my father worked and into a small, snow-filled woods. I went into the woods, where discarded oil drums were rounded out by snow. I went in far enough so as not to be able to see beyond the trees.

When I got home, in the purple evening, I found my mother walking back and forth in the living room, my father sitting, watching her, and my brother Lenard sitting more still than my father, staring out beyond them both. When she reached a wall, my mother hit it with a hand before she turned away from it and walked across the room to the opposite wall.

She shouted, "I don't want to die in this closed-in house. I want to know the outside world."

I felt a thrill, a rush that started at my feet and ran up through my legs and torso and neck and out the top of my head, and I felt lifted out of myself.

My mother went to the door of my parents' bedroom, opened it, went in, and slammed it behind her. I saw my father lower his head and put his hand over his eyes. When my father dropped his hand and raised his head, I, on an impulse, ran to him, and he put his arms around me, and I felt not that everything would be all right—I knew it wouldn't be—but an immense acceptance of everything wrong, immense in its deep, deep darkness. I shook as I sobbed, and my father held me closer. My mother came out of the bedroom to see what the matter was. I didn't want her to come out. I wanted to stay alone with my father, against whose face I pressed my face and sobbed.

Holding me, my father called me *"Tsi gars."*

Lenard, two years younger than I, remained still and silent, staring out beyond whatever was happening in the room.

Our mother led me away, washed my face in the bathroom, then brought me to the bedroom I shared with Lenard and told me to undress and get into bed. I woke when Lenard got into bed with me. Awake, I heard my parents speaking to one another, just the murmur of their voices. They were together in their bed. The headboard of their bed was just behind the lathe and plaster wall that the headboard of my bed stood against, and over their bed, as over mine, hung Christ crucified. I didn't want to know what they were saying to one another, but the low, tired sounds of their voices kept me awake and attentive. Their voices ceased.

I put an arm around my brother so I could fall asleep.

4

MY AUNT—OR, TO GIVE HER HER FULL HONORIFIC, Matante—Cora often spent Christmas at our house. One year, I was given as a gift a toy log-cabin set that consisted of different lengths of brown dowels notched at each end so that they could be interlocked to form corners and walls and, if the builder was good at it, doors and windows. The roof was made of narrow green slats of wood, and there was a wooden red chimney. I made a log cabin in the middle of the living room. After I put the roof on, I had a curious sense, lowering my head to the floor and looking through the doorway into the toy cabin, that very little kept me from being able to go inside and live in that dim interior, where pale strips of light from the living room showed between the logs. In fact, it seemed to me I had lived in there, and I knew that from inside I could look out the doorway, not at the legs of a chair and the toes of my aunt Cora's black shoes, but at a landscape under snow.

My aunt, whose French was greatly more grammatical than her English, said, "Hey, you done a good job."

I turned around and smiled at her. She always wore a green visor to protect her eyes, which were filmed by cataracts, from the light. To see, she had to open her eyes wide and stare, so those whitish eyes seemed to bulge. She kept her hands clasped in her lap and her feet crossed.

She said, "You would have been good at helping to build cabins back then."

Then she told me the story of how her *pepère*, my great-grandfather, had just managed to slam the door to his cabin before an Indian tomahawk hit it.

She was a big woman, with large shoulders and arms, but she sat like a well-behaved girl in a missionary school. Her hair was white, with two white, artificial braids pinned to the sides of her head just above the black band of the visor. Her face was gray-white, and she had long hairs on her chin. The bodice of her blue taffeta dress was cut low to reveal the slopes of her great breasts, and she wore a rhinestone necklace that was as elaborate as magnified, flashing lace through which her flesh showed. The dress had a very full skirt, raised high and pulled onto her lap so her legs were exposed almost up to the knees. She wore orange stockings and black shoes with laces, the kind old women wore.

When she reached for a glass of root beer from a tray my mother offered, she made a kind of arabesque with her wrist and slowly raised her arm, then delicately extended her long fingers to take a glass. At the same time, she uncrossed her feet and separated her legs so her knees opened sideways into her taffeta skirt. Her smile was large and unstrained.

It would not have been unthinkable, given the slow and deliberate way she moved, that she was wearing under her dress something, something unthinkable, to bruise her soft flesh. Her clothes and jewelry were the ornaments on a body in agony.

Her agony was her longing. And her greatest longing, ever since she was a girl, was to enter a convent and become a nun. God had given her a vocation, she was sure—that is, God had inspired in her a longing that could be fulfilled only by her devoting herself to her religion.

She had, when still a girl, been accepted into a convent as a postulant. The job assigned to her was to wash floors and clean toilets. After a year of washing floors and cleaning toilets, she was told she didn't have a real vocation and must leave the convent.

But she knew in her soul that she did have a vocation. What could that longing, which was an agony to her, be but the impulse to give herself up to God and live out her life— even if that meant sacrificing her life to cleaning floors and toilets—only to be with God?

She never explained why she wasn't allowed to stay in the convent and be professed. I wondered if it was because she didn't wash the floors and clean the toilets well enough, but, from something my mother told me, which was "She was too avid," I suspected Matante Cora was asked to leave because she was fanatic in her devotions. She recited her prayers in a voice higher than the others, bowed her head in adoration of the host lower than the others, and kept silences, her lips pressed together, with a greater show of strictness than the others. She washed and cleaned fanatically, mortifying her flesh by using scalding water.

Shortly after she was asked to leave the convent, she married. She knew before she married that the man was an alcoholic and ran around with other women. Marriage didn't change him. He would leave her alone in the tenement apartment house for a week and come back drunk, dirty, and reeking of perfume. He'd be too drunk even to undress, and Cora would do this for him, and as she'd undress him he'd vomit. When he was really drunk, he shit (my aunt used this word) in his pants, and Cora would clean this up as well as the vomit. Naked, he'd lean on her, and she'd stagger getting him to the bathroom. Sometimes he'd fall, and she couldn't get him up, so she'd have to wash his body as he lay, then cover him with a blanket and let him sleep where he was until he woke up. In the meantime, she'd wash his clothes. This happened over and over, and after each time he'd say he'd never do it again, but he would; he'd go off, sometimes for a whole week, and Cora always had him back.

Taking delicate sips from her glass of root beer, Matante Cora told my mother this, which she had told my mother

many times before, and my mother, as she always did because she had to, listened, trying not smile.

Matante Cora said, "He lived off the women he picked
up in bars. When he was out, I'd lie in bed wondering what
woman he was in bed with, where, and how long it would
take her before she finally threw him out. I could always
count on that: that the woman he was living off would throw
him out. And then he'd come back to me."

My mother winced. "He must have smelled of those
women."

"He smelled. He smelled of more than cheap perfume.
Sometimes the smell that came off him made me want to
vomit. He'd say, 'Give me a kiss, give me a kiss.'"

"You didn't."

Matante Cora raised a hand to her bosom in a gesture of,
What else could I do? "He was my husband."

"Yes," my mother said, reflecting, I thought, on her life
with my father. "And that makes me realize how lucky I am
to have the steady, faithful husband I do."

Matante Cora said, "When he started to beat me up, my
mother told me to leave him, to come back home and live
with her. I was always black and blue. Hey, once he threw a
knife at me, but he missed. I wouldn't leave him."

I, standing closer to my mother's chair, asked, "But
why?"

Matante Cora looked at me from under her green visor.
"Because I knew that everything I prayed for, with all my
heart and soul, I could only ever have by staying with him
and suffering whatever God sent to me through him. I knew
that I was earning my eternity."

I stared more closely at Matante Cora.

My mother said, "I've got a husband who doesn't even drink."

"When I became pregnant, my husband would go off for weeks, a month. He'd never tell me where he'd been. If I asked, he'd beat me up—that is, if he wasn't so drunk he was throwing up and shitting and unable to hit me. And when my daughter was born, he became worse."

"For the sake of your baby, shouldn't you have gone to your mother?"

"No. God had sent him to me, and I did what I knew God wanted me to do to be with God after I die. And my mother refused to see me because I didn't go to her. She said what I was doing didn't make any sense. My own mother didn't understand. Everyone refused to see me because I wouldn't give him up, wouldn't even accept help. I was alone once for a period of three months, and I had no money."

"He'd bring you money?"

"I counted on him bringing home the money he got from his women."

"Oh, Cora," my mother said and raised a hand to a cheek. She hadn't heard this fact before. "You didn't take it."

"I took it. I needed to eat, the baby needed to eat. When he was away for those three months, I didn't have money to buy food, and my baby starved to death."

My mother raised her other hand to her cheek. "You let your baby starve to death?"

"I watched her die. She was in her crib, a tiny, skinny girl, and suddenly she began to grow, to grow and grow, her arms and legs especially, and then she cried out and went blue and died. The baby was already buried when he came back."

"And you didn't kick him out after that?"

Matante Cora smiled a wide smile. "No."

"Why?"

"Because I knew that I had to save him for his eternity. No one else would do that. If I'd kicked him out, he'd have died in a state of sin. He was near to dying. He'd have been lost for eternity, my husband, if I didn't save him. I couldn't let that happen."

Lowering hear head a little, my mother said, "Yes."

"And I did save him. When he came back after the death of our baby, he was in a worse state than ever. He was covered in sores. I knew he didn't have long to live."

"You slept in the same bed with him?"

"I washed him, I fed him, I slept in the same bed with him."

"Where did you get the money?"

"He came back with a hundred dollars."

"Cora, my God."

"He died in our bed. He confessed and received extreme unction. He was saved for eternity. He died in our Catholic Church."

My mother turned and stared at me for a long moment, and I stared at her. She seemed to be trying to see in my eyes the disbelief I saw in hers about everything Matante Cora had said.

She asked me quietly, "Don't you want to play more with your log-cabin set?"

I put my hand on the back of her chair to let her know I wanted to stay where I was, listening with her to Matante Cora.

Matante said, "A short while after my husband died, I

found I was pregnant again," and my mother and I waited
for her to go on talking.

After her husband's death, she moved into the apartment
of her mother, who took care of the baby while she was at
work. She got a job in a laundry, which was a half hour's walk
away, and on the way Matante Cora said prayers. By the time
she reached the junction, she would have said her first prayer;
by the bottom of the hill she would have said ten prayers, with
meditations separating them. Most of these prayers were
Our Fathers and Hail Marys, but some she made up herself,
and these were pleas, more and more fervent pleas, to be with
her God, but only if it was God's will that she should be. She
longed to be made helpless in God's will.

Her job in the laundry was to sort out the dirty clothes
that came in canvas bags. She would sit on a low stool in the
midst of the bags, and she'd open one, take out dirty, stained
sheets, dirty shirts, dirty underwear and socks, some of them
so dirty you couldn't believe people had used them until the
time they'd sent them to the laundry, and she'd make sure
each item had an indelible mark on it, and then she'd separate the items into baskets. She would find diapers filled with
shit from a mother too lazy to do anything but wrap it up and
throw it into the bag.

My mother asked, "How could a mother do that?"

Matante Cora answered, "You don't know what people
are like out in the world. You're better living here in the protected world of your own house."

Sighing a little, "I know I am," my mother said.

Then Matante Cora described in detail the condition of
an item of clothing, which made my mother exclaim, "No,

Cora, no, that isn't possible," to which Matante answered, again, "You're lucky to be protected from the world."

Again, my mother said, "I am, I know I am."

I didn't understand what my aunt had described, but, as if to outdo herself in her descriptions, she went on to describe the state of an undershirt in a way that made my stomach turn over, and yet I listened, as my mother, too, listened: the undershirt must have belonged to a man with a terrible disease because the shirt was stiff, *stiff,* with dried blood and pus and whatever else had leaked from his sores and dried on the cloth. One of the colored women who also worked sorting out the dirty laundry found it and swore and wouldn't take it out of the bag. Slowly, elegantly, Matante Cora took it out, held it by its short sleeves, and to show the others she had no fear of what was merely human, with a smile raised it and pressed it to her face. The other women screamed, or some of them did. One shouted that she was crazy. No one in the laundry would have understood her doing this even if she'd explained. No one would have understood that, so sure of the incorruptibility of what protected *her,* which was infinite, she could put herself in the midst of corruption, which was finite, and feel totally pure.

Biting her lower lip, my mother again looked around at me with disbelief. I looked away from her.

Then, with that sudden and surprising demonstration of honesty she was capable of as if in reaction to her own pretensions, Matante Cora said, "Well, who else would do such dirty work, who else but one of us French? We're not called white niggers for nothing." Without addressing my father, but to speak out about what he would not speak about, she, as if in reaction to his pretensions, said, "My brother knows. He knows from working in the sorting room in the textile mill when he left grammar school, there, where all the bloody, greasy, stinking pelts of the sheep had to be sorted out, work that not even the blacks would do, but work we French did. He knows as much as any of us why we're white niggers."

My father appeared not to hear.

He drove my aunt back to her tenement apartment near the parish church after Christmas supper, which consisted of mince pies, and I was alone with my mother, who said, "Cora embarrasses me so much."

"Embarrasses you?" I asked. I was helping her wash the supper dishes in the pantry. "About what?"

"About those feelings she talked about." A shiver of disapproval made my mother's shoulders shake a little. "Those longings."

Embarrassment came over me, as if I myself were guilty of my aunt's longings. I knew I was not, knew that they were —as her Mother Superior, who told her she must leave the convent, knew they were—insincere. It was as though I felt I was guilty of insincere longings.

My mother smiled and said, "And that story about the undershirt."

I, too, smiled.

"What would anyone outside the parish make of her?" my mother asked.

"I guess they'd think she's peculiar."

"More than peculiar. They'd think she was silly—uneducated, primitive, and silly."

"Yes," I said.

"Come to think of it," my mother said, "what would anyone outside the parish make of anyone in it? What would they make of Monsieur le Curé? Or les Mères de Jésus-Marie?"

"I don't know," I said.

"And what did she mean, saying the French are white niggers?"

"I don't know," I repeated.

"Canucks," my mother said.

Then, as we heard my father coming back into the house and in the entryway stomping his rubber boots to get the snow off them before he removed them, my mother, who didn't have much time before he entered and wouldn't be able to joke anymore, said in a whisper to me, "All that talk by Aunt Cora about eternity." She laughed. "Between you and me and the lamppost, I don't think we go anywhere when we die, and I know for sure that once we die we can't come back as ghosts. What do you think?"

"Maybe not," I said and laughed with her.

5

THOUGH BOTH MY PARENTS WERE FRANCO-AMERICANS and Catholics and every Sunday went to Mass together, Lenard and I with them, they belonged to different nationalities and different religions.

This came to me one Sunday morning at Mass with my parents. My mother's religion, I thought, was as American as the American flag that stood to one side of the altar, and my father's religion was Canuck, which had no identifying flag, not even the Vatican flag that stood on the other side of the altar.

At Mass, Monsieur le Curé, whose head looked like a skull with black eyes in the sockets, gave the sermon, a sermon warning us that our temporal lives on earth were nothing but a preparation for our eternal lives after our deaths. The morning sunlight was beaming through the tall, narrow, and pointed stained glass windows onto the congregation as Monsieur le Curé admonished from his pulpit.

Glancing up from my missal, I noted that my mother was paying attention to the sermon and that my father was not paying attention, but, his lips moving a little, he was saying a prayer to himself. It occurred to me that I had never in fact heard my father say a prayer out loud.

The pastor returned to the altar to continue the Mass. I continued to be more attentive to my father than to the Mass. He was no more attentive to the pastor at the altar than he had been to the pastor giving the sermon but, as if alone, always said his prayer silently to himself. I was also aware that while my mother participated in the Mass, my father, though he stood and kneeled and sat with the congregation, didn't.

My mother was light complexioned, with blue eyes. My father had thick gray hair, a square chin, and a broad forehead, and he had the black staring eyes of his half-caste mother.

My father was my father, but, in his silence, I didn't know who he was, didn't even know what his religion was, and who the God of his religion was. He might have been saying prayers that I didn't know. And yet, I *did* know that his religion and the God of his religion existed, and *did* know that the prayers of his religion existed.

After Mass, we went to visit Matante Cora. She had been to the six o'clock Mass, but since then she had said the prayers a nun would say. At the large, round wooden table in the middle of the kitchen, she gave us bowls of tea and crullers from the bakery, and, as if in return for her hospitality, she expected to be listened to—not by my father, who she knew wouldn't listen, but by my mother and me. She talked about her prayers, which were all prayers for cures—especially a prayer (which she herself had thought up) for curing the cataracts in both her eyes, though the cataracts had become worse. "Yes, yes," my mother said. My father sat at a distance from her around the curve of the table, and Lenard and I were between them. "Yes," my mother said and looked towards my father to try to get his eye and indicate to him that it was time to leave. But my father stared out, not at the flue to the coal stove, not even at the silvery coiled wire handle that was used for shutting or opening the flue, but at something that I knew my mother could never see, and that I, too, would probably never see. But I was aware that there was something to see by staring out as my father did, and to my mother there was nothing.

Lenard was staring out as my father did.

Matante Cora took from her room her newest acquisitions of holy cards, spread them on the table, and explained, in detail, what martyrdom each saint had suffered and what prayers she said to each saint for what cure. Saint Lucy held out her eyes on a platter, and Saint Agatha had her breasts held out on a platter by an angel. One card showed the disembowelment of Saint Erasmus, his intestines wound out of him onto a big wheel.

This card made my mother and me look at one another and smile, and I thought that perhaps my mother tolerated Matante Cora to reassure herself that, really, Matante Cora's devotions were not to be taken seriously but were a joke. My mother had the humor, which was not at all Canuck, to laugh, and she liked to laugh. She liked jokes.

Making her expression serious, my mother asked Matante Cora if Saint Erasmus was the saint you would pray to to cure constipation. She could seem serious about this, for one of the most important topics of conversation in the parish was constipation and laxatives. Matante Cora said solemnly, "Why do you think I am so regular in my bowel movements?"

This little joke of my mother's, which I, smiling, got, Matante Cora did not get at all.

Matante Cora placed a card on the table, which was of the Sacred Heart, who held the robes over his chest open with delicate hands to reveal his thorn-entangled, burning heart, and she said, "But if I have to suffer, I pray that all my suffering will earn me my death."

I saw in my mother's face a hardening, and her nostrils tightened. She had had enough of Matante Cora. But she had to stay until my father, as if a trance were broken, looked around the table at us, seeming, for a moment, not to recognize quite where he was or who we were.

His eyes settled on Lenard, who, as if made aware that our father was looking at him, looked up, and they smiled at one another.

Matante Cora was talking about how her mother had collected wild sumac berries from the bushes that grew in the lots among the clapboard houses, to make a medicine to go along with her prayers.

My aunt said, "Last night, I woke up and saw her standing at the foot of my bed," and my father stopped her with *"Tais-toi à c't'heure."* He wouldn't hear my aunt talk about ghosts. And he said to my mother that he wanted to go.

My mother was, essentially, a secular woman. She did not believe in ghosts.

My father, who even at obligatory Mass seemed outwardly not to participate but, saying his rosary, to be alone, was inwardly deeply religious. He believed in ghosts.

6

LIKE MY MOTHER, I DID NOT BELIEVE IN GHOSTS, BUT I remained frightened of their appearing to me even as I grew into adolescence, and I remained particularly frightened of the ghost of a large, dark woman, a Mother, appearing to me. This my own mother could never have understood, and I would never have tried to get my father to express his understanding, for I knew he would no more talk about his beliefs than he would of his ancestry, maybe because ashamed of such beliefs, or maybe for some other reason. Yet I was sure that my father was as frightened of that Mother, that line of Mothers going back and back into darkness, as I was.

During my last year in the French primary school, when I was fourteen and aware that the next year I would have to leave the confines of the parish to go outside to high school, which was Catholic but not French, I became very devout for a long winter period. My devotion to the God of the parish went as deep into the unknown as that line of Mothers, but I felt as secure within this unknowable God as I felt secure within the parish, at least for that winter when, leaving a note for my mother to wake me (which she did reluctantly, asking me, wouldn't I prefer staying in the warm bed), I went to Mass every morning. Perhaps my daily attendance began in reaction to the threat I felt at going outside the parish, the center of which was the church, and perhaps it came too from something one of the Mothers said: that to love God was to love someone who was beyond this life, someone as if dead who knew everything the living didn't and couldn't know, but which the living must die to be able to know. If I didn't hear this from anyone, I thought it, and the thought had to have been inspired in some way by my religion, a religion not of held beliefs, certainly not of conscious convictions, but of a *sense* of God—a strange, enveloping sense barely—and if at all, delicately—in contact with my five senses, a *sense* that came to me and my senses from as far outside as death.

Every morning, despite my mother trying to persuade me to stay in bed, I got up entranced by this sense, I dressed in the cold room entranced by the sense, and, without break- fast because I was to receive Communion and must not eat or even drink water, I went out into the freezing cold entranced by that sense, walked the empty streets alongside the snowbanks heaped on the impassable sidewalks, saw the thin gray dawn light expand into sunlight on the flat, lower and higher levels of cloud, breathed in and smelled and tasted the icy, clear air, and heard the voices of angels singing in the high bare branches of the maple trees, all the while entranced by that sense.

I was entranced, too, by the cold church, the lights not yet switched on, I sitting alone in a pew, each member of the small congregation at that early Mass with a long pew to himself and herself, and focusing on the flame of the vigil lamp flickering in red glass that hung before the altar; I was entranced by the dimness, by the silence, by the emptiness, by that sense that most drew me to itself, so powerfully that I would one day have to give in entirely to it, for being itself dim, silent, empty, for being all outside me, far, far, far outside me. And I sensed this vast outside not in spite of my being enclosed within this French church, but because I was in it. In that time before the lights came on—bulbs suddenly glaring in large lanterns with amberlike glass hanging within the pillar-supported arches alongside of the narrow nave, and, preceded by an altar boy ringing a little bell, Monsieur le Curé entering from the vestry in his chasuble and carrying the chalice under the chalice veil and burse and climbing the steps to the altar where he deposited the covered chalice, and turning to the almost empty church and, his arms outstretched, intoning, "Introibo ad altare Dei"—in that time *before* this, *before* the Mass, did I feel my true devotion, feel it in the entrancing sense that may have had nothing to do with the religion as enacted on the altar at Mass, but with some other religion, other but as unique to my parish as a bird that had evolved over hundreds of years was unique to the forests of North America. If I was a Catholic, I was a Catholic of my parish, and my deepest piety to my Catholicism, isolated from the rest of Catholicism as my parish was isolated from the rest of the world, was not piety towards any held beliefs, any convictions, but piety inspired by silence, by empty space, by death.

Would I have been able to articulate this in those early years of my teens? No, but I did sense it powerfully, sensed it, I think now, fatally.

My mother would have thought, rightly, that I was being morbid.

She did not believe that the ghosts of Indians could appear, but she had a romantic idea about Indians that I knew was as wrong as the belief that they did appear. Clenching her hand into a fist and holding it up to me, and to my brothers, as if she were trying to get us to swear by it like an ancient Roman matron with her name, she would say, "You must be stoic, stoic in the way your Indian ancestors were." Our father, who had no romantic ideas of Indians, never held them up to us as an example of any behavior.

In the same way that she did not understand our religion, and in the same way that she did not understand Indians, I felt she did not really understand me. She thought I would love, as she did, a text about Indians she translated for the son of an Irish neighbor who was studying freshman French in college but who hadn't enough French to do the work himself. The text was a synopsis of Chateaubriand's *Atala*.

She kept her copy, written in pencil in her Palmer Method handwriting, in the Chippendale desk. She signed her translation, as if the original had been written by her: Albina Plante. I found it after her death, and, reading it again after so many years, I was overcome not with my mother's misunderstanding but with her fantasy of the religion she had married into—a fantasy that she hoped I would share but that I didn't.

My mother wrote:

After the discovery of the Mississippi River by Father Marquette and the unfortunate La Salle, the first French who settled at Biloxi, a village on the Gulf of Mexico, about 80 miles from New Orleans, became allies of the Indian tribe named Natchez, who had great power in that country. Among them, an old blind man named Chactas was considered a patriarch to his people. Despite the many injustices he received from the French, he loved them.

In 1725, a French boy named René, led on by the passions and misfortunes of life, arrived at Louisiana. He went up the Mississippi to where the Natchez tribe lived and asked to be admitted as a warrior. After hearing his story, Chactas adopted him as his son and gave him, as a wife, an Indian maiden named Celuta. Shortly after their marriage, the Indians prepared for a beaver hunting expedition. It was in Autumn, and René was elected to go along with them. One night after their departure, by the light of the moon and while the rest of the Natchez tribe

slept, he and Chactas sat down, and it was then that René
asked the old patriarch to tell him of his adventures. He
told him this story.

Chactas recounted to René how, as a young man, he
and other braves of the Natchez tribe, together with some
Spanish, fought an enemy tribe, the Muscogulges, who won.
Wounded, Chactas was saved by an old Castilian man, Lopez, who later adopted him as his son. "One morning, I confronted Lopez, dressed in my Indian clothes, and told him
that I would die were I unable to return to the desert and re-
sume the life of an Indian." Chactas and Lopez parted, and
soon after, Chactas was captured by the Muscogulges, who
chained him—"not too tightly because of my youth"—and
told him he would be burned to death. He was, however,
saved by the daughter of the chief, Atala, who, with "a flut-
tering of her clothes," came to him at night. "Tears flowed
freely from her eyes and by the light of the fire I could see a
little gold crucifix that hung on her breast. She was very
pretty and I was irresistibly attracted to her. I feared being
alone with her, yet when she freed me from my bonds, I hes-
itated to leave her even when she implored me to go away
and save myself. After we kissed, she said these words to me:
'Handsome prisoner, I foolishly gave into your wish, but
where shall this passion lead us? My religion separates me
from you always. Oh my mother, what have you done?'" But
Chactas was indifferent to the death that awaited him and
could think only of Atala. They escaped together into the
forest, Chactas carrying Atala in his arms. He told René he

couldn't remember much of what he said to her, for "the souvenirs of love in the heart of an old man are like the silence that hovers over the Indian's hut at dusk." As deeply in love as they were, however, they did not make love, or so this is understood by Chactas's asking what would save Atala from succumbing to nature—only a miracle, and it happened when she prayed to the God of the Christians. "At that moment, René, I found in that religion something wonderful, something that stayed the flow of passion when everything seemed to favor it, such as the secret the forest would keep, the absence of men and the faithfulness of the shadows. She appeared divine, that simple little savage, who was on her knees before an old pine tree as at the foot of an altar and was offering her prayers to her God for her lover." They were discovered by four Muscogulges warriors under orders to find them, and Chactas was bound to the stake. But the ceremony of the Feast of the Dead, during which no captive can be put to death, stayed his execution, and again Atala saved him. They went deeper into the forest. "She made me a coat from the bark of an ash tree and some moccasins from the fur of a muskrat. When we came to a river, she held on to my shoulders and we swam across. Often, I would notice her looking at me longingly, and then she would become melancholy. I could read in her eyes that she had a secret hidden in her soul. She was always pulling me to her, then repulsing me, thus building up my hopes, then destroying them." After fifteen nights, they entered the Allegheny Mountains. A storm came up, and with the lightning, thunder, and wind, he gathered Atala to him. He asked her what bothered her, and she told him that she was in fact not the daughter of the chief of the Muscogulges, but that her mother was an Indian woman and her father a white man. Her mother revealed to the chief before their marriage that she had conceived, and because of her honesty he forgave her. "When she told me her father was a man named Lopez, I let out a cry that resounded in the solitude, and holding her tightly to me, I told her how Lopez had adopted me and she was greatly confused, yet happy. It seemed to bring us closer, and when we thought our happiness was about to reach the heights, we heard a dog barking and soon after an old missionary carrying a lantern came upon us." Atala, kneeling at his feet, told him that heaven must have sent him to save her. The missionary bade them follow him to his grotto. Moved by the couple, the missionary, Father Aubry, told her that he would instruct Chactas in their religion and, when he was worthy of her, he and she would wed. He made Atala a soft bed, and he and Chactas left for the Mission, where Chactas would become Christian. On the way, Father Aubry stopped at the foot of a large cross in the forest to celebrate the mysteries of his religion—that is, to say Mass—and Chactas felt the God of the Christians descend into his heart.

Upon returning to the grotto, I was surprised, also disappointed in not seeing Atala coming to greet me. Father Aubry entered first, and I followed quickly, and there on the bed he had so carefully made for her lay Atala, her face flushed with fever and her arms outstretched, beckoning me. I looked at her lying there suffering and I thought how weak is he who lets the passions dominate him and how strong is he who reposes in God. She asked the missionary to approach her bedside also, as she said she knew death was near and she had something to tell us.

She was born out of wedlock, and at her birth they despaired of her life, so her mother promised the Queen of Angels that she would consecrate her virginity to Her if her daughter were spared. When she was sixteen, her mother died, and a few hours before her death she made her daughter promise to renounce the pleasures that had troubled her and always remain a virgin, otherwise she would suffer eternal torment. "It was very easy to do as she wished, until I met Chactas." Atala's voice grew weaker and her suffering was intense. She seemed to be waiting for something, and when I told her I would embrace the Christian religion, she uttered: "It is time to call God here." I fell on my knees at the foot of her bed and saw Father Aubry open the chalice and take between his two fingers the host, white as snow, which he placed on Atala's tongue. Then he took some cotton, dipped it in some holy oil, and rubbed her temples. "Father," I cried, "will that medicine give her life?" "Yes, my son," he replied, "eternal life." Atala had expired.

That night, we transported her precious remains to an opening in the grotto. Father Aubry had rolled her in a piece of linen, woven by his mother. Atala was resting on a bed of mimosa and in her hair was a flower from the magnolia tree. The missionary prayed all night. I sat in silence at her head. The next day, I carried Atala on my shoulders and with Father Aubry proceeding up, we marched to her last resting place. We dug her grave, and when it was finished I placed her there and picked up a handful of earth, and taking one last look at my beloved, I sprinkled some over her face until her features disappeared. We finished our sad task, then returned to the grotto. He encouraged me to return to my people to console my mother.

Upon leaving, once more I visited her grave, and falling on my knees I cried: "Sleep in peace in this strange land." Then I departed from the daughter of Lopez knowing that I would forever after live in virtue.

That is my story, René, and many years later I, feeling very old, am looking forward to a reunion in Heaven with my Atala.

I suspected my mother was impressed by this story because it dared, within the world of Indians, a freedom from the strictures of her religion, which, however ultimately spiritual, she could never herself have dared, but which I already knew I must one day dare for myself.

It was not a freedom she could possibly dare with my father. About my father being one-quarter Indian, my mother would say in his presence, "He didn't tell me until after we got married. Would I have married him if he'd told me before?" She'd look at him and, if close to him, put her hand on his head. "Would I have?" He'd shrug.

And I would wonder if there was anything of my father's religion in mine, which was without a story—without words—to express it.

7

MY MOTHER'S MOTHER HAD BEEN AGAINST HER marrying my father. *"Tu verras,"* she said, *"il est un vrai Canuck. Je les connais, les Canucks."* My mother, who in marrying my father had married a real Canuck as if she herself, being French, were not, retained the feelings her mother had about the breed.

Though she didn't like Canucks, my mother had to see my father's family, which, once a year at least, gathered in clan meetings. There were no such clan meetings among my mother and her brothers and sisters, not one of whom was married to a Canuck. The meeting of my father's clan made the local newspaper.

PLANTE FAMILY REUNION IS HELD

Annual Affair Conducted at Orchard Farm, Harmony
More Than 100 Attend
The 17th annual reunion of the Plante family was held at Orchard Farm, Harmony, the home of Mr. and Mrs. Omer Plante, where more than 100 enjoyed a chicken and chowder dinner served at tables under a canopy in the yard. Bingo and Sports Events on Program. Some come from far Sister Thérèse Marguerite of Outremont Convent, Montreal was a guest. Other relatives were present from Seattle, Providence, Arctic Center, North Grosvenordale, Conn, and Chepachet. Three families were represented by three generations.

This clipping was saved not by my father but, oddly, by my mother. I recall this meeting of the whole Plante clan, the last there was. Cars, with rounded hoods and fenders and running boards, were parked in a grass-grown field among trees, and, like an encampment, folding tables were set up among the cars with bottles and cardboard boxes on them. The center of the camp was a low, brown, clapboard house with a big screened-in porch, which no one was allowed to enter. In front of the house, in a wide, bare yard, was the canvas canopy, and under it were long wooden tables with benches attached.

I sat with my parents at one of these tables. My aunt Cora stood at the end and served into bowls with a ladle from a big pot, what was always known in my family as a *chudron,* not clam chowder, but pea soup she had made with hominy, as thick as porridge. My father said, *"C'est ça, la vraie soupe aux pois."* My mother didn't like hominy and thought the soup too thick, the way Indians ate soup. She laughed a lot at the clan reunion and joined in the games, the races in potato sacks, in a way my father didn't, but when I saw her sitting alone at the end of a bench, the table empty, I went to sit by her. She put her hand on my head. All the people around us in the farmyard, almost all unknown to me, relatives removed two and three times, seemed strange, as if, suddenly, I didn't know where they had come from. Though they wore the same clothes that everyone else in America wore—the women cotton housedresses and the men khaki trousers and big sports shirts with wide sleeves that hung to their elbows —there was a slowness of movement among them, and sometimes they seemed to stand completely still, my father among them.

I sat closer to my mother. For once, the strangeness of my father and his people made me feel distant from them, and I wanted to be close to my mother, who was as different from these people as a white woman from a Protestant country among natives of a country who had never heard of Christianity.

She had given up her country when she married my father.

But she had one Yankee Protestant friend, a woman named Eliza Tanner, whom she had met when, before their marriages, they were telephone operators. This remote period my mother sometimes referred to as the happiest in her life, and she retained from it a particular, elongated enunciation of telephone numbers, so "nine" became "ni-un." After she married, Eliza moved to Maine with her husband but visited her relatives in Providence, and on these visits she came to our house in the parish to see my mother. She came for a cup of tea in the afternoon, while my father was at work in the factory. I'd sit with Eliza and my mother at the kitchen table and wonder at the vivacity and clarity with which Eliza spoke. Her English did not have an accent, or, if accented differently from the English we spoke, the accent was, I thought, American. With her, my mother herself became vivacious and clear, and I saw in her someone I never saw otherwise, someone who had her own ideas about such issues as the marriage of priests. It always surprised and pleased me that my mother could see beyond what she as a Catholic had been taught to believe to what a Protestant believed, and to respect, and even to agree in principle with, the Protestant belief that married ministers better understood the problems of married couples than bachelor priests. That Eliza's daughter had married a Protestant minister, which made Eliza herself foreign to me, my mother found not at all foreign, as if she had, at some time in her life, been a Protestant and was familiar with their ways. Eliza always left before my father returned from work.

8

WITH MY MOTHER'S PROTESTANT FRIEND AND WITH Irish friends from the Irish parish where she would go once a week to join a group of women who sewed dressings for a hospital, I began to see how lonely she was in our parish, though she was supposed to be, herself, French. I saw how lonely she was in our parish and how she longed to get out of it, though she knew this was impossible for her because my father would never leave, and she would never leave my father. And she was as intimidated by the world beyond the parish as I was.

On a Saturday afternoon, after one of those confrontations in which my mother accused my father of closing her up in our house as in a tomb and he, on his part, said nothing—confrontations I had learned to withdraw from by going into my room and shutting the door—she came into my room and asked me if I'd go downtown shopping with her. Feeling how badly she needed support in her longing to get away, downtown Providence being as far as she ever got from our parish, I put down my book and said yes. It was the March end of the long, cold winter during which I'd been going to daily Mass, but I was losing the entrancement I'd so strangely sensed, and I too wanted to get out of the parish. We went by bus downhill from Mount Pleasant through increasingly dilapidated clapboard tenement houses towards the center of the city, and farther downhill past the white-domed and pillared State House in which, my mother told me, her brother, one of my uncles, had an office (he was, I think, state school supervisor), and farther down, steeply, into the small city, where we got off at an underpass below the train station. We never mentioned my father.

Whatever my mother came to buy was found in the big department stores, especially the Outlet Company, which had bare wooden floors and varnished wooden counters.

Going into a fancier shop, where she would go only if there was a sale on, she'd whisper to me, "This is an exclusive shop," and then bite her lower lip as if shamed by and also defiant of that exclusivity. A halo of self-consciousness would descend on my boy's head the moment we entered the exclusive shop, carpeted and with indirect lighting and full-length mirrors. My mother would whisper even more softly to me, "We've only come to look around."

On that Saturday, my mother stopped at the window of one of the fancy women's clothes shops and said she wanted to go in to have a look at the coats on sale. A black rubber runner with slush on it led to a glass door with a glass handle, and before I opened the door for her my mother informed me, with no one else to hear, of the shop's exclusivity. We crossed, in our overshoes, the carpet to the rack of coats on sale, and as soon as we got to it a saleslady came silently over to us. She was wearing a simple black dress and an imitation pearl necklace she kept touching with one hand as she unhooked with the other a coat from the rack that she held out for my mother to look at. My mother, who wasn't allowed a choice by the saleslady, stared at the coat in silence. She couldn't say she was just looking. The saleslady was taking too much trouble for my mother to disappoint her, or even offend her, by saying she was just looking. "I think this would suit you," the saleslady said, but still my mother, staring at the purple coat spotted with black dots, was silent. I thought the saleslady, because she was of that high class of people who worked in exclusive shops, had to be right. I wanted my mother to agree with her that it suited her. I wanted my mother to say she would buy it. I thought my mother shouldn't ask the price, which, on the level where we now were, shouldn't be an issue. The saleslady was doing my mother a disinterested favor by showing her a coat she, the saleslady, knew, with authority, would be my mother's best coat. I said, "It's a nice coat." My mother nodded. The saleslady said, "It doesn't cost anything to try it on," and this comment lowered her from the high class I had imagined her at, where money was irrelevant to real taste. Then I thought she said this to put my mother at ease.

As my mother took off her old coat, I saw, at the side of her brown dress, large black stitches where she had sewn up a seam that had come undone. The saleslady, I was sure, noticed the stitches. My mother had no doubt forgotten about them; otherwise she would never have taken off the coat and revealed them. That halo burned about my head and a sweat broke out on my small body. My mother handed me her old coat, and I watched her turn around so the saleslady could help her on with the new. "Have a look in the mirror," the saleslady said, and the three of us moved over to a three-way, full-length mirror, my mother in front, the saleslady to the side, I to the other side—all of us reflected in the angles of the mirror. My mother was wearing a woolen scarf tied under her chin. She swayed from side to side, so the purple coat with the black dots swung. "What do you think?" she asked me. She had to buy the coat, I thought, as buying would be the only way to excuse those stitches in the eyes of the saleslady. I said, "I think it really suits you."

For a moment, in the soft lighting of the shop, my mother, I saw, did think it suited her. Again, she swung the coat from side to side, and she raised her chin and turned her face from side to side, too, to look at herself.

Her face was smooth. "You really like it?" she asked me. "Yes," I said, "I do." Then she turned to the saleslady with a sudden fullness of confidence and said to her, "My son knows." The saleslady smiled at me. My mother said, "He is going to be a dress designer." I didn't say yes or no. The saleslady kept her smile on me. She said, "The best design-ers are men." "He says the coat suits me," my mother said. "I know he'll be a good dress designer," the saleslady said; "he's got taste." I wiped my cold, wet hands on my mother's old coat. My mother looked back at the mirror and opened the coat to see the lining, and in doing so she exposed the big crisscrossing stitches, which might have been the stitches of a great wound. Holding the coat open for a moment, she stared at that wound. Then she let the coat fall.

Silent again, my mother paid for the coat. I carried it in

a box. As we were leaving the shop, she said, having thought about what had happened, "I don't care." "No," I said. "She doesn't know who we are," my mother said. "No," I repeated. In the falling snow, we walked along the sidewalk, banked with snow that had been shoveled along the gutter. I said to my mother, "It's a long time since I decided I wouldn't be a dress designer." "You used to draw women's clothes," she said. "That was a long time ago," I said.

After we got home, my mother tried on the coat in her bedroom and looked at herself in the cheval mirror there. She frowned. My father, in the room too, said he thought the coat was beautiful, really beautiful. I was sitting on their bed. "Yes, it is," I said, but I knew that the coat was ugly and that my mother knew it too. She had bought—had, against her will, been made to buy—an ugly coat. She always ended up with ugly coats, the ones the salesladies couldn't sell to anyone else, the ones they knew they could sell to her, dumb cluck that she was, will-less as she was. A look of bitterness came over her face. "It's a good, warm winter coat," I said. I saw her face go smooth again, and she sighed a little. I resented that she had to wear that coat and felt she should not have to resign herself to it as she did. It wasn't her fault that she had to wear it, and perhaps it wasn't altogether mine.

9

WITH SPRING, WHEN I FELT THE GROUND UNDER MY feet where the ice had melted and when there seemed to rise up from the very earth a stirring restlessness, I not only wanted to get out of the parish, I felt I *needed* to get out, needed to get out of the darkness. And the more I needed to get out to go somewhere bright where the restlessness would be satisfied, the more there appeared in the darkness images from the houses and yards, the stores, the streets. These images appeared *because* of the surrounding darkness, were made vivid *because* of the surrounding darkness: a forsythia bush in bright yellow blossom, a dog in an empty cement driveway sitting quietly in its own shadow, the window of a closed grocery shop in which hung, by a string, a large bunch of grapes that shone in the brilliant sunlight.

I began to write down images. I wrote in English.

But behind my English was the French that was my native language as taught by the Mothers. And that native French was so much the language of our religion that my first reading book—*Mon premier livre de lecture,* with two copyrights: Droits réservés, Canada, 1935, and Copyright, Washington, D.C., 1940—made us believe that the very letters of our language had been given baptismal names. In the last few months of my last year of the parochial school, and distanced enough from those lessons as I grew older, I found them more interesting than when I had been taught them. I translated a lesson into English:

> All beings here on earth, men and things, have been baptized, that is have received a name that serves to identify them. The sounds that have been taught also have names, baptismal names.
>
> The sound that resembles a drop of falling water, *ddd ddd,* is called *D.*
>
> The sound that resembles an echo responding to little girls, *leu, leu, leu,* is called *L.*

The sound that resembles that made by a baby with his lips, *bbb bbb bbb,* is called *B.*

The sound that resembles that of a naughty child who cries pushing away something, *nnn nnn nnn,* is called *N.*

The sound that resembles that made by a little girl with her lips to show that something is good is called *M.*

The sound that makes you think of a passing wind, *vvv vvv vvv,* is called *V.*

Sounds of dropping water, echoes, wind, were given baptismal names in my first language.

Writing compulsively, I noted, on scrap after scrap of paper, the images—the sights, the sounds, the feel, the smells and tastes—of spring: the winged, pale green seeds whirling as they fell from the maple trees; a record heard through an open window; the damp, even steamy warmth of the sun; the smell of grass; the taste of a lime rickey at a soda fountain. Though I wrote in English, there remained within this language the baptized letters of my French religion, letters that always promised the invisible; but, as much as I tried, my English could not fulfill that promise, nor, really, could my French, not any longer, for I was losing my French. Because I was losing it I looked more and more often at *Mon premier livre de lecture,* which, more and more, appeared to have been the first reading book of a boy who was becoming a stranger to me. Yet, I continued to write, more compulsively than ever. Perhaps the impulse to write was the need, inculcated in me, to make the invisible visible and therefore possess the vast invisible. Because I would never be able to make the invisible visible, however, the need became a need to possess everything that was visible, and not only everything visible, but everything heard, everything touched, everything smelled, everything tasted. I must get everything in, everything.

And all that images demanded of me was to be aware of what occurred in the darkness around me, in which awareness I found a strange freedom, confined as I was by the darkness of my parish.

More and more, I saw emerge from the darkness mostly images of abandonment, as if abandonment were, finally, the fulfillment of the history of the parish. If I didn't ask myself then, I ask myself now why my observations were especially excited by a world that I imagined had already disappeared, the palisade fallen apart, the grapevines entangling the decaying timbers, battered pots and cracked plates in piles of trash, old trunks broken open to rotting clothes.

IO

MY MOTHER HAD A BROTHER WHO WAS A CHRISTIAN Brother, an order not of priests but of lay religious who taught young men. His name was Brother Leo. He had died before I was born, but she kept his photograph, which was on his funeral memorial card, on a shelf in a glass-fronted cabinet atop a desk.

This desk had a sloping front and drawers below, and above the cabinet of bookshelves was a pierced pediment. It was the only piece of furniture in the house that had any value beyond mere utility. My mother called it Chippendale. In one of the pigeonholes of the desk was a stack of envelopes containing locks of hair from the first haircuts of her sons, the name of each son written in pencil on an envelope by my mother: Robert, Donald, Raymond, Roland, René, David, Lenard. My parents had seven sons, the five oldest ones in college or in the armed services when Lenard and I were growing up. As a keeper of family records, my mother saved school report cards, a scrapbook of cuttings from high school newspapers in which my brothers' names were mentioned, and photographs. In her last years, she threw out most of this memorabilia.

In the photograph on his funeral card, Brother Leo, in a black robe with stiff white bands projecting from his neck, merged into a vagueness in which he appeared to float, but his eyes, staring out from behind rimless spectacles, were intensely focused. The photograph was propped against the books he had given to my family. Before this gift, meant to educate a family he evidently thought needed to be educated, there had been no books. These included such works, in small, decorated volumes, as *The World's Greatest Orations*. The fiction was in French, novels by Ludevic Halévy, Alphonse Daudet, and Prosper Mérimée, as though Brother Leo had appealed to what he assumed to be the native culture of the family. My father said about these French novels, *"C'est ça, la vraie littérature."*

As an expression of his elevated stature as a Christian Brother, that shelf of books gave Brother Leo enough authority in my family to convince my father that, though it would cost him, his sons should go, after graduating from the parochial primary school, to the high school where he taught, La Salle Academy, which was outside the parish.

After graduating from Notre Dame de Lourdes, I went on to the all-boys' high school at La Salle Academy, which, despite its name, was not French, for the Christian Brothers were an Irish order.

La Salle was a good half hour's walk outside the parish, and from within the world of a Christian Brother education, which was very strict, I now thought of our parish as being a little village in remote Gaul where, from time to time, a prefect with directives from the Imperial City of Rome would come to check up on us, but who left us, on his departure, to our own old ways and our own strange religion, a religion evolved over generations in such a remote, disconnected place. The prefect, in our case, was the Irish bishop of Rhode Island, who came to our church only for confirmation and whose attempts at French, with an Irish accent, we made fun of. At La Salle, I was no longer in that remote pagan village but in Rome, and the religion of the Christian Brothers was that of the Imperial City.

The Christian Brothers informed us of our obligations to obey the laws governing sex. The command was simple. A brother with a crew cut of bristling black hair and a stark black cassock, known for his strictness as Black Jack, shouted at us as if we were in boot camp: "Hands off!" He didn't have to explain what he meant, though not one of us would have admitted to another that his understanding of what Black Jack meant came from experience.

Another, gentler brother, his cassock always streaked with chalk dust, told us not to stay in bed on Saturday mornings, however warm and pleasant that was, but to get up as soon as we awoke and start a day of healthy and vigorous physical activity.

When I complained to my mother about the strictness of the brothers, under whose will my will would be subjugated for four years, she said, "One day, when you're out in the world, you'll be grateful." This obviously meant that out in the world I would always have to subjugate my will to the will of others in authority, even over my very body, which was no longer free. Her brother Leo had convinced her that going to La Salle Academy was a good preparation for me in my life. And if I said to her that sometimes I missed the parochial nuns and their stories, my mother would tell me, as one of the teaching brothers might, to shape up, I was too old for such stories, and this, coming from her, shocked me.

The Militant Roman Church, of which the Christian Brothers were soldiers, supported, absolutely, all the obligations of American law, in terms of which I must try to live my daily life. And my mother was, above all, American.

She didn't intend it, but her God won out over my father's God. Not that there was a decisive battle between them —my father's God simply, unassumingly gave into and became invisible within my mother's God, in the same way that the Canuck tribal parish, weak and helpless, simply and unassumingly gave into and became invisible within the englobing country of America. My father's Canuck God became, in its dark invisibility, more and more a shadow lost within my mother's superseding, all-too-bright, and knowing American God. Finally, God became for me an altogether American Catholic God, magnified by the globe that made him as visible as a shining, all-seeing eye high among the clouds of the American sky, aware of me for the civic and even military duties I was bound, as an American, to fulfill.

I was still a believing Catholic because I believed I had no choice. To believe in God was a civic and, again, a military obligation imposed as much by the Vatican in Rome as by Washington, both of whose combined power I was more than ever subjected to, for the penalty of disobedience to the laws of the Vatican was mortal sin and eternal torment and those of Washington imprisonment. I was an American Catholic because I kept the laws.

There were no ghosts, not even forests, in this Catholic America.

II

AFTER FOUR YEARS AT THE CHRISTIAN BROTHERS' high school of La Salle, I went on to Boston College, where I was taught by Jesuits. I expected the Jesuits to be more daunting than the Christian Brothers, but when, in my first class, I stood to answer a question, the Jesuit teacher told me I didn't have to stand at attention but could speak sitting, and this relaxation of the rules I was used to came as a surprise. The laws there were different.

At Boston College in 1957 courses in theology and philosophy were required. The courses in philosophy—logic, epistemology, and ontology—interested me a lot. They were all based solidly in the writings of Saint Thomas Aquinas, whose *Summa theologica* was the great and authoritative reference book.

(The philosopher whose writings most had to be refuted by Scholasticism because the writings were most contemporary to our times [by some three hundred years or more] was René Descartes—for his mechanistic view of the human, in whom the soul was reduced to the pituitary gland. But this view did not need refutation by me, for I simply had no interest in him. And yet I knew I was, inspired by Scholasticism, as regressive as someone who believed the earth was the center of the universe.)

Saint Thomas was above all reasonable and demonstrated the existence of God in five proofs, but even he said that his reasonable demonstrations could not of themselves convince a person who did not believe in the existence of God that he must now believe in him. All reason could do was to bring you along a road up a mountain to a deep gap, but to leap across the gap to God required an act of faith, which was beyond reason, and so beyond law and authority. This was where freedom was.

I read Saint Thomas with a sense of discovery and found something in the *Summa* that made me feel he, in all his reasonableness, was the saint who had the most to say to me as someone who wanted to believe in a God whom I would willingly leap over to with an act of faith, for this God would allow me freedom.

Incorporeal things, of which there are no images, are known to us by means of their relation to sensible bodies of which there are images. And so when we understand something about incorporeal things, we have to have recourse to the images of bodies, although there are no images of incorporeal things themselves. (*Summa theologica*, Ia.84.7.*ad* 3)

This not only made it impossible to think about God except in terms of images of him (even the most intangible of

images such as light and space), it also made all images em-
bodiments of a bodiless sense. I wanted to believe in a God
who was not only embodied in an image but also infused cor-
poreal images with all the grace of the incorporeal. He was
a God whom we could love only through images.

In winter-cold, snow-deep New England, I wanted to be
in the light of God, in the brightest, warmest, sun-tanning,
world-illuminating light of God. It seemed to me that, standing at the narrow gap that the road of reason had brought
me to, if I leaped over, I would find myself face to face with
a new God, that God whom I would see in the clearest images of brightness. And this was what I wanted.

In the circle of lamplight at my desk in my dormitory
room, I tried to think of images that would glorify this different God.

One winter day, this happened.

I was walking down by the pond below the campus. The
pond was frozen, the pine trees around it covered in snow,
which from time to time cascaded and sent a slight shudder
through the still, misty air. Through the trees I saw the
gothic tower of Gasson Hall, and I had the sudden, strange
sense—a sense more than a thought—that I didn't have to
search for an image of God because the image would occur
to me of itself. It was wrong of me, really, to search for the
image, because searching was a kind of intention, and no
image that revealed God could be had by intending it. What
I must do instead of looking for an image of God was to
forget about God entirely when I wrote down images that
struck me, such as the gothic tower of the college building
showing through the snow-cascading pine trees. I must, in

fact, forget that any image had any meaning at all—I must concentrate only on making images as clear and vivid as possible, and if there was any meaning to them, it would occur of itself beyond my intention. If God was in any way revealed in them, God would occur in them beyond my intention to see God revealed. My concentration on an image must be so pointed it must exclude any possibility of that image having any meaning—and exclude, even more, any possibility of revealing the glory of God.

I concentrated on images:

A book turned down on a pillow.

The way my roommate, Bob, crossed his delicate, long-fingered hands across his chest as he slept in the bed across the room from me.[1]

The soft heap of sheets taken from the beds of all the dorm mates by the women bed makers and piled at the end of the corridor, under a window through which the winter morning sun shone.

Such images drew me closer and closer to my senses, because the most vivid images were the ones that most vividly invoked the senses. And the images became all eyes, ears, mouth, nose, and touch. I wrote about images of the body that God as I knew him and at his most powerful would have condemned for having nothing to do with him, but only with the body. But if this powerful God still kept me from fulfilling my longings in sexual acts—acts that were as vague as

1. I did not understand my attraction to Bob, whom I loved. But I found my love most expressed in our kneeling side by side at the Communion rail in the chapel attached to the dormitory, receiving Communion, and, back in our pew, bowing our heads together in prayer.

my longings, but potent for being so vague—he could not keep me from inscribing images that struck me with a greater power than he had over any of my acts. I recall coming from a class along a path to the dormitory on a hill at dusk, again through falling snow and pine trees from which snow cascaded as I passed them, and seeing, outside a building in which were the changing rooms of the football team, a fellow student, illuminated at his back from light coming through an open doorway, standing naked in the falling snow, his body emitting a cloud of steam. This image made me stop for a moment to take it in with wonder at it, wonder beyond meaning, beyond even sexual meaning. I thought: I'll remember this for the rest of my life. It seemed to me there had never before occurred to me an image that dared me as this one did to fix it, to regard it, to revere it, to be the center of desires, making it more an image to devote myself to than any holy image I had ever seen.

If I couldn't have a God who blessed me in my senses of sight, hearing, taste, smell, and touch, I didn't want a God.

I certainly didn't want the American God, the God who saw all and, in his wisdom, privileged some and reduced others to niggers, white and black—niggers whose imposed duty was to serve the American God.

My realization of my God, now only potentially a God, depended entirely on an image. But what image?

12

BOSTON COLLEGE, IN A SUBURB OF BOSTON, WAS populated by the Boston Irish, a large, self-enclosed sect unto themselves, among whom I was clearly not Irish. And I did not know one other Canuck on campus, not one. I wouldn't have wanted to know any, for I was as far outside of the parish as I had ever been, and I insisted to myself that I would stay outside.

Alone, I often took the trolley from the terminus at the bottom of College Hill to go into Boston, which to me was a Yankee city. No one knew who I was. Out in the public among people who were most likely Yankee, I could, myself, have been Yankee.

I would get out of the M.T.A. station at Copley Square, and, thinking that no one would know I was not a Bostonian, I would go into the Boston Public Library, climb the shining marble stairs up to the reading room, and sit at a table and look up and around at the marble busts on the top of the surrounding shelves, all illuminated from below their chins, and there would come over me a sense of great possibility. Those possibilities, as numerous as all the books on the shelves, possessed me in just the way I was possessed by the aching need to read all the books. I would read them. I would possess my possession. I wanted, and I would have, everything.

But, sitting in the quiet, the movement of people soft blurs about me, I would suddenly find myself thinking of my family in the parish, and the person I most thought about was my father. I didn't want to think about him who had perhaps never been into a library, and certainly not the Boston Public Library. And an equally sudden awareness of myself pretending to be someone I wasn't would come over me, and I would leave.

This happened all over Boston.

Passing the equestrian statue of George Washington within the gates, I would enter the Public Garden thinking everything was possible for me. The garden would be dusky, almost deserted on an autumn afternoon. The peripheral traffic would sound hundreds and hundreds of miles away, so that, crossing the little bridge over the pond, I would pause at the railing and, placing a hand on it, feel that I was hundreds and hundreds of miles away, looking out over the water from which a thin mist rose. It would always come to me as a surprise to focus on a Japanese stone lantern on the brink of the pond, behind it dangling willow branches dissolving in the mist. Then, unaccountably, I would think of my father, and the belief that everything was possible for me would suddenly go in the knowledge that nothing was possible for me, however much I insisted it was.

(Instead of an inner resentment towards the Yankees for their superiority, for their having dispossessed the French of their earlier claim to possess the New World—years before the arrival of the Pilgrims [Plymouth, Massachusetts, had been claimed as Port Saint-Louis by Samuel de Champlain] —my father was in fact in awe of them. There were very few situations in which he had dealings with one or another of them, and when he did he was always the indentured servant grateful for his master's attention, eager for his master's approval, agreeing with everything his master said.)

In Boston, I would climb the steep incline of Beacon Hill, imagining I was rising to a level above myself, but a level at which I'd be indistinguishable from everyone who lived there. I would walk along the brick sidewalks, passing the fences of iron pickets before the brick houses with granite steps and many-paned windows, and I would imagine that were I invited into a party in one of those houses, I would be immediately assimilated in my Ivy League suit.

(That very suit, however, made me aware of my father. Before I left for college, my father and I went downtown together, perhaps the first time this ever happened and no doubt on my mother's insistence, to go to the Outlet Company to buy me a suit, as I didn't have one. I tried on the Ivy League suit, narrow, with narrow lapels and a thin stripe, and, looking at myself in a full-length mirror, I already saw myself as another person, a person who would have everything. But when, raising a sleeve to look at the price tag, I saw how much it cost, I shook my head and said to my father, "No, it's too expensive." My father said, "You'll have it." He was strangely excited.)

Walking around the fenced-in garden in Louisburg Square, which I knew was considered by the Yankees who lived there to be the hub of the hub of the universe, I would feel that I was at the hub of the hub of the universe, and that everything the Yankees had I must have. What that "everything" was I couldn't say, but it possessed me, and, more and more, I ached to possess that possession. Though I couldn't say what it was, my sense of the Yankee everything was of a brightness, not darkness; of great openness, not small confinement; of a world not limited by law, but made open by law. I would then notice a stain on the sleeve of my suit, and I would be overwhelmed by the awareness of my father's excitement at my having it, however expensive, and I would see myself dressed up to pretend to be a real Ivy League student —say, a Harvard student—rather than one at a Catholic college with fake gothic architecture. And I would revile myself: I'd have nothing.

(In the factory where he worked—the Nicholson File Company, which manufactured industrial files—my father was always on the side of management, centered in the owner, whom my father called The Old Man. Whenever there was any industrial dispute, even to the point of breaking a strike by his fellow bench operators, my father supported management. With, to me, embarrassing pride, he would, at our supper table, say, "The Old Man called me in today." The Old Man, a Yankee, was eager to get my father to organize an independent union among the workers to stop the takeover by the A.F. of L. My father wasn't successful, and by siding with the Old Man and breaking the strike demanded by the more powerful unions, he lost his job, and eventually the Old Man lost his factory.)

I would descend from Beacon Hill into the narrow, dim, traffic-tangled streets behind. I would peer through the iron picket fence into the burial ground of soot-black King's Chapel, then go down dark Court Street to the Old State House and the site of the Boston Massacre, commemorated by a plaque worn smooth and golden by automobile tires, which I'd look at hurrying across the street when there was a lull in the traffic. Passing down Congress Street, I'd go into Dock Square, circled by pushcarts selling tomatoes, oranges, lettuces, to Faneuil Hall, into the basement of which men in bloody smocks would be taking sides of beef and lamb, the protective gauze stained with blood. As I'd climb the steps to Faneuil Hall, a man in a gray dust jacket would open the door for me, and, inside, all puritan white, he would draw back the covers from glass cases to reveal early versions of the Declaration of Independence, with many blots and lines scratched out; reveal letters, coins, snuffboxes, and, in one small glass case, the very small, flowered, and frilled silk suit of Thomas Jefferson.

How, I would wonder, had the Yankees achieved such openness, as I imagined them to have, in the law? On a wall inside a spacious, simple, and light-filled Yankee church, marble tablets carved with the Ten Commandments, with its incised Roman numerals gilded, would appear to me not to threaten condemnation of the devout for their actions, words, and thoughts but to liberate them. How? And why did I believe they were open in a way I wasn't? Was their religion, their American religion, so very much theirs that I could only long for the same openness with no hope of ever having it, because to me America was a country of enforced laws under the American God who took away freedom? Did I imagine they belonged to another America simply because, unlike the people I was born and bred from, they had been born and bred in wealth and power and could do in their America everything that I couldn't do in mine? Did I imagine that *their* American God privileged them and enslaved me? Of course I wanted to belong to their America, of course I did.

(And so did my father. He always voted Republican because the Republican Party in New England was led by Yankees. He knew that the Irish, who were disdainful of the French, led the Democratic Party. The Yankees who led the Republican Party went to the French, who were disdainful of the Irish, for votes. More and more, the Yankees depended on the French for votes. No less a Yankee than Senator Henry Cabot Lodge, of Beacon Hill, assured the French that they represented one of the oldest settlements of the continent, that they had been Americans for generations, that their coming to the United States was merely a movement of

Americans across an imaginary line from one part of America to another, as if America were all of North America and altogether frontierless forest. But the Irish won the elections.)

I would, in Boston, go to places no one else seemed to go to, at least not at the times that I went, for I was alone in these places. I went up Hull Street to the top of Copps Hill and into the small cemetery on the crown. The bare branches of trees shook in the high, cold, whistling wind, and the long, wet, yellow and brown grass swayed. Over the rooftops of the surrounding brick buildings I saw the docks and ships, and, farther out, the gray ocean, from which a smell of salt and seaweed blew in. I had come to see the black tomb of the Mather family within its enclosure of iron pickets, and I envied all those Americans who were able to trace their ancestry back to this tomb, to this cemetery, to this center of the New World that they had inherited as that world's rightful claimants. I believed that I had no way of tracing my ancestry, which, in any case, would not allow me either the wealth or the power to claim anything. I was the son of a working-class immigrant from French Canada who did not know, or did not want to know, anything about his ancestry.

(Not only was my father a Republican but, as silent a man as he was, he ran for office, a minor office, but one that he was encouraged to run for by the party because he was in fact eloquent when addressing a rally in French. He ran over and over again, from 1930, when he was a young man of thirty-three, to 1954, when he was fifty-seven. He never won. In 1938 the man running for governor of the state was named Bill Vanderbilt. My father had a letter from Bill Vanderbilt, thanking him for the great effort he'd made during the campaign and letting him know that although they had not been successful in their quest, in pointing out the things that were wrong in the present administration, they had done their civic duty. This letter meant a great deal to my father.)

In Boston, I often went to the Museum of Fine Arts and, outside the main entrance, always stood to look for a long while at the green statue of an Indian brave on a horse, his arms outstretched, but loosely, as if he were facing his death, as if he were accepting that he would be a ghost. This statue drew me to it with a sense of what I could allow myself to expect, which I was otherwise not allowed to have in Boston.

I knew through my father that to romanticize the Indians, as not only my mother did but the Yankees did, was to falsify them; at those moments when I wondered about his Indian ancestry, I would see in him, much more than in myself, everything he was not allowed in the United States, for though my father made attempts to enter into Yankee America as a political supporter of a party that was alien to him just because it was Yankee, I believe he always knew that he would be defeated. He was not a Yankee; he was a quarter-breed Blackfoot Indian, which put him at an even greater remove from Yankee America than being French did, and as such, however much he never admitted this, I sensed in him a fatalistic acceptance of all defeats. My mother was right about Indian stoicism, but not as she understood it—never seeking redress for injustices done to him, my father stoically accepted defeat, and he did so without ever showing any emotion, by remaining silent, sometimes with a sullen impassivity that made his handsome face appear as stark as stone. I saw myself in him, but at the same time I did not understand his silence, which struck me as the silence of someone doomed who, eyes unblinking, accepted his doom.

He was a North American, but he came from a country that no longer existed, that had already succumbed to its doom—a country with no defined cities, without churches, without libraries, without courthouses, where no records were kept. And at a deep level he continued to live in that nonexistent country.

13

I WANTED TO GET OUT OF AMERICA.

In 1959, at the age of nineteen, I left America to go to Europe to study.

On the ship from New York to France, I met two people I was to see after the voyage, each of them so different from the other that my friendships with them could have meant only that I was divided; I was two people, as different in myself as my parents were from each other.

One was a teacher from a state college in the Midwest named June, and she, in her quiet way, seemed to me original. June had an oval, pale face, closed in by her dark brown hair that was parted in the middle of her head and that drooped down over her cheeks and was drawn back below her ears into a single plait at her nape. She hardly ever moved her head on her thin, exposed neck, but, to look from side to side at the other people eating at the table in the dining room I was assigned to, she moved her entire body, as if she didn't allow herself much movement. Her smile, too, seemed to be constrained by her facial muscles. She was serious. We sometimes walked the decks together without talking, or, after dinner, sat at a table in the bar, our talk serious. She always left to go to her cabin once the band started to play. Maybe— I'd sometimes think—she was not original but someone I had to respect because she was so serious.

We didn't see one another at disembarkation, though I looked for her on the platform of the train station at Le Havre while waiting among other passengers for the boat train to Paris.

When, in Paris, I saw a man, at a table next to me in a cheap restaurant, eating *boudin*, I thought: my God, my father relished *boudin*, which I had thought existed only in the parish. The sight of a man eating the thick black sausage brought me right back to my Canuck parish. And when, at the end of my meal, I asked for *une crème de glace*, the waitress, not understanding, turned to a woman at another table who said that *crème de glace* was the proper way of saying *glace*, and the waitress turned back to me to say that I was teaching her French. I was speaking the old French of my parish.

But I hadn't come to Paris to be brought back to my parish. I'd come to Paris for what I'd believed existed neither in the parish nor in America, and which, to me, was centered in the image of a bottle of wine on a café table with two wineglasses and, maybe, a nosegay of violets sold by an old toothless woman who passed among the tables with a basket on her arm, and who stopped before me, smiled, tapped me on the cheek, and called me *mignon*, which attention had never happened to me before.

My first Sunday there, I, obliged to go to Mass, went to a church, and in the voice of the old priest giving the sermon I heard the voice of Monsieur le Curé, the pastor of my parish church, and once again I was brought back to my parish, but now with an added pull that I resented. I had come to Europe to be free of the American God, but, to my horror, my Canuck God, who I'd thought had disappeared altogether, became exposed like a ghost that first Sunday in Paris in the shadows of the old gray stone church that smelled of incense and dampness. But the momentary apparition passed, and I left the church before the end of the Mass, which I had never before done, and went to walk in the Luxembourg Gardens.

Walking, I met June. She was, as I was, alone. We went to a café for something cool to drink. Paris, soot black, was very hot, and she, moving as little as possible as we sat at the table, appeared clean and cool in a white linen dress. She was of Danish descent and was thinking of taking a trip to Copenhagen to see where her ancestors had come from, and she asked me, with a slight frown, if I would be interested in going to Copenhagen with her.

I had never heard of an American whose "nationality"[1]

1. When, at the French consulate in Boston, I had applied for a visa to study in France, I wrote in the space on the form where "nationality" was asked for, "French," for that was what I thought my nationality was. The woman on the other side of the counter, looking over the form, said, "Then you don't need a visa." Puzzled, because I had always considered my nationality French, in the same way I considered friends whose parents came from Italy to have Italian nationality and those from Ireland to have Irish, I simply stared at her. She asked, "Where were you born?" "In America," I answered. She said, "Then you are an American and need a visa."

was Danish, so I considered her, simply, American, American in a way I wasn't: middle- or even upper-middle-class Protestant American, and, as such, equal to any American for whose political and religious privileges America was founded by the Protestant Founding Fathers—men whom I could never quite see as the founding fathers of my native country, but whose country overcame mine. I felt privileged by June's asking me to go to Copenhagen with her, and I said, sure, I'd go.

The trip took a day, a night during which we slept sitting up in our seats in the hot compartment, and another day, part of which we spent on a ferry across a northern sea.

Most of the time, we were silent because June was silent. When we arrived, I left it to her to find rooms at a tourist office in the train station. She couldn't speak Danish and had no relatives she knew of in Denmark.

Our rooms were in the house of a huge asthmatic man who told us, wheezing, that he didn't like his guests to visit one another's rooms. His eyes bulged so all the irises were visible in the bloodshot whites around them. "No, no," June said, and I said nothing, allowing June, as her right, to speak for me.

As tired as I was, and maybe because I was so tired, I felt open—as open as the vast northern summer evening—to the delicate strangeness and adventure of having, only a few hours earlier, arrived in a foreign city. June and I went out to eat, and I saw everything, even the knives and forks in the restaurant, as the center of great possibility, detached from anything as definite as knives and forks.

June was silent throughout our meal. I wanted to talk, but

I knew she didn't want to, and I tried to respect her silence, in which I had sensed all her originality by remaining silent, too. After we ate, I didn't want to go back to our rooms. However, June, very tired, said she must go to bed. The high sky was still light. I could have said I'd walk around on my own, but, as if I on my own wasn't allowed to walk the streets, I said I'd go to bed, too. We walked along a cobbled street where children, in a gang, were shouting at one another in Danish. As an expression of the sense of great, detached possibility I felt, I said, "I'm going to learn Danish." June said starkly, "You're not going to learn Danish." I said, "Just enough to get by." Irritated, she said, "You want to do everything, but you can't." I became irritated in return. I said, "I can," but gently, so as not to show my irritation. Suddenly, June had stopped taking me seriously.

We were passing a café, and I asked her if I could offer her a glass of wine before we returned to our rooms. She said she really was too tired. But I was determined to set right what was wrong, whatever it was that was wrong, and I said I was tired too, but, please, just one glass. She sat still with her glass of wine before her, and when she raised it with the stiff movements of her arm, it was just to take two or three sips.

All sense of possibility went. The realization that nothing was possible was always beneath the exhilaration I felt from time to time—now that I was *away*, more *away* than I had been in Boston—that everything was possible. The lights of the café shone in my glass. Nothing was possible, but I still felt that longing for everything to be possible, and this longing, because nothing was possible, was, as always, my agony. June could not in any way understand that agony, which, had I tried to express it to her, she would have seen only as wanting something that I should have known I couldn't have, that I should not have allowed myself.

I thought the only way I could put right what had gone wrong was to enter into a subject with June that was as serious as any subject could be. I said, "Sometimes I wonder —"

Frowning, she asked me, "What do you wonder?"

I could not have been more serious, more sincere, than when I asked, looking at her, "Do you believe in God?"

She answered, "I never have."

I didn't sleep well that night, sweating under the eiderdown. In the morning, I found June at breakfast in the dining room, my place set across from her. Breakfast was bowls of milk coffee and slices of bread with butter and peach jam. June asked me what I was going to do that day. I had thought we'd come to Copenhagen to be together. I had no idea what I would do on my own.

Perhaps seeing the bewilderment in my eyes, she said, "After breakfast, we can take a walk around."

"I'd like that," I said.

We didn't talk as we walked around Protestant Copenhagen, I with my umbrella, though the sky was clear. When I noted that the doors of a church were open, I went up to them to look in. I saw lit candles and an altar rail, and I said to June, "I think this is a Catholic church." She asked, "Do you want to go in?" and I said, "Yes, I do." She, Protestant, motioned that I should go in before her. I heard her footsteps behind me on the stone paving as I went to the altar rail, where, impulsively, I knelt and bowed my head. I prayed, if it was a prayer, to have my impossible longing, my agony, removed from me. When I stood, I looked at June, but she turned her head away from me quickly to study the altar.

I said, "I feel better now," but she seemed not to hear me, and I suddenly felt in her presence entirely false in what I'd done. As if she sensed my falseness, she turned and walked slowly back down the aisle, and I, embarrassed, followed her out of the church. In the street, she looked at her watch and said she'd like to do some shopping on her own. "Oh, sure," I said.

I hardly saw June the three remaining days we were in Copenhagen. By the time I got to the breakfast table, she was gone, though her empty bowl and plate with bread crumbs and smears of jam were still there. Perhaps she had gone out to see in Copenhagen, in the old part of the city, the streets, the buildings, the doorways and steps and railings she imagined her ancestors saw before emigrating, to try to connect, if only in terms of just one ancestor walking down such a street, passing such a building, walking up such steps, trailing a hand along such a railing. And she might have gone down to the ocean to see where her ancestors had departed from.

As intimidated as I was, I went out to see the city on my own, always carrying my umbrella with me and the notebook in which I kept my diary. I wrote that the bread was served with butter as thick as the slice of bread itself, and the women smoked small cigars. I wrote about being alone in the Tivoli amusement park at night, where I walked among crowds of people I didn't know, staring at couples with pale white skin and black hair who walked with their arms about one another and sometimes stopped to kiss. I noted the side of an amusement stall painted with stylized flowers and leaves, cables of red and blue lights strung from tree to tree, the dense darkness of the leafy trees above the lights and the scuffed, bare earth below.

I saw June at breakfast on our last day, but she said she would like to spend the day alone and left before I had finished. I wondered why she didn't like me and wished I could make her like me. Maybe she didn't like me because she saw how deeply insincere I was. It was her right not to like me, and her right to find me insincere. I took my time over breakfast. The house, with frosted glass doors between the rooms and a high, narrow entry and steep, uncarpeted stairs, seemed, as always, completely empty except for me.

Again I went out with my umbrella. I stood on a corner and studied a map of the city, but I couldn't concentrate. I stared up at a shop sign, a pipe painted on a board hanging from a scrolled wrought iron bracket above the doorway, and I thought I must put the image into my diary.

Then the longing, which I knew I would never be able to realize and that every attempt I made to realize would be realized only in a self-incriminating pretense because I *knew* I couldn't realize it, overwhelmed me.

I leaned against the shop's building, a plain, stucco building whose walls went straight down to the cobblestone paving.

After a moment, I studied my map once more and figured out how to get to the Rundetårn. Admission cost half a kroner. The tower had not steps but a curving stone ramp, and the inside walls were whitewashed. I walked up slowly and came out onto a view of green copper steeples and domes and sharply pitched red roofs, the gray-blue water of the sound beyond them. The sky was clear and the gulls wheeled around and around in it.

No one else was on the tower. I hung my umbrella over the railing, sat on a bench, and began to write in my diary. The bells of the city rang. It was eleven o'clock. I shut my diary and closed my eyes and thought, There is no God.

A sudden elation made me stand, and, feeling very light and bright, I walked around the top of the tower. The spaces appeared to open up more and more, open up with the greatest sense of freedom I had ever had.

Only the world existed, and in the world I would realize all my longings, realize them in all the vast, vast wonders of the world: in foreign languages, in gleaming knives and forks on either side of a bright white plate at a restaurant table, in glasses of wine lit up by café lights, in bowls of milk coffee and dense yellow butter spread thickly on bread with peach jam, in women smoking thin cigars, in fun fairs with stalls painted with stylized flowers and birds and with red and green bulbs strung through dark trees, in shop signs and shop windows and antique shops and bookshops, in squares and fountains, in pictures and statues, in everything I would see and note in the different cities of different countries all over the vast world. I would keep everything I saw, heard, touched, tasted, smelled, in my diary.

14

JUNE HAD GONE TO COPENHAGEN BECAUSE IT WAS THE capital of the country from which her ancestors had left to go to the United States of America. When I returned to Paris, where I rented a room in the apartment of an elderly woman, I was aware as never before that I was in the capital of the country from which my ancestors had left to go to North America, maybe not even then North America but La Nouvelle France. But I had no idea where in La Vieille France they were from.

In Paris, I felt I was, with my old French, a provincial colonial who, after generations, was in the capital to see the sites—the palaces and monuments and bridges—that his ancestors had seen. So, as I had imagined June walking about Copenhagen imagining her ancestors seeing what she saw, I went around Paris trying to connect the person I was with the person I had been when, say, the Louvre was still a royal residence, when the old shoe I saw in a glass case in the museum of Cluny was worn by someone, when the old vellum pages of hand-copied Gregorian chant for sale in the *bouquinistes* along the Seine were once bound together and used to sing in church services.

And even if L'Arc de Triomphe, Les Champs Elysées, and La Tour d'Eiffel had been built after my ancestors left, these all meant something special to me, more than they could mean to an ordinary tourist, *because* I was French, a Frenchman who was losing his provincialism, and the God of that provincialism, in the big capital.

Like a provincial determined to assume the dress and manners of the capital, I bought a cheap French suit, the jacket short and the trousers tight about the ankles, and shoes with very narrow pointed tips; I used my hand to start counting, not with my index finger but with my raised thumb; and when separating after hours in a café from the students who also had rooms in the elderly woman's apartment, I waved not by raising my palm towards them but by turning my palm away and folding my fingers into it. I was leaving my parish behind. Both a sudden focusing back on the parish and an equally sudden expansion away from it occurred to me when, in the Louvre, I came upon *The Burial of Atala*, the immense painting by Girodet, with Father Aubry holding Atala's shoulders to lower her into her grave and Chactas clasping her legs. It came to me as a vivifying shock, the sight of the painting whose meaning had been entirely closed in by my French parochial world but that now opened into the wide world of French history because it unexpectedly appeared within the Louvre, that vast, contextualizing depository of French culture. This wide and deep culture included my ancestors, wherever they had originated from in France, included their emigration from La Vieille France to la Nouvelle France, included French Canadian ancestors, and included, too, my half-caste French Blackfoot grandmother. I had every right to consider myself French.

I read a lot in French to make of my Canuck French what my aunt Cora called "the real French French, Parisian French." My Canuck French contained words that I was sure did not exist in French French, in Parisian French, such as an expression my father used when talking to his sons, an expression that I thought must have originated with him: *tsi gars.* He would say, "Your hairs"—a direct translation from the French—"need cutting, *tsi gars.*" I understood that *tsi* was a contraction of *petit,* but I had no idea what *gars* meant. I wanted to free my French of such parochial words.

Also, wanting to read into the large scope of French society and history, which I imagined I had the right to claim, I read the whole of the *Chronique des Pasquier* by Georges Duhamel, I read many of the interconnected novels of Emile Zola, and I set out to read *La Comédie humaine* of Honoré de Balzac.

In his novel *Les Chouans,* I found this passage, which I translated into English:

The word *gars,* pronounced *gâ,* is a remnant of the Celtic tongue. It has passed from Low Breton into French, and is, in our present language, the word that most reverberates with the past. The *gais* was the principal arm of the Gaels or Gauls; *gaisde* meant "armed"; *gais,* "bravery"; *gas,* "strength." These parallels prove that the word *gars* originated in the expressions of our ancestors. The word has an analogy with the Latin word *vir,* "man," the root *virtus,* "strength, courage." Patriotism justifies this dissertation, which will, perhaps, rehabilitate, for some people, the words: *gars, garçon, garçonette, garce, garcette,* generally banished from discourse as unseemly, but whose origin is so warlike, and which occur here and there in the course of this history. Brittany is, of all France, the country where the Gaullist customs have left the strongest imprint. The parts of the province where, to our day, the savage life and superstitious spirit of our crude ancestors have remained, as it were, most flagrant, is called the country des Gars. When a canton is inhabited by a number of savages similar to those who have appeared in these pages, the people of the country say: Les Gars of such and such a parish, and this old name is like a reward for the fidelity with which they strive to preserve the traditions of the Gallic language and ways; moreover, their lives retain deep vestiges of the beliefs and superstitious practices of ancient times. There, the feudal customs are still respected. There, antiquarians discover Druid monuments still standing. There, modern civilization is frightened to penetrate through the immense, primeval forest. An unbelievable ferociousness, a brutal stubbornness, but also faith in oaths taken; the complete absence of laws, of our language, but also the patriarchal simplicity and heroic values, make the inhabitants of this country's people as intellectually poor as are the Mohegans and Redskins of North America, but as lofty, as cunning, as hard as they. The place that Brittany occupies in the center of Europe makes it a greater curiosity than Canada. Surrounded by an enlightenment whose healing warmth does not penetrate, this country is like a frozen piece of coal that remains hidden and black in the bosom of a bright hearth.

I hadn't been wrong to imagine my parish as a remote outpost in Gaul. A little research revealed to me that the "country" where my ancestors came from was ruled by Romans from the time of Julius Caesar's invasion until the fifth century, after which refugee Celts moved in from Britain, bringing with them their language. That the "country" was originally named Armorica gave an ironical base to the revelation. Balzac offered me, however vaguely and however romantically, the distant right to claim France in one word that until my reading of the passage had seemed to me to have been exclusive to my father's limited vocabulary, and I tried to read my character into the character of those people Balzac described. Though a line from the Canadian anthem that I thought I had forgotten but now recalled claimed Canadians were born *"d'une race fière,"* I was not very strong or brave, and I didn't see myself at all as warlike. I could not see myself as unbelievably ferocious or brutally stubborn or with any faith in oaths, nor was I a person of heroic virtues. Where I did imagine an affinity with the people of the "country" was in my retaining deep vestiges of the beliefs and superstitious practices of ancient times, but this affinity was reduced to insignificance by the far greater affinity I imagined I had with them in their living lives in the complete absence of laws. That was how I thought of myself living, not only in France, but in the whole of Europe.

In Europe, I was free.

But my Europe, in which I assumed such total freedom, was not the Europe of Europeans I met; it was entirely mine. In their Europe, Europeans were subjected to laws I was unaware of, or, if aware of them, I didn't think they applied to me, such as the laws, stenciled with the dates on which they were put into effect, *Défense d'afficher* on soot-black walls or *Défense de cracher* in the Metro stations (I was not going to stick any posters to the walls or spit). Europeans had to carry identity cards and could be stopped by a policeman and asked for them; I reserved the American right not to carry identification, especially in Europe. They had to deal with complicated bureaucracy, even when sending a package by post;

I, in Europe, didn't live a daily life, had no social security number, did not pay taxes, was not duty bound by the military, did not owe loyalty to the state. Though I tried to look European, my romance with Europe was not that of an ancient, lawless Breton but entirely that of an American foreigner who wanted to be free of America. Whatever claims I imagined I could make, I was not French, I was not European.

But however pretentious I was, my pretensions allowed me happiness for the first time in my life.

I had more than a month before I was to start the academic year at the Catholic University of Louvain in Belgium, and I would, I told myself, take the fullest advantage of my European freedom. I would travel. I would see everything and record everything in my diary. I was an explorer, and I would discover my country.

Yet, rereading the passage I'd translated from Balzac's *Les Chouans,* which I kept in my notebook so that I would come across it often, I would, at the moment when Balzac compares the country of *Les Gars* to the inhabitants of Canada and Redskins, feel come over me a strange and at the same time familiar pull, drawing me back from my pretensions and making me see through them, to look away from Europe and out over the Atlantic Ocean to North America, not to the United States, but to Canada and the Redskins. I felt that I was drawn to a center and through it and then out of the other side of it into a vast dark space that was, perhaps, the country I lived in truly.

That was where my father lived.

In my letters to my parents, though addressed to both of

them, it was my mother I most thought of as I recounted my experiences. I wrote that I had been to Montmarte and seen in a nightclub *Les Nues osées,* which I knew would amuse her, both for my having been and for her pretending to warn me of the temptations of the flesh. Never having known it, she nevertheless had a sense of the freedom of being away, especially in the Paris she imagined, which was the Paris I wanted her to imagine: of wine, of cafés where everyone was a freethinker, and of dancing, daring nudes in *boîtes de nuit.* As a joke, I wanted to titillate her, but, really, I was not interested in the Paris I titillated her with any more than I knew my father would be. Not that my father condemned the temptations of the flesh; he seemed never, ever to be tempted, as if the flesh and its appetites were simple facts of life that need never be questioned.

I loved her, I loved my mother, and with her I could be light-spirited in a way I could never be with my father, so why, I asked myself, was I not drawn to her country in the helpless way I was drawn to the country of my father?

15

THE OTHER PERSON I MET ON THE STEAMER TO Europe, *le paquebot Le Liberté,*[1] was a singer named Gloria Stewart, whose passage was paid for in exchange for her entertaining the tourist-class passengers. She was traveling

---

1. The article *le,* I learned, was used because the feminine gender of the noun was determined by the masculine *le paquebot.*

with her two children, Harold and Debbie, and with them was going from Paris to Spain to sing in a jazz club in Barcelona. Every evening, just as the band began to play in the lounge, June would leave to go to her cabin. I stayed on, and I got to know Gloria. I did, I think, because she was so different from June.

Gloria was brilliant black, and, singing at the microphone, she wore a tight, white satin strapless cocktail dress spangled in silver. Her bare shoulders gleamed, as if lightly smeared with Vaseline, as did the slopes of her breasts, which appeared not to be supported by but to be loose in the pointed cups of her stiff bodice. Her entire dress appeared a fraction separated from her thin, soft, tender, black body, which moved within the stiff dress. Her black hair was dense, almost solid, and at the back looked as if pulled out in jagged points from the density. She wore dangling silver earrings. The spangles on her bodice shaking as her earrings did, she looked about the lounge as she sang, not at me but, maybe, for someone she was expecting, her irises as black as her pupils and little flecks of black in the whites.

When she stopped singing, I asked her to dance. She laughed and said sure.

I danced with her every night, after June left the lounge. Before debarkation at Le Havre, Gloria told me to write to her care of American Express, Barcelona.

Back in Paris from Copenhagen, I dared myself to write to Gloria to say I was coming, and I was surprised to have a letter from her telling me to come to a little town called Sitges, outside Barcelona, where she had found an apartment, cheap.

On the train, I was in a crowded, second-class compartment. Night came. Sweating, I tried to sleep sitting up among the others in the same compartment, illuminated only by a dim blue bulb overhead, but couldn't. No one could. From time to time one of the men lit a cigarette, and in the light I saw the faces of the other travelers. The women wore black kerchiefs and had callused, square hands they held crossed in their laps. A chicken in a burlap sack on the luggage rack moved. I couldn't imagine Gloria existing. Next to the window, I stood and pulled it open to breathe in the cold night air. All I could see was the looming outline of a high, dark mountain.

I understood when one of the women complained that the open window caused drafts, so I shut it and leaned my head against the dark, shuddering pane. I was two divided people, and each side was pitted against the other; the outcome, I knew, would be so violent it would destroy me altogether. That there could be no reconciliation between the two halves filled me with the nauseating possibility that the half that obeyed the laws and insisted on imposing the same obedience on the half that didn't would win, and I would lead a life of subjugation. And then, amazingly, the one who was lawless in me won, and I rested my head against the headrest, closed my eyes, and fell asleep. It was absolutely right that I should be going to stay with Gloria, the most lawless person I had ever met.

But, waking at moments and not knowing where I was, I felt, more than ever before in my life, alone and lost, felt, more than I had ever imagined it was possible to feel, *dépaysé*.

At the Spanish border, the Spanish passengers I had traveled with were, I noted, held up in long queues by the border police to have their documents examined, and I, my American passport in my hand, was shown to an entrance where there was no queue.

Spain was a country of laws imposed by a Fascist regime that I was mostly ignorant of or, if I knew of it, that I ignored.

From Barcelona, I took a local train with wooden seats. The sea appeared in the bright Mediterranean light. I had come very far. And it was odd that in coming so far I was going to Gloria. At every station, I stood to look out the window at the names of the towns. Coming, as I did, from a country of pines and oaks and birch, I saw, for the first time, palm trees.

As the train slowed down at a station, I spotted Gloria, in a man's white shirt, untucked and with the collar turned up at the nape, and tight black pedal pushers and espadrilles, waiting with Harold and Debbie. I waved, and they, laughing, waved back; I became excited and, on the cement platform, dropped my bag, put my arms around Gloria, and kissed her cheek. She, too, was excited, and she moved as if jiving. The kids, too, were excited, each in turn carrying my bag along the narrow streets through the white town. I was about to ask how they knew what train I'd be on, but in my excitement I forgot to. The sunlight on the white walls was so bright it seemed suddenly, as if shining beyond the possibility of the brightest brightness, to become darkness.

As if it were an expression of her excitement, Gloria said, "This place is a dump."

Gloria, I learned, always put down, offhand, the place where she was: Sitges was a dump, and they should move to Barcelona; Barcelona was a dump, and they should move to Berlin; Berlin was a dump—

I said, "But look at the flowers in pots everywhere."

"Yeah," Gloria said.

The apartment had tile floors and stark white walls, and all the furniture in the living-dining room, including the dining table, was covered with clothes, mostly evening wear, cocktail dresses and gowns and even a ball gown, and the floor was littered with shoes with stiletto heels. There were also large, glossy, black-and-white photographs, some curling at the edges and torn, of Gloria wearing the clothes thrown around, and one of the photographs showed Gloria, with a bouffant wig, turning so the gown swirled out about her. She pushed clothes off the dining table, and Harold and Debbie went out, then came back with plates, knives, forks, and a cold Spanish omelette. Debbie wore wooden clogs that rang against the tile floor.

Harold asked me, "Will you climb the mountain with us?"

From the open double windows at the side of the room was a view of a purple mountain.

"Yes," I said.

"Can I come?" Debbie asked.

"We'll all go," Gloria said.

She always said they would do things they never did do, but the kids didn't seem to mind not doing anything and sitting in the apartment, Debbie brushing her long frizzy hair and Harold drawing the mountain.

Gloria said to me, "I'll show you where you'll sleep."

I followed her down a long corridor with my bag, and I saw, through open doorways to the left and right, bedrooms with clothes thrown everywhere. Gloria opened a door onto a room that had in it only two beds and a chair between them. She and I stood together in the room, both looking about as if at what wasn't there.

She had to say something. She asked, "What bed will you sleep in?"

I felt a strange looseness in my body. "Any one will do."

"What about this one?" she said, pointing with a long, thin black finger with a long, clear, manicured nail.

"That's fine."

She looked about the room again, then at me, and asked, "What would you like to do now?"

"Oh," I said.

If she had not left it to me but had said, Now we're going to lie on your bed and have sex, I would have done it, there where I found myself.

"The kids are going to the beach," she said.

I looked at her.

She, too, looked at me, looked at me closely, and as if she felt a little sorry for me, she said, "You must be tired."

Hunching a shoulder, I said, "Not really."

Gloria put a hand on my hunched shoulder and, still more sorry for me, said, "Why don't you go out to the beach with the kids."

"You won't come?"

"No, I've got a lot to do here," she said.

Released from whatever it was she might have wanted

from me, I wanted, spontaneously, to put my arm about her and hug her and kiss her.

"Go on," she said.

The beach was three streets away, beyond a road along the seafront and below a stone seawall. Fishing boats were pulled up on it, and people in bikinis lay on the sand among the boats. My large swimsuit had a tartan pattern. High above the seawall was a tawny church tower, and as I, with Harold and Debbie on either side of me, ran into the sea, the church bell rang.

"People just got married," Harold said.

Lying between boats on the beach were two men, hairy and fat, one with a skimpy green bikini and the other with a skimpy blue bikini, which were shoved into mounds by their penises, the fingers of their hands extended towards one another and intertwined. The sight amused me a lot. Really, I thought, anything could happen here—two men, as I had never seen them do before, could hold hands while lying on a beach.

When the kids and I got back to the apartment, Gloria wasn't there. I said I'd have a nap and, in my room, wondered if I should shut my door or not. I left it open. I woke in the purple light of after-sunset. I found the kids in the living room, sitting quietly among all the clothes.

"Where's your mom?" I asked.

"Gone to Barcelona," Harold said.

Debbie explained, "She's gone for the afternoon show at the club."

"What club?" I asked.

"She sings in a club."

"Then she should be back soon," I said.

Debbie laughed, a high, delicate laugh from a delicate girl. "Afternoon means night here. She gets back about five or six in the morning."

"If she doesn't stay in Barcelona," Harold said.

I took the kids out for something to eat, and then we sat for a long while in the restaurant, sat in the stupor I imagined they often spent hours and hours in and that I was already getting used to. Finally, Debbie said it was time to go home, and she led Harold and me. In the living room, we again sat in a stupor until Debbie said it was time to go to bed.

In bed, I lay thinking that Gloria was free to do exactly what she wanted, as I was free to do exactly what I wanted. But, free as we both were, I suspected that Gloria had, until I arrived, seen in me a companion in her freedom; then, on my arrival she had seen that even before the mutual freedom was tested, I was not the companion she'd imagined I'd be. I had no idea what life she led in Barcelona, and I was jealous of whatever life it was, for I couldn't imagine it.

In the morning, I was woken by Debbie shouting at Harold, reprimanding him for something he should or shouldn't have done. She came to the doorway of my room and, as if reprimanding me also, told me it was time to get up. She led the way to a café for breakfast, then to the beach. She and Harold left me.

I rose up from the damp sand when I heard Gloria call me. Her white clothes making her look deep black, she was coming towards me with a white man. She was jumping around a little as they came forward. They were laughing.

As though I were part of her family, she said to me,

"We've got a guest," and she introduced me to the man—or at first I saw him as a mature man.

I held out my hand to the guest, who took it. He had close-cropped hair and black eyes with delicate lashes, and his lips, faintly curving at the corners into a smile, were full and yet delicately defined. Holding his dry, warm hand, I asked, "What did you say your name is?"

"I'll spell it," he said, and he spelled, slowly and with a strange accent, which was partly English and partly something very far from being English, "*O*, umlaut, *c*, cedilla, *i*, dot—Öçi," and he smiled despite himself.

Very seriously, I asked, "Öçi?"

"That's right," Öçi answered.

Öçi was in fact only two years older than me. He was twenty-one.

The kids came running across the beach to their mother, who had returned from Barcelona with someone they didn't know, which I imagined happened often but which excited them. Debbie immediately asked for his name with a tone of interrogating him, and on his telling her, she asked, "What kind of name is that?"

"A funny name," was all he answered, smiling.

We all watched—as if he were there to do exactly as he wanted—Öçi undress, stripping his body to a brief European bathing suit. With a slow leap, because he was capable of jumping in a slow and lazy way, Öçi ran to the sea and dived in.

Squinting in the sea glare, Gloria asked Debbie to give her her straw hat, and she put it on and rolled down the sleeves of her white blouse.

Debbie asked her mother, "Who's he?"

"I don't know," Gloria said. "I met him in Barcelona and asked him to come stay."

"What did he say his name is?" Debbie asked.

"I didn't understand," Gloria said. "Something like Archie."

"Öçi," I said.

"Oh," Gloria said. "I don't think I like him after all."

"You don't like him?" I asked.

"He's weird."

I didn't understand what she meant—so many people were weird to Gloria, and sometimes this was a compliment and sometimes it wasn't.

Gloria told the kids they had to go home with her. The priest would be there soon to give them lessons, and she bet they hadn't studied. They were going to grow up knowing nothing. Maybe she'd made a mistake taking them to Europe and should have left them with her mother in Harlem. Their father wouldn't look after them. They dressed silently and followed her across the sand.

When she reached the beached boats, she turned back to me and, as if remembering something she'd forgotten, called, "Are you all right?"

"I'm all right," I called back.

Then, turning away, she seemed to forget me.

Alone, I sat and watched Öçi emerge from the sea. As he came towards me, I thought he looked right at me, and I sat up more. Dripping, he sat before me, his legs crossed. His wet body shone as with a fine oil, an unguent lightly smeared all over his skin, and this shine made his body appear very solid. When he spoke, I was as attentive to the liquid pink inside his mouth, his tongue and teeth, as to what he said. Though he had never met me before, Öçi leaned towards me as if he had always known me.

"You're American," he said.

"I am," I said, aware of my own smile as he smiled.

"What kind of American are you?"

"What do you mean?"

"Well, all Americans are Irish or Italian or Jewish or Negro."

"I'm French," I said. And then I said, "I'm also Indian, American Indian, Blackfoot."

The look Öçi gave me made me realize I was more exotic to him than he was to me.

"Have you been to America?" I asked.

"No."

I asked, "Where are you from?"

With a slight sigh, Öçi lifted some sand then let it run through his fingers, and he said, "From everywhere."

"Where do you live?"

"Now, in Spain."

"Why?"

Öçi said, "I don't know myself, really." He brushed his hands against one another. "And so I'll leave Spain."

"And go where?"

Öçi turned towards the sea and said, "I would like to go to America." When he turned back to me, he smiled his smile with the fine corners of his lips.

I, smiling also, lowered my head.

He said to me, "Tell me about Gloria."

"I don't know much about her."

"You don't?"

"I got here just yesterday."

The fact that I had arrived only the day before interested Öçi. He asked, "Didn't you know her?"

"Oh, sure," I said. "I met her on the boat from New York to France. We became friends."

"I see," Öçi said.

He said we should go to a café, he wanted a drink.

The sun was setting when we got back to the apartment house. As I didn't have a key, I rang the bell without a name, and the door clicked open with no one asking who was there. The door to the apartment was open. In the late, deep violet light of the dining room, Debbie and Harold, at a corner of the dining table, were writing out lessons. Debbie said her mother was sleeping. Öçi and I sat in the living room, not talking. The room became dark, and though the kids turned on a light in the dining room, Öçi and I continued to sit in the dark until Gloria, yawning, came in and switched on a light. She was wearing a blue silk *robe de chambre* that clung to her sharp hips and was open deep between her breasts. Her hair stood out in points.

She dropped into an armchair, the back of it draped with a black dress hanging upside down so the straps trailed on the floor, and she asked, blinking, "So what do you all want to do?"

"Aren't you going to the club today?" Debbie asked.

Gloria made a gesture with a hand, which she left hanging loosely from her bent wrist. "That club is a dump. I keep telling them to get rid of the whores, but do they listen to me? But, yes, I'm going. I was asking, what do you all want to do?"

She had, it seemed, suddenly left Öçi out as a companion

to her freedom. He simply smiled, a smile that was slight but that accepted everything that happened as amusing.

Gloria left for Barcelona, and Öçi and I took the kids out to eat, after which they said they wanted to get back to the apartment; the priest was coming to teach them Spanish. This made Öçi smile one of his smiles. He asked what I'd like to do, and I, assuming as much as I could his smile, said anything he'd like to do. It was a hot night. He'd like a swim. We walked in silence along the empty streets, lit by dim bulbs under fluted tin shades attached to the stucco walls of houses, down to the sea, and, over the sea wall, to the empty beach. Öçi kicked off his loafers and quickly undressed and, naked, ran into the sea, from where I heard a splash, a sigh, and the exclamation "Oh, the delight." As I undressed, I became aroused, and, holding my top-heavy erection against my stomach, I ran into the sea, where I couldn't see Öçi, who had, in all the darkness, disappeared. He appeared, emerging wet and gleaming, near me, and in the pale light from the seafront I saw that smile. He then swam back to the shore, leaving me in a state of amazement at what was happening. When I got back to the beach, he was dressed. Turning away from him, I dressed quickly, my clothes sticking to my wet body, and turning back to him I now smiled. And, not with cold, I began to shiver.

The kids had gone to bed. My clothes still sticking to my wet body, I followed Öçi down the passageway to my bedroom. The door was shut. Öçi and I reached for the handle together. He put his hand on it first, then he went still. I, my extended fingers almost touching Öçi's hand, also went still. Öçi opened the door.

I began, more than to shiver, to shudder with an excitement I had never experienced before. Öçi shut the door behind us.

Moonlight shone through the one open window of the room, creating a wide beam that made the rumpled sheets of one of the two beds in the room phosphorescent; the other bed was in shadows. I said, pointing to the bed with the shining sheets, "I've already slept in this one," which made Öçi smile at me as if I were a child claiming his right to his bed against the threat of its being taken away. He gave me a little push, his hand on my shoulder, towards my bed, and he drew back into the slanting shadow cast over the bed on the other side of the narrow room. I stood in the bright moonlight, so bright I couldn't see Öçi beyond it, though I knew he could see me. I stood for a long time and heard him undress, throw his clothes on the floor, and lie on his bed, and I knew, by I had no idea what instinct, that lying on his bed with his hands behind his head he was watching me, probably smiling, aware that, trembling as I was, I was unable to expose myself to him naked—because to undress before him had to be to make myself vulnerable to him in the most exposing way possible, as if anything less would have him lose all interest in me, as little as I felt that interest must be. Maybe this was the moment in my life that required my daring myself as I never had before to do something that I had for years wanted to do, had for years believed would give me everything, everything, everything that I wanted; and I would do it, I would do it; I would, with shaking hands, unbutton my shirt and slip the sleeves along my arms and let it fall to the floor, kick off my sandals, unbutton the top button of my trousers and the buttons of my fly, feeling the cool air around my belly and groin, and lower the trouser legs and step out of them. I did it, and not only did I stand naked in the beaming moonlight, I stood with a full, lopsided erection that, as if already in anticipation of an orgasm, jerked a little. And then I lay on my bed, lay on top of the rumpled sheets.

Now I had to leave everything else to Öçi, and I had to because I was frightened that if I did anything more—if I got up and approached his bed, invisible to me—he would, laughing, say I had misunderstood him, and this most daring moment of my life would be the all-defeating moment of my life. I looked into the shadows where Öçi was in his bed, and a shock went through me when I saw him emerge from the shadows and stand, himself naked, in the moonlight. The shock engorged my entire body with daring, so I sat up. He stretched, raising his arms high above his head, and he yawned. He did not have an erection. I lay back slowly, the shock suddenly not one of risk but of utter defeat in the risk, when I saw him turn away and walk towards the open window. His elbows on the sill, he leaned out of the window, and I saw his head of bright, dense hair, his nape, his shoulders, and, as he turned away, his profile edged in moonlight, and I saw him walk through the streaming beam of moonlight towards my bed, towards me, his erection preceding him. My defeat turned immediately to the glory of the onrushing realization of everything, everything, everything I had ever wanted, with no possibility now of anything being held back, and I held out my arms to him.

No sensation, none, had ever been or would ever equal the sensation of his body in contact with my body. No sensation had ever been or would ever be as revealing of everything, everything all together, as his warm, wet mouth on my mouth. Nothing had ever been or would ever be as revealing of the wonder of awareness as our lovemaking.

In that narrow bed, the sheets twisted about us as we twisted about each other, the wonder was that with all my senses alive, they were alive, every different one of them, to every different part of him, so I saw, now, one of his eyes, then his clavicle, then a nipple, then his navel, then the glans bulging the foreskin, then a knee, then the heel of a foot; so I heard a faint but deep moan, heard the sound of bubbling saliva, heard the pull of sweating skin pull away from skin; so I touched, touched, then grabbed and then clenched the nape of his neck, his wrist, his cock, his ankle; so I tasted salt, sweat, armpit; so I smelled sun lotion, garlic breath, pungent body heat. And in having so much, I wanted more, and the more I had the more I felt that everything would come together into something complete, something even more complete than a body, something that, as if it enveloped the body, gave the body its completeness. I made love, made love with a passion that amazed me, for that completeness, for that more, for everything. I think my lovemaking amazed Öçi.

I made love for the completeness of everything beyond us, of everything out in the world there was to see, to hear, to touch, to taste, and to smell—so, making love, I saw, in flashes, a suitcase on a train station platform, saw a view of a palm grove from a train window, saw the sea through the palm trees; heard footsteps along stone-paved, empty streets, heard singing from an open doorway, heard low waves seething on a pebbled beach; touched the fibrous trunk of a palm tree, held a huge bunch of ripe grapes, dug my hands into the hot sand of a beach; tasted hard, spicy sausage, tasted tannin-tanged wine, tasted seawater; smelled burning bees' wax candles, smelled frying olive oil in a seaside restaurant, smelled sea breeze. And all of this would suddenly come together—everything, everything, everything would all come together, from the present and the future and the past, which past flashed with the image of a dog sitting in its shadow on a sunlit driveway, a flowering forsythia bush, a heap of mown grass, the maple trees shading my parish streets.

Making love, I was free, joyously free, in the sense of everything coming together of itself, far beyond my ability to bring it together.

I woke to the sunlight blazing through the open window onto the empty bed on the other side of the room with its sheets neatly folded on the mattress. I fell back asleep. I woke again, and it seemed odd to me that the sheets were still folded on the bed. The apartment was very quiet.

Naked, I got up, went to the window, and leaned out, and in the sunlight my body smelled as it warmed of a pungent odor, and I turned my head and pressed my nose into my shoulder to smell the odor more deeply. I didn't smell of myself.

Showered and dressed, I went into the sunlit living room, where Gloria, sitting in a square of light through a window, was combing her hair with an electrically heated metal comb attached to a socket by a wire, so steam was rising from her head. She was wearing her blue silk *robe de chambre*. Her face severe, she looked at me as I came into the room as if to reprimand me for having slept late, or for something.

I asked, "Where is Öçi?"

"He just left to go to Mass with the kids," Gloria said.

"Just now?"

"You want to go to Mass with them? If you hurry, you'll catch up with them in the street. But you've got to wear a shirt with long sleeves."

I put on a wrinkled shirt with long sleeves and hurried out and caught up with them as they were entering the church. Debbie's head was covered in her black lace mantilla, and Harold and Öçi were wearing long-sleeved shirts. Harold and Debbie each took one of my hands, and Öçi, carrying a *sac de plage* that was his overnight bag, led the way. We stood at the back, and I watched, over the heads of the congregation, the priest I had met the day before, in a green chasuble with a gold cross on it, saying Mass at the candlelit altar. Men and women were fanning themselves with open fans.

I whispered to Öçi, "Are you a Catholic?"

"Yes," he said.

I wondered not what the Mass could mean to me so much as what it could mean to Debbie and Harold, and, more, what it could mean to Öçi. If we were both Catholics, we were different kinds of Catholics, because his Catholicism allowed him, after a night of lovemaking, to receive Communion, and mine didn't. He went to the Communion rail with the kids, and when he came back he smiled at me and I smiled at him.

After Mass, the kids went to see the priest, and I walked Öçi to the train station.

He asked, "Did Gloria tell you that I'll come back next weekend?"

"I didn't really speak with Gloria."

"Then I can tell you—I'll come back next weekend."

We didn't say good-bye.

Gloria was still in her *robe de chambre.*

She said, "I've prepared breakfast for us on the balcony."

On the balcony a table with a white cloth was set. The cutlery and china gleamed. She told me to give her five minutes to get dressed. I went out onto the balcony and leaned against the balustrade, towards the sea, and I knew that if I leaned farther forward, leaned so far over that I wouldn't be able to draw back, I wouldn't fall but would fly out over the sea, more amazingly free than I had ever thought it possible to be. I turned back only when I heard Gloria pull a chair away from the table. We didn't talk as we ate but kept looking down the street at the sea, where the waves rose to points that flashed, over and over, in small, brilliantly luminous globes. Gloria poured more coffee into my cup and asked, "Did Archie have sex with you last night?"

"He did, yes," I said.

"Boy, did I get him wrong."

Gloria pressed her lips together and drew them in so they disappeared, and the space between her nose and her upper lip swelled out far, the two ridges of the narrow concavity forming a half circle. I thought the black flecks in the whites of her eyes jumped about. Her round nose twitched, and she rubbed it with a knuckle. She glanced away, looked back at me, glanced the other way, and looked back, considering me. Again her nose twitched and she rubbed it, then she kept her finger crooked over the bridge. She had painted her long fingernails red. She asked, "Was it your first time?"

"Yes," I said.

Dropping her hand from her face and letting it hang loose in the air, she asked, "Did you like it?"

I laughed. "I liked it."

She made a face. "I should have known," she said. "I should have made him go away. I should have protected you. That's the deepest feeling I have for you, you know—to protect you."

"Thanks," I said.

"Well, I guess you're on your own now."

"Thanks again," I said.

"Do you think about what your mother would say if she knew?"

"I don't think about that, no."

She laughed and said, "I'm your European mother, and I guess I say it's all right."

Harold and Debbie came in from Mass, Debbie still wearing her black mantilla over her head.

That afternoon we all climbed a mountain.

The next day, having said nothing to me, Gloria went to Barcelona, as the kids informed me when I got up. I asked them if they'd like to go to the beach with me, and they said they wanted to stay in and play. I could never make them do what they didn't want to do. I went to the beach alone.

Back in the apartment, I found Harold and Debbie walking along the corridor, he wearing one of his mother's strapless cocktail dresses and wigs, his lips coated with red lipstick, wavering on stiletto heel shoes. The bodice of the dress slipped down his smooth chest below his nipples, and he raised it. Behind him, Debbie, her hair shoved under a knitted cap, was wearing my clothes, a shirt and trousers rolled up at the bottoms, and my shoes.

"What are you two doing?" I asked.

Debbie said, "We're playing queers."

From my bed, I heard Gloria come in, singing, as dawn was rising. I thought I heard a man's voice in the midst of Gloria's singing, and I listened, but I imagined I'd made a mistake, as I didn't hear it again. But I did hear Gloria laugh.

Again, I slept late, and when I awoke, Gloria again was gone. So were Harold and Debbie, who, I felt, lost interest in me and went off on their own, I didn't know where.

I was alone most of the week. Saturday, I went in the early afternoon to wait in the train station, though I didn't know if Öçi was supposed to arrive. I saw, past the ticket controller, the trains pull into and leave on the platform. Whenever a train stopped, I went to the entrance and onto the platform. The doors opened, people descended with bundles, then the doors slammed shut and whistles blew, and the brown, dusty train with dirty windows started off slowly. Many, many trains stopped and then left.

The sky clouded over and rain fell. I stood at the entrance to the station facing the square. The rain was falling heavily, so the drops exploded on the square as if in silver flashes, and through the flashes a young man on a bicycle pedaled fast in one direction, and going in another direction an old man, holding a burlap sack over his head with one hand, was goading the donkey he was riding to go faster.

I stared out, and as I did I sensed myself more and more removed from what I saw, but the greater my sense of removal the more acute became my awareness of what I saw. I stared, as if from a far, far distance, at a lottery ticket on the ground near me, at a burnt matchstick, at the petals of a crushed geranium blossom. I thought I wouldn't be able to touch the stone of the wall I was next to if I reached my hand out to it, because it appeared to me so far away, and yet I was aware of the faint chisel marks in it.

The rain stopped, and I thought, Öçi isn't coming and walked back to the apartment.

Debbie was brushing her hair. She asked, "Where were you?"

"I was out."

"Archie came," she said.

"Did he?"

"He waited for the rain to stop, and then he went out to buy some food for supper. Harold went with him. We didn't know where you were. Archie wondered if you were gone."

"Gone where?"

"People go," Debbie said.

I heard the door to the apartment open and Öçi's voice speaking to Harold in Spanish. Harold came into the room first, and he turned round to Öçi and said, "Here he is," and Öçi came in.

I traveled with him around Spain, staying in cheap hotels. I remember a funeral procession, the black, plumed horses pulling a glassed-in hearse through which the black coffin showed, and the line of mourners, in black, following, all along the avenue above a beach, where we lay side by side, our shoulders touching. I remember the smell of suntan lotion from loosely clothed people in narrow, white streets, and the feel of the paving on bare soles and the sensation of dry salt on sunburned skin. I remember a large fish on a table. I remember waking in the morning to the wailing singing of a man on a donkey passing below the balcony of the hotel room. I remember a basket of oranges.

I remember a walk to a village without electricity and the candlelit windows of the small houses. I remember coiled rope. Patches of machine oil on cement. A rusty pickup truck. An iron grille gate. Dusty cactuses. Shrimp tails dropped on the pavement under café tables. A shoeshine boy. The window of a taxidermist's shop filled with stuffed animals. The shadows of a colonnade. A lawn in a square. A canary in a wooden cage. A flower stall. A fat woman with small hands and feet, dancing with quick, taut gestures while a man tapped a table and called out, "Olé." A bicycle in a courtyard. A Gypsy woman with ear lobes shredded because of earrings that had been pulled through them, the gold rings now piercing the sides of her ears, she carrying a baby in a sling. An earthenware jug. Two fried eggs. A bread roll with chocolate. I remember disordered sheets.

I remember going with him to visit the high, vast chapel in a mountainside to honor the Fascist dictator; it was dug by Republican prisoners of war forced into slavery. The chapel was dominated by a cross.

16

I WENT NORTH TO BEGIN MY SCHOLASTIC YEAR AT THE Catholic University of Louvain, Belgium, and I wished all the while that I was in Spain. I lived in a room with a chamber pot in a cabinet beside the bed, the French windows of the room looking out over a sandy square on the outskirts of the old town. Though I got to know other students—in particular three other Americans—I was different from them, I felt, because I had been to Spain and fallen in love and they had not. I so often talked to them about Spain, my Spain, that they said something must have happened to me there, more than one attendance at a bullfight, to make me want so much to go back. Had I fallen in love? I laughed and said no, no.

The Belgian autumn was motionless with gray mists, and every morning started with my looking out a window through that motionless mist at a cabbage patch in the back garden. I walked through the morning mist to the lectures, given in a small, cold, wood-paneled lecture hall, the professor of philosophy at a podium that was like a pulpit (his first lecture was on the origins of Greek philosophy, which he said had begun with the ancient Greeks pondering sea waves and wondering how things change and yet remain the same), and while the other students, wearing scarves and suede jackets, took notes, I thought of Spain.

I thought that the philosophical problem Spain posed was that objects—a beach pebble, a bunch of grapes, a coffee cup—appeared, in the Spanish sunlight, to be so intensely unique, how was it possible to generalize from them into an idea that included all beach pebbles, all bunches of grapes, all coffee cups? It was as if the harsh, dry, brilliant sunlight of Spain gave to each and every object of Spain—the pebble on the beach, the bunch of grapes on the vine growing over the stone wall, the coffee cup left on the café table—the hallucinatory impression of there being *only* that pebble, that bunch of grapes, that cup. In Spain, the sunlit particularity of every object denied the reality of the very *idea* of pebble, grape, cup, so the presence of each object appeared totally, amazingly unique, incapable of being abstracted into an idea. And in Spain I had made love for the first time ever, which resisted every attempt I made to give it a meaning.

In the university lecture hall, where there were nuns and seminarians attentive to the professor, I, longing to be back in Spain, was attentive to my own metaphysical query of how the experience of lovemaking, which had been the most amazingly unique experience of my life, could never, ever be anything but a unique experience, could never, ever be abstracted from the bodies making love into even a real recollection of lovemaking, much less a *concept* of it.

The reality of our lovemaking was so much unto itself that I could not even imagine it repeated; it was *fixed* in the details of a stark, white-walled hotel room with a Spanish-tiled floor, of a bentwood chair on which were thrown light summer clothes, of a scattered pair of leather moccasins and sandals, of a dog barking outside in the far, moonlit distance—all of these *fixing* the event as having no other event in the past to refer itself to what was in any way similar, as having no other event in the future to refer itself to what would be similar, as having no other event in all of human experience to refer itself to what would be similar. To categorize the event in any way—as, say, sex between two boys —never occurred to me.

Öçi was Öçi, and even his sex was his sex and no one else's, and he, being uniquely who he was, made me, at least in terms of his attraction to me, uniquely me. Our sex was ours and no one else's, and I loved him as passionately as if we in all the world were the only two people to be mutually attracted to one another sexually, and who had met and made love as no two people had ever, ever made love.

As desperate as I was to make love again, I could imagine lovemaking only with Öçi. I was in love with Öçi and could not love anyone else. And yet, I had had, making love with Öçi, the overwhelming sense that *something* would occur in the lovemaking that would give it a universal meaning, that some sixth sense would unite all my five senses and make lovemaking all inclusive, make complete the many, many details I recalled of our nights, our mornings, our afternoons in hotel beds together: the thin gold chain, without a medal, hanging about his neck.

But the more I tried to understand *something* about my love for Öçi—*something* about our making love over and over, slowly, our skins as if made smooth by an exuding unguent—the more closed in on itself it became and, as the days and weeks passed since I had left Öçi, the stranger our lovemaking became in my imagining it. Why did something so real become so strange?

Was it because the beach pebble, the bunch of grapes, the coffee cup, and the act of lovemaking had, in fact, their own reality, a reality that appeared to me unreal because, being unique, I couldn't get to it with my generalizing mind, so the reality existed with great and singular intensity but was impenetrable to me? The pebble, oval and smooth and gray and slightly porous, had a profound meaning, but, because the meaning was closed to me by the pebble's uniqueness, the meaning was beyond comprehension, and the very incomprehension made the pebble unreal. And so, too, did the act of lovemaking, for its total uniqueness, have a profound but incomprehensible meaning.

On my arrival in Louvain, I had written to him in Spain, where he lived in the town of Reus—doing what, I wasn't sure, because Öçi kept what he considered the least interesting aspects of his life, such as work, vague—but he hadn't yet responded. That I didn't have a letter from him made me imagine that, instead, he would appear in Louvain. I imagined, even, that he missed me so much—more than I missed him—he had to come to me. At a lecture, thinking of Öçi on the beach at Sitges, I would suddenly imagine that a student in a suede jacket and scarf around his neck in front of me had the same head as Öçi; or, in a café with my American friends drinking *vins chauds,* it would strike me, with a pointed sense of its being about to happen, that Öçi was going to enter; or, on my return from a lecture, I would find him sitting in the narrow park I passed through every day, where, even when the sun shone, mist hung in the shadowed bushes, and we'd sit together under the brick tower of Jansenius and talk and then go to my room and undress and get into the large, sagging bed and make love.

If I heard in the student restaurant a table of students speaking in Spanish, the sudden impulse would come to me to go, myself, to Spain, to Reus, and knock on Öçi's door. I started lessons in Spanish, and I kept on the table in my room that served as a desk a little earthenware Spanish jug, a saucer from a Spanish café, and a shell from a Spanish beach, all of which kept me in touch with not only Spain but Öçi in

Spain. He had given me the little jug; the saucer came from a café where we'd had drinks, which were accounted for by a pile of saucers, each saucer representing a drink; the shell came from the beach where I had lain next to him, our shoulders touching, as always when we lay together.

The intensity of the particularity of these objects should have made the very objects unbearable to themselves, to their very particularity, should have made them expand beyond themselves to become generalizations of themselves, to become forms, forms that rose and rose and rose from every single object to meet in those Platonic forms that made it possible to have such ideas as earthenware jug, saucer, seashell. But there were no such forms, there were no such comprehensive ideas as earthenware jug, saucer, seashell. There was only getting every earthenware jug in, every saucer, every seashell, each and every one unique; there was only getting everything in, the only alternative being to leave everything out.

From Ernest Hemingway's *Death in the Afternoon:*

If I could have made this enough of a book it would have had everything in it. . . . It should make clear the change in the country as you come down out of the mountains and into Valencia in the dusk on the train holding a rooster for a woman who is bringing it to her sister; and it should show the wooden ring at Alcira where they dragged the dead horses out in the field and you had to pick your way over them; and the noise in the streets in Madrid after midnight, and the fair that goes on all night long, in June, and walking home on Sundays from the ring. . . . It should have the smell of the burnt powder and the smoke and the flash and the noise of the traca going off through the green leaves of the trees, and it should have the taste of horchata, ice-cold horchata, and the new-washed streets in the sun, and the melons and beads of cool on the outside of the pitchers of beer; the storks on the houses in Barco de Avila and wheeling in the sky, and the red-mud color of the ring; and at night dancing to the pipes, and the drum with lights through the green leaves and the portrait of Garibaldi framed in leaves. . . . There ought to be Astorga, Lugo, Orense, Soria, Tarragona, and Catalayud, the chestnut woods on the high hills, the green country and the rivers, the red dust, the small shade beside the dry rivers and the white, baked clay hills; cool walking under the palms in the old city on the cliff above the sea, cool in the evening with the breeze; mosquitoes at night, but in the morning the water clear and the sand white; then sitting in the heavy twilight at Miro's; vines as far as you can see, cut by the hedges and the road; the railroad and the pebbly beach and tall papyrus grass. There were earthen jars for the different years of wine, twelve feet high, set side by side in a dark room; a tower on the house to climb to in the evening to see the vines, the villages and mountains, and to listen to hear how quiet it was. In front of the barn a woman held a duck whose throat she had cut and stroked her gently while a little girl held up a cup to catch the blood for making gravy. The duck seemed very contented, and when they put her down (the blood all in the cup) she waddled twice and found she was dead.... No. It is not enough of a book.

Students in Louvain gathered in a dive, where they drank Stella Artois and got drunk, and I could have gone there with the intention of finding *someone* who might have gone there to find someone like me. Or I could have taken the short train ride to Brussels to search out cafés where I might have found *someone*. But this never even occurred to me as a possibility, one I would have been too shy to have acted on in any case. I didn't want to make love with *someone*. I wanted to make love with Öçi.

I wrote to him again but got no reply.

I wrote day after day in my diary—the entries, as October darkened into November, more and more desperate about sustaining my sincerity in truly loving Öçi. Sustaining this sincerity exhausted me, made me unable to sleep, reduced me to lying on my bed and weeping. But no expression, no gesture I could think of, even an attempt to kill myself, could, I knew, convey the sincerity, not, certainly, to myself, and there was no one else to whom I could try to convey this sincerity but Öçi—and even if he were present, he would be the last to believe it.

The moment I tried, obsessively, to find that expression, that gesture, it would come over me, with a sudden sense of weakness through all my body, that as the expression and gesture had to come from *me*, and as everything that came from *me* was false, any expression, any gesture, no matter how passionate, would be false. For the expression and gesture to be true, some force from outside me, much vaster and stronger and greater than I was, must overwhelm me and *force* from me the expression, the gesture.

I had no letter from Öçi, but I had many from Gloria.

Gloria wrote that her husband, in America, had been jailed for two to three years, she didn't know why, so it was left to her to support her family, which meant having to sing at a jazz club in Barcelona every night for five bucks, just enough to keep the apartment at Sitges and feed the kids and pay her fare back and forth from Sitges to Barcelona. Maybe she should leave Spain and go to England, to London. Then she wrote she'd stay in Sitges after all because she was having an affair with the priest who was teaching the kids. After a gap, I had a letter from her in which she wrote that she was in a Spanish prison: some people from the club, people I had met and played craps with at the club bar, had planned to rob a grocery store, one of them with a gun just to threaten the grocer, but when the grocer pulled out a knife, the guy with the gun shot and killed the grocer. The police rounded up everyone at the club, innocent or not, and put them all in jail, including Gloria. Being in jail on suspicion wasn't so bad— she just refused to sew mailbags, and no one forced her to— but she was worried about the kids, who were living alone without money. She hoped the priest would take care of them. She was, she wrote in another letter, released from prison but was made persona non grata, and she had to leave Spain with the kids. She'd be taken with them to the Spanish border, from where she'd somehow get to Berlin, where she thought she'd be able to get a job singing in a club. But, really, she wanted to go to London. In all her letters, she wrote that she missed me a lot and wished that I could go to Berlin with her, where she would take care of me. She wondered if I had a girlfriend yet.

Then I had a letter from Öçi, in a thin blue envelope with British stamps.

We are two different persons. I accepted you as you were, although perhaps I would have preferred you to be different, and I will continue to accept you as you are and as you will be, I never did and never will expect you to change from what you are.

I noted that his English was awkward. What he had to say about me was incidental to his being in London, where, tired of being a stateless person with only travel documents that made him persona non grata in most countries and gave him trouble in countries where he was nominally persona grata, he would try to get a British passport, and if he got it he would, with that in hand, eventually go to America.

As he was in London, there was no other place for me to be but London also. When I wrote to him that I would come, he wrote back—with calm acceptance of what I wanted to do—that I should telephone him when I arrived.

Victoria Station, vast, seemed to be constructed of high, black iron girders that supported nothing but darkness above; all the light there was at about eye level, yellowish and dimly diffused in the cold, soot-smelling air. At a row of telephones, I asked an old woman next to me to please help me make a call, and she instructed me to insert, just a little way in, my large tuppence coin into a slot, then dial, and when I heard a *peep-peep-peep* to press the coin all the way into the slot. Öçi answered, and with the sound of his voice, the foreignness of which I had forgotten, I felt London, the immense and unknown city of London, open up about me with a great sense of possibility.

But he closed down that sense of possibility by saying that as it was late, I should find a hotel, and we would meet the next day.

My mind went blank, and I thought: You were a fool to come.

He suggested a hotel in Dorset Square, where I slept so late into the next day someone knocked on my door to make sure I was all right. I waited in the small lobby for Öçi to appear, which he did from the winter dusk. Seeing him, I began to shiver, which he must have sensed when he embraced me briefly and kissed me on both cheeks. He stepped back and said we'd have a meal together, then go to the theater. I would do anything he said, anything.

In the Indian restaurant, my silence was heavy and weighed down, and it reduced to silence every effort he made to talk. But what he wanted to talk about—plays, ballets and operas, films, books—I had no interest in. And he made it clear that he did not want to talk about what I wanted to talk about.

The central image of the play was a white horse appearing in darkness.

On the underground train to Baker Street, we sat side by side in an empty carriage, our shoulders touching. I had to hold myself back from putting my arm around his shoulders and often felt my elbow jerk with the almost irresistible urge to do just that. But I stared at him while he, his head lowered, stared at the floor.

Outside the Baker Street station, he said he would take a bus to Swiss Cottage, and I waited with him at the stop, near a street lamp. We were standing close, our breaths steaming in the damp air. I continued to stare at him and he continued to stare away.

Suddenly I said, "I have to kiss you."

He turned and walked away. I followed. We walked together.

He said, "I hadn't intended to bring this up."

"I know," I answered. "I know it was a stupid thing for me to come to London, but I couldn't help myself."

We were walking quickly, or he was and I was keeping up with him. He said, "I have to insist that I can't be anything towards you but a friend."

"I know."

"I can't help you."

I stopped and he stopped with me. "I wish to God you could."

"You have the wrong idea of me. I'm not what you think I am."

"I don't have any idea of you, none. All I have of you is you, here, standing here."

"I could act in a way that would give you an idea of me that you wouldn't like, that would make you see I'm not what you imagine I am."

"You couldn't. You'd remain what you are to me."

"But do you want to remain as you are, wanting something that you know you can't have?"

"No," I said, then, "yes, yes, I do."

"I could make you stop wanting it."

"No, don't do that."

We were speaking in flat voices.

I asked, "Where do you get your bus?"

We walked on to the bus stop in silence, and again I waited with him.

He asked, "What is it about me that makes you feel the way you do about me?"

I shrugged my shoulders.

"You don't know?"

"No."

As we waited, he walked restlessly back and forth. "You don't have to wait," he said. "Why don't you go back to your hotel?"

"Yes," I said.

He tapped me on the shoulder.

"I don't feel sorry for you," he said.

"I'm not asking you to."

"Will you ring me tomorrow?"

I didn't answer but walked away. I was halfway down the block when I heard him call me, and I turned and waited. He walked towards me. He said, "You won't do anything stupid, will you?"

Smiling, I said, "No, of course not."

He said, smiling also, "I thought I saw the white horse coming out of the darkness," then he left, running to get back to the stop because the bus was approaching, and I, very tired, returned to my hotel room. I slept deeply.

Ringing Öçi the next morning, I woke him. He said he

didn't know what he was going to do that day and that I should ring him again around noon.

I said, "I feel much better this morning," though in fact I felt worse.

"That's good," he said quietly.

I said, "You sound tired. Please rest."

"Yes," he said, as if surprised by the presumption of my solicitude, "of course I will."

I hung up telling myself that this must be the last time I would talk to Öçi, that I must not give in and telephone him again because he did not want me to telephone him again.

I thought, I've got to stop loving Öçi, I've got to.

I waited until noon but didn't telephone Öçi, though I hoped he would telephone me. I'd give him a half hour past noon, I thought, still hoping he would telephone me. He did, and asked if I'd like to meet him and some of his friends in a pub, and I suddenly did feel better, so suddenly I was surprised.

This is what happened.

I met him and his friends in a pub off Saint Martin's Lane. His friends were all from different places—Israel, Hungary, Pakistan, Holland[1]—and they all seemed to like me, like me so much that with Öçi smiling his smile as he watched, they joked with me, calling me an American beauty and touched me on the shoulders, the chest, the hips. One, the Israeli, with an effeminate, undulant movement of his entire body, swung

---

1. Öçi, I learned, was originally from Turkey, but of a Greek mother from the Pontus and a father from Hungary, which was as incomprehensible to me as his statelessness.

the end of his long scarf lightly across my face. And the Dutch young man, tall and slender, with clear, bright features and wearing a dark blue blazer and a striped tie, asked me, rather formally, if I'd like him to be my guide in London, which I, with a lilt in my own assumed formality, said I'd like very much.

But each time, I made love with someone different—made love with someone in a bed, over a night, over a day and a night, each of us fully and unreservedly exposed to each other in our naked bodies, as happened in London, as happened later in Paris, as happened on *Le Liberté* on my way back to America after the year abroad—I had the overwhelming sense, a sense that I sometimes thought was the very reason for my making love, of all the details coming together with the promise of everything in the world coming together, but coming together in a way I would never understand, because everything was too much for me. I would never be able to get everything in; but neither would I be able to leave everything out.

17

THE FIRST SUNDAY AFTER MY RETURN A YEAR LATER, I went to Mass with my mother and father. My younger brother, Lenard, was away at college, and my older brothers, most of them now married or retired as bachelors, lived in different states. Monsieur le Curé had died and was replaced by a young pastor who gave his sermons in English, not French, and who did not talk so much about eternity as about the teachings of the Church on matters of contraception and abortion. All the while he spoke, I kept my eyes closed, which I wanted to be interpreted as also closing my ears.

Away on my own, I had stopped going to Mass, but back home with my parents I had to go with them. I kept from them that I hadn't been to Mass for a year as I kept from them that I had also stopped going to confession, so I was, according to the Roman commandments, in a state of sin and could not receive Communion without committing the mortal sin of sacrilege. But, there in my parish, I in no way felt I was in a state of sin, though after the elevation and consecration of the host, I didn't, as I would have done normally in the past, go to the Communion rail to kneel and receive. My mother went, but my father did not. Watching the parishioners walk along the aisles to the Communion rail and kneel and open their mouths for the host, my mother among them, I recalled that the grammar-school nuns—who sat in their heavy black robes and veils in the front pews of the church with their present classes of students, fewer than when I'd been one of them—had told us that if we received Communion in a state of mortal sin, our bowels would burst asunder in outrage at the sacrilege.

The Mothers looked old. What, I wondered, would Mère Sainte Flore—she, appearing to me old, from time to time adjusting the stiff white bonnet under her black veil, which swayed with her movements about her stooped shoulders—think of me if she knew about me? Was it possible that she would not be surprised—if she had known of what I believed to have been my most fulfilled longing—to find, if I did go to the altar rail and Communion, that instead of my bowels bursting asunder, I would emit a glow from all my body for having come alive in all my senses? Able to imagine, with delight in my imagination, being in my own beatific state, I felt very far away from a state of sin, but I wouldn't put my imagination to the test by receiving. I was wary of the beliefs of the Mothers, who could pray for strange miracles to occur, which would transform a person in ways only they knew about. The Mothers struck me as funny, but they made me want to withdraw from them in fear.

At the end of Mass, I watched Mère Sainte Flore limp past me out of church and back into the convent of the Mothers.

As my mother and I walked side by side to leave the church, my father just behind us, my mother took my arm. I knew she thought I was a good-looking young man who a few days before had come back from a long stay in Europe, and she wanted to show me off to the other parishioners as her son. Stepping out of the foyer, she whispered to me, as if to let others who were looking at us think that we shared a secret intimacy, "Did you see how Mère Sainte Flore couldn't keep still?"

I said I did.

My mother tried to suppress her laughter but didn't try very hard. "Do you think she was trying not to fart?"

This old joke between my mother and me about the Mothers farting seemed flat to me, and I didn't laugh.

"What's the matter with you?" my mother asked. "Have you lost your sense of humor?"

I had embarrassed her by not laughing with her, and so I did laugh.

My mother looked around. No one would have known

what we were laughing at, and she liked that we were united in a way other people might wonder at.

At the top of the flight of granite steps that led from the brick church down to the street, we stopped to turn to my father. "Are we going to visit Cora?" my mother asked him.

A slight puzzlement came over his face. Why would we not visit Cora?

"Do you want to see her?" my mother asked me.

"I would, yes," I answered.

It was a warm, early-autumn morning. While my mother talked for a short while with some women—the women she would deride for their hats, she, as always, wearing the simplest of hats—I stood to the side with my father.

In our silence, I had a powerful sense of his bodily presence, and the exposed details—the hairy lobe of one ear, a tensed muscle in his square chin, his smooth, broad nape below the line of his close-cut but thick white hair, his large, big-knuckled hand with one finger stunted by an accident at the factory that had taken off half his nail—struck me with the amazement of my never having noticed them before.

My mother had asked me lots of questions about my year traveling and studying abroad, all based on what she imagined, say, Paris to be, but my father had not once asked me anything.

When I searched for something to say to him to start a brief conversation while my mother was talking with *les bonnes femmes de la paroisse,* all I could think of to say, in French, was that I had remarked in Paris that people in restaurants ate *boudin,* the blood sausage my parents ate at home, and which I had thought existed only in our parish.

My father answered, also in French, that his mother used to make good blood sausages.

It occurred to me that my relationship with my mother, which always seemed to me rather obvious in our love for each other, depended a lot on our talking to each other, but my relationship with my father, whatever that was, had nothing to do with our talking to each other. Though it had happened in the past that my mother and I had discussed our differences, which we both assumed we could articulate, I had never even considered such discussions with my father, as if our differences could not be articulated. I could, I imagined, *explain* my relationship with my mother, but in no way that with my father, and once again, as happened when I was a little boy, which I recalled vividly, I felt towards my father a greater pull than I had ever felt towards my mother.

I asked him, "Did you know that our French ancestors came from Brittany?"

He raised his eyebrows. "Is that so? How do you know?"

A sudden embarrassment about my surmise, taken from a book he would not have heard about, made me say, "I don't, really."

How easily I could be made to feel I was intruding on my father's privacy. (When, on my return, I used the familiar *tu* with him, he responded with, *"Je n'ai jamias tutoyé mon père."*) He withdrew into his private self.

The three of us went to Matante Cora's with the usual crullers my father bought at the bakery.

Her long, thin, white braids hung down from the headband around her green visor to her shoulders.

Matante Cora said, "Les Mères de Jésus-Marie are getting

old now, and they're not being replaced by younger Mothers. There must be a lot of moans and groans in the convent when the floors are being washed. I'd like to go over and help, but I know they won't have me. They'll be dying out, and soon they'll all be dead, and that will be the end of the parochial school and the end, too, of the parish."

"The Irish will come in," my father said, as if he had been following a train of thought that had nothing to do with what my aunt was saying.

"That's right, the Irish will be coming in and taking over."

My mother asked, "What's wrong with the Irish?"

Neither my father nor my aunt answered her.

"Well, soon we'll all be dead," Matante Cora said.

"You're always talking about death," my mother said to her.

"Isn't that what we live for? My mother used to say, whenever I asked her if she'd like to have my father back from the dead, 'No, we work too hard to die.'"

"That's terrible," my mother said. "I don't live to die. I live to live." She looked at me. "Isn't that what I should say, that I live to live?"

"Yes," I said.

"I want you to live to live, even if that means going far away from me. I was never able to go anywhere, but I want you to go everywhere, all over the world."

"Thanks," I said.

My terseness made my mother withdraw, as if she felt I was not really accepting her show of positiveness, which she believed was the only show I would accept.

Matante Cora talked, and all she could talk about was the way the Mothers in the convent were getting too old to teach, too old to take care of themselves, too old even to take care of the church and the flowers for the altar. And then she started to talk about how she was sure she had had a vocation, and was still sure she had a vocation, to become a Mother. She continued to express her devotion in her prayers. She told us, as she had told us many Sundays in the past, about her prayers, most expressively about the prayer she had composed for her eyes to be cured of the yellowish cataracts that were thickening on her wide, staring eyes.

My mother said we should go, and my father got up from the big, round, wooden table in the middle of the kitchen.

There was, I saw, no point in coming back to see Matante Cora alone. Whatever she had to tell me about her mother and her mother's mother I had already heard, and she had, I was sure, nothing new to tell me.

I walked back to our house between my mother and father. The maple trees were just beginning to go yellow and red, and some leaves dropped about us as we passed along the almost trafficless streets.

My mother said, "Cora lives in the past."

I asked, "You think her beliefs are outdated?"

"Oh, I don't doubt her faith. She has such strong faith. But her ideas about her faith are outdated. She should have an operation for her cataracts instead of praying they'll go away and she'll be cured."

"Right," I said.

"What do you think?" she asked my father.

He was frowning with his deep thinking. He said, "I don't know."

I suddenly thought of the prayer, as recounted by Matante Cora, that my father was supposed to have been given by his mother to cure burns, and wondered if my mother had stopped him not only from using it but from believing in it. And there was no way I could have asked my father to pass it on to me, whatever my mother thought of it.

My parents napped in the afternoon, and I, restless, went out for a walk around the parish. I had said to myself there was no point in returning to Matante Cora, but I found myself climbing the worn wooden stairs up to her tenement apartment.

"Tell me more about that prayer Mémère passed on to my father," I asked.

All Cora said was, as I had heard before, "She should have passed it on to me."

My parents' house was deeply quiet when I got back, so quiet I had the impression that it was empty, and, made apprehensive by that sensed emptiness, I called, "Momma?" Immediately, I wondered why I hadn't called my father instead.

She called me from the pantry. "Come and look." She was standing at the pantry window, which was over the old sink, and she was looking out at the sunset.

The sun was halfway down behind a distant hill called Violet Hill, which was now a deep violet, as were striations of thin clouds above it. In the spaces between the clouds, the light reddened as the sun quickly sank, then the red gave way to a far, far bright green.

My mother said to me, "You've changed."

"I hope so," I said, not wanting to be serious with her.

"I'm not sure I like the change. You used to be so devout."

"I used to force myself to be devout."

"Who was forcing you?"

I could talk to my mother about such matters only if I laughed. "You were."

"*I* was?"

"Yes."

My mother said, "But I went to Communion every Sunday while you were away for your intentions."

I said, "What do you think my intentions might have been?"

"I prayed for the good of your soul, that God would keep you safe and sound and strengthen your faith by your being away."

"Maybe I had other intentions I wish you had prayed for."

"Don't joke with me," she said. "I noticed you weren't paying much attention to the Mass and were deliberately not paying attention to the pastor when he gave his sermon."

"Neither did Dad."

"Your father never does."

"What does he do, then, if he's not paying attention to the Mass or, even less, the sermon?"

"He prays."

"What prayers?"

"Don't try to get me away from what I wanted to say to you. Never mind your father. *You* didn't pay attention."

"I was saying my own prayers for my intentions."

"And what were they?"

I knew I would shock her, which was what I wanted to do. I spread my hands wide on either side of my face and smiled. "Prayers for all my bodily senses."

But she was more amused than shocked, though she had

to put on a show of being shocked. She couldn't help herself from laughing, but she tried to speak with a severe tone. "You didn't learn that from me."

"Maybe not, but haven't you ever wished for such a prayer?"

She laughed more, then said, more severely, "Stop it."

Faint stars appeared in the far green space.

I said, "The fact is, Momma, that I don't go to church anymore."

Sighing, she placed her hand on the side of my face and looked into my eyes for a long while; then she said quietly, "I understand you, as you understand me. We've both got blue eyes." She dropped her hand.

I asked, "Where is Dad?"

"He's still napping."

"He sleeps a lot."

"He does." My mother bit her lower lip. "Yes, he does."

"Is he all right?"

"I hope so. He'd never go to a doctor. You know how he is. It's in his Indian blood, his trusting his mother's medicines and not a real doctor's. But I pray he's all right."

My mother, I noticed for the first time, had aged.

She asked, "Tell me, why should I have ever wanted more than what he has given me? He's always been a good provider, a good husband, and good father. Why should I have ever wanted something more than our lives together in this house? Why, do you think?"

"I wish I could tell you," I answered.

My mother went out to visit a neighbor, an Irish friend of hers, and I, in the dark kitchen, sat in the rocking chair in the corner and read by the light of a dim lamp attached to the wall. I didn't at first see my father when he came into the kitchen, and when I did I realized that, as if he were still half asleep, he seemed not to know where he was.

I said, "Dad."

He appeared in the pale, round light of the lamp in his robe and slippers. I got up from the rocking chair to let him sit there, in what everyone knew was his chair. I sat on a kitchen chair near him. His head lowered, he rocked. The veins about his ankles showed.

I asked, "Are you all right?"

He passed a hand over his face. My father's English was studied and totally without idiomatic expressions, as was mine. He said, "Your mother tells the truth about Cora's beliefs. They are outdated, all of them superstitions, and they are best forgotten."

"Yes, they probably are," I said.

That night, I went to bed in my old room, the window open not to a lot of woods but to a neighboring clapboard house that had been built on the other side of a privet hedge. The longing I had was not a sensual longing, however great my sensual longings were. But because God did not exist, I was unable to call it a longing to be with God. It had to be a nameless longing.

18

MY MORTAL SIN WAS ENVY, ENVY THAT SOUGHT ITS satisfaction in the depth and breadth of my possessiveness, which was to have everything, to have nothing less than everything.

After I returned from Europe, I, wanting to fulfill my ambitions, went to live in New York, where I stayed for five years. To go into what happened during those years would be to go back to years of total failure—failure because I became possessed by people who rejected my attempts at possessing them and, more, because I rejected, with a crudeness I had never imagined I was capable of, those people who seemed to be possessed by me. I had fantasies of killing or being killed. In the midst of such fantasies, which were generated by sex, the only decision I was able to make was that I must withdraw from everyone, and withdraw especially from sex. I moved to Boston, where the very few people I knew dated from when I was in college there, old friends I didn't want to possess any more than they wanted to possess me.

In Boston, I taught English to foreigners in a language school, and, as if it were the fulfillment of an ambition I had always had, I found a room in a house on Beacon Hill. The house was an old, gray clapboard, the angles slightly askew. My one small room smelled of soot, and coal dust was impacted in the cracks among the wide, warped floorboards. There, I spent my weekends trying to write stories.

To get to the school where I taught, I crossed the Boston Common. One balmy afternoon, as I entered the Common, a smell hit me across the face: that of sea, warm stones, and suntan lotion, and I had no idea where the smell came from, but it was the smell of Sitges. It did not bring with it any surge of nostalgia; I did not want to be back in Sitges, nor did I miss Sitges or Spain. I didn't miss Öçi. And yet, everything I had felt for him came back to me as on a gust of wind. Even the sensation of touching him, seeing him, hearing him, tasting him, and smelling him came back but as though I were sensing in all these something vaster than he was, as vast as the gusts across the Common, which, as invisible as they were, made the trees shake. In that vast and invisible wind I missed that something terribly. Overcome, I sat on a bench.

A guy passing looked at me, stopped, and quickly sat on a bench across the cement path. In a minute I realized he, maybe in a hurry but also unwilling to let an opportunity go by, was staring at me. He wore two-tone, brown and white, brogues. I didn't find him attractive, and I thought, How can you be attracted to me? You don't know anything about me but the way I look. But I did know how he could be attracted to me for nothing but my looks. I got up and walked away. At a turning in the cement path, I felt suddenly awful about leaving that guy. I wanted to go back to him to say, "Look, I understand, I do, and I'm sorry, but I've got to go now." The guy wasn't there. I knew I wouldn't have gone back, and I told myself that he might have been relieved that I'd gone because he was in so much of a hurry.

All the while I was in Boston, I longed to return to Europe.

In my reading of Henry James, which became a world to me, I associated the writer with my longing.

From time to time, I visited his grave, across the Charles River in the Cambridge Cemetery. One afternoon, after a snowstorm that left a heavy silence and stillness everywhere, I went to the cemetery in that state of agony of longing for more than to return to Europe, for more than I could possibly have said, which longing was my eternal state of being. Just within the gates, on a number of plots without markers, were small American flags stuck in the snow and frozen flowers half buried in drifts. The snow up to my shins, I trudged up a hill, past the dead of the Second World War, then, farther up, the graves of Polish and Irish and Italian immigrants, then the graves of the First World War dead. Beyond were gravestones with such names as Fannie Cutting and James Stenson and William Wilde, Yankee names, and in their midst was the monument to the Civil war, a cannon surrounded by listing gravestones. The James family plot was on a ridge overlooking the Charles River, on the other side of which stretched snow-covered Soldiers Field, with a polar pink sky low over the winter-bare trees.

The plot was small, with a brick wall at the top, like the headboard of a bed, the bedstead made of granite curbstones, the whole blanketed in snow from which the individual stones stood out. Buried there were Henry James Sr. and his wife; their daughter, Alice; their son William and his wife and their children; and their son Henry. On his stone, the incised letters were inlaid with ice:

HENRY JAMES, O.M.
NOVELIST, CITIZEN
OF TWO COUNTRIES.
INTERPRETER OF HIS
GENERATION ON BOTH
SIDES OF THE SEA.
NEW YORK, APRIL 15, 1843
LONDON, FEBRUARY 28, 1916

I made my plea. If I couldn't, because I couldn't afford it, go to Europe, I could, and I did, write.

But the agony of writing was to find in it a secret—a secret that was, like some inner bright globe, touched on but that remained, however much one's touch penetrated it, inexhaustible. To have everything in that secret—"to have the far-off hum of a thousand possibilities, the shimmering of the whole circumstance, the bigness, big with the breadth of great vague connections"—was what writing was about. To be possessed by that secret and to possess that possession, that was what writing was about. To bring that secret up out of its depths beneath any blankness, to make it seen, heard, felt, smelled, tasted, that was what writing was about. To believe, above all, that there *was* a secret to be brought up and out into images—into, simply, *one* image—that referred themselves—that referred *itself*—back to the existence of the inner globe of that secret, that was what writing was all about. And Henry James assured me of this belief.

During a winter thaw, one afternoon after classes in the language school, I climbed Beacon Hill with legs made heavy by the steep incline, tired but determined to go on with a story once I was back in my room. I stopped when I saw a black girl sitting on a granite stoop to one of the narrow brick houses and assembling a miniature log cabin on the brick sidewalk. She was humming and did not look up at me, even though I was standing in front of her. Only when I said "I had a log-cabin set when I was a boy" did she glance up at me and smile, but, as if I had disappeared, she went back to assembling the cabin, humming again.

Why did I think that this so public sight of the black girl

assembling a toy log cabin on a sidewalk of Beacon Hill contained a secret? As I walked away, I thought that the secret existed more in the memory of the world than in my memory. But how could that be? How could a secret be public? As deeply as the sight of the miniature log cabin being assembled on a sidewalk of Beacon Hill by a black girl referred me back to my assembling one just like it on the floor of the living room of my family house years before, I was all at once made aware that it referred much more to the memories of thousands and thousands who had assembled toy log cabins in thousands and thousands of different places; and that instead of the repetition diminishing the sense of the toy log cabin having a meaning, a meaning that *should* be private to be at all engaging, the repetition of it everywhere expanded the meaning and, in expanding it into the public world, in fact made it more engaging, because there in the world —there in the memories of the vast public—it was truly enormous, enormous with the breadth of immense vague connections. It struck me as the image of a secret that was public rather than private, and it was a secret because, for being so small and yet being so enormous in what it connected with, it could never be exposed in its entirety; and it was public because, like a potent image of a national religion, it shimmered with the whole circumstance of the country. I imagined that it, like the image of a national religion, possessed the whole country more than it possessed me, possessed the whole country to interpret it. But it would never be fully interpreted. The connections that would have to be made to expose its meaning were, in their very vagueness, too vast.

To know, to be sure, that there were connections to be

made that would reveal the meaning, that would reveal everything all together as cohesively as that central and bright globe, but also to know, to be absolutely sure, that these connections, as much as the country tried, would never be made or the revelation occur, filled me with a profound sense of reassurance.

I was wrong to associate Henry James more with Europe, where he had heard the far-off hum of a thousand possibilities in the air that seemed, itself, to have echoing dimensions, than with America, where he had heard nothing.

On his return to his country after twenty years of living abroad, he asked himself in *The American Scene*, "*Were* there any secrets at all, or had the outward blankness, the quality of blankness, as it were, in the air, its inward equivalent as well?"

There *were* American secrets.

19

BUT I WAS SAVING TO GO BACK TO EUROPE, WHERE, AS if usurping my Europe, my parents went before I could.

My brother Donald, retired as a major from the Marine Corps and not yet ready to marry, went to live in Paris for a year. Why he did this had nothing, I think, to do with our French ancestry and an attempt to connect with a France that had—neither he nor I knew since when—been disconnected from us; he just wanted to spend some free time in what he called, because that was what everyone called it, the City of Lights, and there he invited my parents to join him for some months. He had rented a small apartment in the tenth arrondissement, a working-class quarter of the city.

All their lives, my parents had been only as far as New York, where they went on their honeymoon, my mother not knowing even on the ferry from Newport to Manhattan what the marriage act was, a revelation that had to depend on my father. Back in Providence, back in the parish, they didn't leave except for occasional afternoon excursions to see their married sons in Massachusetts. My father didn't want to go to Paris, and because he didn't, my mother, who was one with him in the marriage act, couldn't go.

Donald's invitation raised my mother's spirits because it offered her a way out, at least for a time, but the sustaining of those raised spirits was up to my father, whose very silence made it doubtful the invitation would be accepted; and because my father's silence continued over days, over those days my mother's spirits began to fall. The brothers who knew how our mother's restless walking about the house from room to room, sometimes hitting the walls with her fists, could break down to her sitting in a chair and rocking back and forth, wrote to my father that, with all due respect to his being a homebody, our mother's health was in danger if she didn't get out of the house, which they were sure she would be pleased to return to after having been away. They had informed our mother about the letter, so she knew when she gave it to him, addressed to him alone, the message it contained. He read it carefully. He lowered it and thrust out his jaw for a moment, then said, "All right," and my mother threw up her arms and shouted, "I'm getting away."

Except for Donald, who was waiting for them in Paris, we

all went to the airport at Boston to see them off, as if their trip were a family event. As there was, then, no security, we stood on the tarmac, and they waved to us from the top of the gangplank. We watched the plane take off and become a diminishing red light in the sky.

In Boston, I received frivolous, joking postcards from my mother. "I'm going alone to see Frou Frou at the Moulin Rouge. You father and Don are too tired to come, the old poops. Whoopee for mama! I've changed so much!" She signed herself Fifi.

In a letter to me, Donald wrote that he had taken our parents to a small restaurant in the *quartier*. Though we had grown up without any alcohol in our household, not even beer, in Paris Donald learned to drink wine with his meals, as I had. In the restaurant, he ordered a small carafe. My father didn't drink any of the wine, but my mother, who had probably never imbibed any form of alcoholic drink in all her life, accepted a glass of wine against my father's disapproving frown. She was in Paris and could do as she wished. Donald warned her not to gulp the wine, but she did and immediately became tipsy; she began to joke with the waiter, not in French but in English, which he did not understand. She held out her glass for more wine, which Donald, amused, poured out for her, though, he wrote, père frowned more with disapproval. She now joked with the waiter *because* he didn't understand, which he took as an insult; and, as if her freedom allowed her to be unrestrained as never before, she made fun of him in French, calling him *Ma petite crotte noire,* which, translated as "My little black snot," was a Canuck expression of endearment. My father found my mother as unfunny as the waiter did, and he said it would be best for everyone if our mother got back to the apartment quickly. Once inside, she dropped onto the bed and fell asleep, snoring lightly. Laughing, Donald said to our father, *"Voilà votre femme."* And our father said to him, *"Voilà ta mère."*

As my brother Donald was devout, he organized for himself and my parents a pilgrimage to Lourdes, which was especially significant because our parish church was called Notre Dame de Lourdes. My mother wrote that the pilgrimage would be the greatest event in her life, though I read into her enthusiasm a depth of falseness, for to go to Lourdes was perhaps to return to the parish in a way that exaggerated everything she had wanted to escape from. But she *had* to make a show of enthusiasm, however false, as if to compensate for her real enthusiasm at being in Paris—for the spiritual *must* be shown more devotion than the temporal. In her religious devotions, my mother, who was really a secular woman, was something of a hypocrite, an accusation that she, shocked, would have fervently denied.

They went by train, in a compartment of French people, commanded over by an old woman who refused to open the window, however stifling, because *les courants d'air* were dangerous. My mother tried to show her goodwill and asked her, *"Vous n'êtes pas tanée?"* *tanée* being a long-, long-outdated word for *fatiguée*, which at least made the old woman smile, though she still refused to open the window, even a little. A little girl in the compartment was carrying a doll in her arms, and, among the dour French, my mother tried at least to engage with her by exclaiming, *"Quelle belle petite catin que tu as,"* which had the girl's mother say to my

mother, *"Madame, on ne dit pas ça,"* my mother not knowing that the word she used for "doll" had for hundreds of
years been used to mean whore. But this got a Frenchman in
the crowded compartment to ask my parents where they
were from that my mother used such old French.

My father, as if this was his right, answered for her:
"L'Amerique."

Where in America?

My father told him, and the man said, *"Monsieur, vous
dites que vous êtes americain, comment ça se fait que vous avez
un accent normand?"*

When I found this out, I thought: Well, Normandy is
close enough to Brittany for them to have some similar accent and to share some expressions, such as *tsi gars.*

From Boston, where I was living, I went to Providence in
my parents' absence and, alone in the house, searched for the
list of ancestors in their bedroom. It could only have been
in my father's wardrobe, in half of which his dark suit hung
from the time of his mother's funeral, and in the other half
of which were drawers of shirts, socks, and underwear, and,
in the top drawer, boxes: a box containing foreign coins,
mostly Chinese; a box containing old watches; a box containing bits of mineral samples from a mine he had once been
persuaded to invest in by a shyster who lost him his money;
a box of old cuff links. And there was a folder. I took it out
and, sitting on my parents' bed, placed all the papers from
the folder on it: his nationalization papers, the death certifi-
cate of his mother, the record of mortgage payments for the
house during the Depression—from 1937 to 1941—amount-
ing to $13.00 a month. The list was not there, and I was more

sure than ever that for some reason of her own, Matante Cora had wanted me to believe that my father had what she should have had. Then I wondered if he had hidden it. But why? Did it reveal information about his antecedents that he truly was shamed by? I lifted the lining papers in the drawers to look under them but saw only blank wood. No, I thought again, he didn't have the list. I put everything back carefully, and, wandering about the house again until darkness fell, I felt that the rooms were haunted; so instead of spending the night as I had intended, I left to return to my room in Boston.

In her last postcard from Paris, my mother wrote about the little boy who played in the courtyard and wanted, he told her, to go to America and travel in *une diligence* to the Far West, and she did not have the heart to tell him that in America no one now traveled in a covered wagon.

They returned to the parish with many clear plastic bottles of water from Lourdes, the blue label printed in black with the image of Bernadette praying before Our Lady in her grotto. But, when I was alone with her, my mother whispered to me, as though I was the only one who would understand her, that all she had really got out of being at Lourdes was sore feet, walking in the endless candlelit procession, singing, again and again, "Ave, Ave Maria."

And she told me that in the taxi from Paris to the airport she looked out at the city she was leaving, and tears came to her eyes.

As I expected, my father said little about Paris, as if there his attitude was that of a provincial who had decided beforehand that he would *not* be impressed by the capital. The *boudin* bought at the butcher in the parish was better than the *boudin* served in Paris restaurants.

20

WHEN, IN 1966, I HAD SAVED ENOUGH MONEY TO return to Europe—$3,000—I decided not on Paris but on London. I decided on London because Öçi was still there. We had exchanged letters, friendly letters. He had managed to get a British passport and was now planning on going to New York, his life's ambition. I wanted to see him because I had, in Boston, finally given in to the greater and greater longing for, if not love, sex, and, always too possessive in what I wanted, I'd been rejected, brutally so. I didn't and I don't know why, but that brutal rejection made me want to see Öçi.

I also had another reason for being in London. There, I made my visits to the Henry James sites: Old Chelsea Church, on the Chelsea Embankment of the Thames where his memorial service was held, and, farther along Cheyne Walk, I paced back and forth before the block of flats, Carlyle Mansions, where he died. And I went on a pilgrimage to Rye, East Sussex, to see Lamb House, where he retired after his disaster as a playwright in London and where he wrote his greatest novels.

I had, in response to a letter on my behalf from an Englishman I'd met in Boston, an invitation from the then occupants of Lamb House, the novelist Rumer Godden and her husband. Part of their agreement in renting the house was that they would show visitors around, a duty I felt they found imposed on them a little when it came to a young American who had nothing to offer but his curiosity about the former occupant and scant interest in them, though I did say I had read Godden's novel *The River* and had liked it very much. She gave me tea in the sitting room and said, as if to make her own presence more felt to me, that all the furniture in the room was hers. I recall chintz-covered armchairs and misty white net curtains over the windows, through which the trees outside were diffused into bright green blurs.

I had no sense of the presence of Henry James—none at all—and wondered what I had expected. In fact, according to Godden, there was very little in the house that had belonged to James, and all of what remained was in one room, just off the entry hall, which James called the telephone room because the telephone receiver was kept there. This was, if the truth be told, the only room normally open to visitors, at certain hours. I asked if I could see it. Godden said, "You won't see much," and she and her husband let me go on my own.

The door to the telephone room was open. I looked at what had been recovered since the 1940s, when most of James's possessions had been sold at auction: his desk, some photographs, a walking stick, a cigar cutter, books from his library. Feeling low, and feeling, too, all the pretensions of my expectations, I left the room and closed the door. My hand on the door handle, it occurred to me that James had held the same handle and closed that same door, and a shiver passed up my arm.

On returning to the sitting room, I saw that the tea things had been cleared and Godden had gone. Her husband was standing there. I knew I must go. Perhaps to make up for something, Godden's husband, whose name I hadn't heard, told me there were still books from Henry James's library— old, uncut French novels—which I might find in secondhand bookshops in Rye, if I cared to look. He also said that James's knife boy, Burgess Noakes, was still alive, and if I went to a certain pub, I'd be bound to see him—a small, crumpled man, who would talk for a pint. I wasn't sure what a knife boy was and learned later that he cleaned the knives before stainless steel was invented and also did errands. Godden's husband did warn me, however, that if I did speak with Noakes, I'd find he remembered very little about Henry James.

I thought I wouldn't go to the pub, but I happened to pass it on my way down the hill on which Rye is built, so I went in. The inside was musty and hardly lit with sunlight through the small windows, and a small, crumpled man was standing at the bar, alone, wearing a hearing aid and blinking. I thought he must be Burgess Noakes, but I was too shy to approach him, and anyway, I told myself, he had had, in the long course of his life, almost nothing to do with James.

I had fantasized coming to London to be a minor Henry James, but that fantasy was completely superseded by someone who came from a world that as far as I knew—and I thought I knew Henry James's writing very well—had nothing to do with James's world. My reason for staying was Nikos Stangos, a Greek born in Athens, a city that seemed to have been of no interest to James.

I'd been given Nikos's telephone number by a mutual friend in Cambridge, Massachusetts, where Nikos, at the time I was an undergraduate at Boston College, had lived as a graduate student in philosophy at Harvard University. When I telephoned him, he asked me to come to tea. At four o'clock, I arrived at the town house in Wyndham Place, behind an iron picket fence painted black, where he lived. I rang the bell of his flat, waited, rang again, waited, but no one came. I rang once more. A net curtain was hanging over the ground-floor window through which I couldn't see. Recalling the old French expression for having tea, *fivocloquer*, I thought that Nikos, who, coming from Greece, might be more continental than British, must have meant me to come at five o'clock.

I went to Hyde Park, where I got lost. It was a warm afternoon, and people, some embracing couples, were lying on the grass. By the time I found my way back to Wyndham Place, the time was five-fifteen. I rang the bell and heard a door behind the street door open and footsteps; then the street door was opened by a young man with a narrow, delicate face and short, black, curly hair. He was wearing gray trousers and a darker gray cardigan over an open-necked white shirt. His face appeared stern, but my first reaction to him was to think, as if in confirmation of my first hope about how he would be: *oh, yes.*

For no reason other than the way he looked, I was pleased to have telephoned him, however much he had sounded annoyed; and I was pleased to go into his flat with him, which appeared to be all browns, with highly polished English furniture.

Hanging at a tilt on the living room walls by long wires attached by hooks to a high picture rail were many pictures —prints, etchings, drawings, gouaches, a few paintings—by contemporary English artists whose work I had seen in the new acquisitions room at the Tate Gallery.

There was a deep stillness in the flat that made me feel still. While we had tea, Nikos asked me many questions about myself, and after I answered one, he seemed to think for a long while before asking another. What he questioned me about was art and music and poetry, and he began, after a while of carefully considering what I answered, to tell me what I was misinformed about, or what I didn't know, or even what I affected to know and didn't know, all of which he did with what seemed to me calm and calming disinterest. His disinterest seemed to come from his being in a very light trance, and, listening to his soft but precise voice, I felt myself go into as light a trance. In my light trance, I accepted his disinterested comments totally. I also knew that at some deeper level, he was interested and not at all annoyed that I had telephoned him.

He told me how much he liked America, how much he liked Americans, who were, he believed, the only people capable of true originality.

I asked him why he was living in London.

Because, he said, his job in the office of the press attaché was the only job he had been able to get that would allow him to leave Greece. He hated his work, but he tolerated it because it allowed him to live away from Greece. He would never again in his life live in Athens.

We talked, again, about art and music and poetry, and, talking with him, I felt myself, again, go into a trance, but a trance that was in no way vague but depthlessly clear, as his thinking seemed to me in no way vague but depthlessly clear. He was, I knew, more intelligent than I was, more cultured, and better educated, not only about art and music and poetry but also history and politics, but, beyond these, there was that deep clarity to him which appeared in the very clarity of his face.

He saw me clearly, and he was able to tell me, so that I was able to see myself clearly, how much I didn't know about art and music and poetry, and how very much I didn't know about history and politics. I certainly didn't know anything about the history and politics of modern Greece.

I told him I wanted to write. I told him, because, however candid he had been with me in making me aware of how much I didn't know, I knew he took me seriously. He was serious, and he took me seriously. He asked me questions about my writing.

Then he showed me one of his poems, written in English. It was called "Pure Reason," and it was a love poem addressed to "you." The poem read almost as if it were arguing a philosophical idea with the person addressed, the terms of the argument as abstract as any philosophical argument, and without one image, metaphor, or simile in it. The philosophical idea was reasoning at its purest. What was remarkable about the poem was that in conveying, as it did, intellectual purity, it conveyed, more, emotional purity, and

it centered the purity—intellectual, emotional, and moral—
in the person to whom it was addressed, in the person with
whom the poet was so much in love.

When Nikos switched on a lamp on a desk in a corner of
the room, he asked me if I was free to have dinner with him.
I didn't want to leave him. I said I was free.

I was wearing a jacket and tie. He asked me to wait while
he went to change. Alone, I looked about the living room,
where I could not see one recognizably Greek object.

Nikos came back into the living room wearing a white
Carnaby Street suit with flared trousers and a tightly fitting
jacket, a pink shirt, and a wide, gray tie that had large white
circles on it like moons. It was as though he had changed into
a different person, and yet in his stillness he was the same
person. I, who always wore the most conventional of clothes,
my ties traditionally dark and narrow and knotted tightly between the wings of my collar, could never have imagined
dressing as he was dressed.

Not as an excuse, but a statement of fact, he said that the
Russian Soviet ambassador had been to Carnaby Street and
approved of the clothes because they were an expression of
working-class culture.

As if lost, I didn't know my way, and he showed me out
into the street and hailed a taxi.

Looking at him across the restaurant table, I noted there
was a slight Asiatic—maybe Byzantine—cast to his eyes.

He paid the restaurant bill and asked me if I'd like to return to his flat with him. There was nothing pressing in his
asking me. In fact, he seemed to ask me with the same disinterest with which he had questioned me about my apprecia-

tion of culture. I assumed that by asking me in so offhanded a way, he didn't want me to think he had made any assumptions, but, on the contrary, I must feel free to leave him. But I made all the assumptions. I had been looking forward to his asking me to go back to his place, so much so that the anticipation of it was for me one of the main pleasures of the evening. I said I'd like to.

In the taxi, he made a point, I thought, of telling me he was not rich.

We were standing still together in his living room, he a little turned away from me, and I reached out and put my hands on his shoulders. He didn't move for a moment, then turned to me slowly and smiled.

He said quietly, "You know, I saw you when you rang the bell at four o'clock."

I frowned.

"At four, I looked out the window, and when I saw you approach the front door, I thought you must be the person I was expecting. I saw you ring a doorbell, but the bell in my flat didn't ring. So I thought you weren't the person I was expecting. After you left, I went out to check my bell and found it wasn't working. I thought, well, he won't come back. I wouldn't have come back."

"Why?" I asked.

"You thought it was your fault that no one answered. I would have thought it was the fault of the person who didn't answer, maybe deliberately didn't answer, because he'd decided he didn't want to see me, and I would have been offended."

I said, "That never occurred to me."

"I know it didn't." He looked at me more closely, at my ears, my temples, the sides of my neck. He said, "I repaired my bell, and, shall I tell you? I was sorry it hadn't worked, I was sorry you'd gone and I wouldn't see you again. And, shall I tell you? I was happy when you came back."

Again, I don't know how else to say what I felt except that I was entranced by him, and this made me feel very calm. And in that calm, I wanted to have sex with him, entrancing sex. It had been so very long.

I asked, "Can I make love with you?"

He didn't speak but smiled more. I waited. He put his arms around me and said quietly, "No," and this made me feel even calmer and more entranced by the calm, and even more so when he pressed the side of his face against mine.

He led me to the sofa, where we sat side by side. He said, "Tell me more about yourself."

"I don't know what to say."

"I want to know."

"I'll tell you anything you want to know."

"Tell me about your childhood, tell me about your growing up, tell me about anything you want."

I told him about Öçi, and as I told him, Nikos studied me and was attentive, it seemed to me, more to my face than to my words.

He said, "He was your first love."

"Yes," I said.

"And do you still love him?"

"I did."

"But not now?"

"I think that I'd have to see him to find out what, really, I feel about him."

"You came to London to see him. Does he know you're waiting?"

"I wrote to him, but I'm not sure he got my letter."

Nikos kept studying my face as if for expressions I myself was unaware of.

"May I see you again?" he asked.

I wanted to ask him what the point of that would be, as he didn't want to make love with me, but said, "If you would like to."

"I would like to," he said.

I saw him the next night, and the night after, and the night after, but I knew that our lovemaking must be up to him. If he didn't want to have sex with me, I felt he wanted something more from me, and it was this something more that, time after time, entranced me.

One evening, as I, from the direction of the top of the street, was approaching the house where Nikos lived, I saw him approaching from the bottom. He was wearing a dark business suit and carrying a briefcase, returning from the office of the press attaché at the Greek Embassy. Having been in his flat so often, I, even though I didn't live there, felt I was coming home.

Meeting me, he said, "If you'd come a minute earlier, you would have rung and, again, no one would have answered."

"I'd have come back," I said.

I followed close behind him as he opened the doors with keys into his flat, so close I bumped into him when he paused just inside to turn to me to ask me, his face so near mine I could have leaned just a little forward and kissed him, but I drew back. He said he had thought of going, that evening, to a cello recital by Rostropovich at the Royal Festival Hall. Would I like to go with him?

During the recital I was attentive to his attention to the music. His attentiveness appeared to be a delicate presence about him, as if his calm soul extended delicately around his face, his head, his entire body.

After the recital, he remained silent. I, too, was silent. As delicate the calm was that appeared to extend all about him, I felt, within him, a gravity of thought and feeling; it was as if that gravity caused the outward, trancelike calm by its inward pull. Silent, we crossed the Thames on the walkway over Hungerford Bridge. The trains to the side of the walkway made the bridge sway. In the middle of the bridge, Nikos reached into a pocket of his jacket and took out a large copper penny, which he threw down into the gray-brown, swiftly moving river far below.

"What's that for?" I asked.

"For luck," he said.

The evening was still expansively light. We walked from the Embankment at Charing Cross up to Trafalgar Square, all the while silent.

In Trafalgar Square, he suggested we sit, and we walked among the people standing in groups to the far-left corner, behind a great, gushing, black fountain, where there was no one else. We sat on a stone bench. The jets of the fountain rose vivid green and white from the center of the huge black cup and splashed into the water of the basin below.

Nikos said he had thought very carefully, and he wanted me, too, to think carefully, about what he was going to say. It was very, very important that I be totally honest.

"Yes," I said.

"I would never, ever want you to feel for me what you don't feel."

"No."

He said, "We're very different, you being American and I Greek, and maybe that makes it impossible for you to feel as I feel, for you to feel for me what I feel for you. I wouldn't want to impose my feelings on you, expecting you to feel for me what I do for you. You must promise me that you won't let me do that."

I was blinking rapidly.

"I've been involved with an older man, an older Englishman, for over a year now. He's away in America, in Washington. When he returns I'll tell him that our relationship must change. I've decided that. Even if you never see me again after this evening, I'll tell him that our relationship must change. What I feel for you has made me decide this, but, even so, you must not think that this means my feelings for you make you responsible for them, make you responsible for me. You must not consider that if you don't feel for me the way I do for you, I'll be hurt. I will be hurt, but my hurt is not something for you to consider, because it would be wrong if you said yes to what I want to ask you just because you may hurt me. It would be dishonest of you." He said, "I love you and I want to ask you to live with me."

I began to rock back and forth, amazed by what he had asked me. "Live with you?" I asked.

"Live with me."

All I could do was nod.

Nikos was twenty-nine, and I was twenty-six.

I spent the entire night with him, making love.

When, after ten days or so after my arrival in London, I saw Öçi, he greeted me in his bed-sitter so warmly, kissing me on the mouth and holding me for longer than I held him and, I felt, pulling me towards the bed with many embroidered and tasseled Turkish cushions on it, I almost gave in to him. It was as if he assumed I'd come to see him in London for just this, and perhaps I had; but I told him I had moved in with someone I'd met, and I was surprised and amused by his sudden jealousy. As he was preparing to leave for New York, I saw little of him, and only briefly. And then he left.

Nikos and I became life partners.

With Nikos, I felt that *I* had no history, but that *he* had a history.

His parents were refugees in Athens, his father a Greek from Bulgaria, his mother a Greek from Constantinople. He remembered the Second World War, when German air force officers were billeted in their house, which was near the airport. He remembered his parents listening to the news transmitted by the BBC World Service on a radio the occupying Germans outlawed but to which the German officers listened with them. He remembered the deaths of the officers. He remembered seeing a German soldier shooting a boy for stealing a potato. He remembered hiding under the table with his mother and the maid during bombardments of the airport, and the shard of a bomb breaking through the roof and chipping a bowl on the table. He remembered moving into the center of Athens, an open city, to stay with an aunt and uncle, and from the terrace watching the flares light up the airport in preparation for the British bombardments, and, the nighttime sky glaringly white, frightened that he had lost his parents, who had stayed in their house to save what they could of it. He worried about his cat, which he had had to leave behind. He remembered coats made from blankets. He remembered, during famine, that a turkey was kept on the balcony and fed precious corn until one day the turkey broke loose from the cord that held it and fluttered down into the street, where a passing man saw it, picked it up, and ran into a side street, and though his uncle bolted out of the apartment and down to the street to run after the man, he didn't catch him, and the family lost the turkey. He remembered men, early in the morning, wheeling barrows through the streets and calling, "Bring out your dead." He remembered the day the Germans left Athens, which was the day his father died. He remembered that during the civil war that followed the world war, he and his cousin would go out onto the balcony after a fight between the Communist and the Royalist Forces and collect the empty bullet shells. He remembered the Communist maid who, every afternoon, would put on her uniform and gun and go out and fight, and who sometimes took Nikos to Communist rallies.

If *I* didn't have politics, *he* had politics.

A boarding student at Athens College, as president of the student council, he had the key to the office with the mimeograph machine, and he would go after the lights were out to print Communist propaganda, which he would then throw from the balconies of cinemas, an act for which, because the Communist Party was outlawed, he would have been arrested if caught. A member of the Communist Party, he, at a cell meeting, had to submit for criticism his poetry, which was found to be too formalist.

A year after we began to live together, there was a military coup in Greece, and a dictatorship of colonels was enforced. The king fled to exile in London. Nikos resigned his job before he was fired, as he knew he would be, not only for his political beliefs but for the politics associated with his family name, for he had cousins who were famous in Greece as left-wing journalists.

We moved to a small flat south of the Thames, on the top floor of a mansion block in Prince of Wales Drive, overlooking Battersea Park.

I joined Nikos in a demonstration against the dictatorship. We stood together outside the Greek Embassy, among a large crowd of demonstrators, with policemen and police vans in a circle around the crowd; we shouted up at the windows of the building, over which the curtains were drawn. A hand separated the curtains and gave us the finger.

Soon after, Nikos got a job at Penguin Books, hired by the founder, Alan Lane, as editor for poetry, art and architecture, and philosophy. He told me I must write.

He had a religion he lived.

After seven years of dictatorship in Greece, the colonels fell, which meant Nikos and I were now free to go there. In Athens with him, on a visit to his mother, I took account of everything in his family apartment that would, I thought, identify him as different from me. I noted the papyrus diploma awarded to his mother at Robert College in Constantinople, the rugs that his parents had taken from Constantinople when they were forced to move to Athens at the time of the exchange of populations, the ceramic fruit bowl with a large chip in it caused by the flying piece of shrapnel during World War II.

When Nikos asked me if I wanted to go with him to church services during the Orthodox Easter Holy Week, I said that of course I wanted to. On Holy Friday, the church bells tolled all day. In the evening, Nikos took me to a church in Plaka. Sweating in the heat of the church, which was filled with the smell of melting candle wax, incense, and perspiration, I stood by the open door, but Nikos penetrated into the crowd so I couldn't see him. Over the heads of the solemn congregation, I saw flower petals thrown up and perfumes sprayed from silver phials. I moved to the side to let the bearers of the *Epitaphios,* the Holy Shroud of stiffened silk velvet embroidered in gold with pearls, out of the church, and got a glimpse of it, held by young men as on a wooden stretcher, covered with petals and splashed with perfume. The church was as filled with chanting as with incense. I waited until I saw Nikos at the end of a procession of people carrying candles and joined him. He had a candle for me. We followed the *Epitaphios* out and around the church, through a garden of flowering lemon trees, where an old woman was pulling ropes to toll the bells in the belfry. Rain started to fall.

On our way back to his family's apartment in Athens, I asked Nikos, "Do you believe?"

He answered, "That is a question I never ask myself."

The next evening, we went to a small Byzantine church

near a football stadium. Fragments of broken marble from ancient buildings were lying about the churchyard, where, the church being small, most of the congregation stood, I beside Nikos, both of us holding unlit candles. The small church was illuminated with candles, and from time to time someone stuck his head out of a low doorway, and it was as if I were looking at one of those Byzantine mosaics in which gigantic people lean out of the doorways or windows of tiny buildings. At midnight, just at the moment when Holy Saturday became Easter Sunday, the priest in bright red robes came out of the church into the courtyard and called out *"Christos anesti!"* and everyone shouted *"Alithos anesti!"* which meant Christ had risen from the dead, and people lit their candles, those near the paschal candle of the priest lighting theirs first and then passing the flame on to the rest of the congregation, so that the flame spread out from a center through the crowd and people's faces were lit in the darkness and the light shone between fingers held about lit candles, and bells rang and firecrackers exploded out in the street.

The God of these people seemed to love the temporal, loved rose petals and gold-and-pearl-stitched vestments and vials of sweet-smelling scent, seemed to love all the rich images of devotion to him.

In the streets of nighttime Athens, some people in groups walked with lighted candles to try to get them home and mark in the smoke of the flame crosses on the lintels of their doorways.

In London, Nikos worked as a publisher while continuing to write his poetry, and I published my first novel, which I called *The Ghost of Henry James,* meant to be about five young Americans who, without history, politics, or religion, floated in an unattached world.

With something of a reputation as a writer, I received a letter asking for a donation for a memorial stone to Henry James, to be laid in the floor of Westminster Abbey. I sent five pounds and was invited to the ceremony.

The dean of Westminster, Leon Edel, Stephen Spender, and a professor from the Sorbonne, all with red carnations in their lapels and led by James's great-grandnephew carrying a laurel wreath, processed down the aisle to Poets' Corner, which I, from where I sat, couldn't see. I had to imagine James's great-grandnephew unveiling the memorial stone in the floor and placing the wreath over it. I heard, over loudspeakers, Stephen Spender, the professor from the Sorbonne, and Leon Edel speak, then I heard the dean ask everyone, "Pray for the soul of Henry James."

After the ceremony, a pink ticket let me into the abbey's Jerusalem Chamber for sherry. I saw the great-grandnephew of Henry James standing alone, and I went to speak with Alexander James Jr., who was twenty-six . His charcoal gray suit from the 1950s was, he said, borrowed, as he didn't own one. He wore a white shirt with a button-down collar and a thin tie. His long hair was parted in the middle and combed back over his ears, and he had pure features—a strong forehead, nose, jaw, and neck—and pale but very intense eyes. A great-grandson of William James, he was studying to become a clinical psychologist. He loved to garden. He said quietly, "I'm not at all used to the kind of attention I'm getting here." It occurred to me that he was a perfect example of the kind of Yankee I had once thought lived at the center of America, and then it occurred to me that that center was gone, not only in America but in Europe. It had floated away.

Living with Nikos, I pretty much had stopped reading Henry James, who no longer seemed relevant to me. (Nikos's favorite work of James was *The Sacred Fount,* which he liked because he thought it "crazy," a novel he was sure the surrealists would have found fascinating.) If I picked up a volume, usually not of fiction but of autobiography or of letters, it was to glance at a page as though to see, in that glance, whether something might quite spontaneously strike me for the commonplace book I had begun to keep. In a letter to his friend Perry, this sentence jumped out at me from James's collected letters:

I would like to see a country in a state of revolution.

Nothing, I thought, could have been more un-Jamesian, but it pleased me to find it in James because it might have been something Nikos said, he whose vision was of the world made socially just by a revolution in the unjust world.

I took from Nikos the criticism that my great weakness in my writing, as well as in my life, was a self-indulgent lack of engagement with the world.

21

EVERY YEAR, I VISITED MY PARENTS IN THE PARISH, but Nikos never came with me.

In their last years, after having lived well over half a century together, the differences between my mother and father seemed to separate them more and more.

I recalled my oldest brother, Robert, once saying that our mother and father should never have married. They were too different.

And yet, in their differences, they had raised seven sons into manhood.

Finally, since they were incapable of taking care of themselves in their old age, Donald came to live with them in their clapboard house and dedicated himself to caring for them until their ends.

When I asked him how he could take on such a responsibility with such a calm commitment, he answered, "It's easy if you take a vow."

On my visits, I tried to relieve my brother of his duties by caring for my parents myself—preparing meals, washing dishes, making their beds, for they now slept in separate beds, which my mother had insisted on and my father had had to agree to, their single beds an indication of some deeper separation.

And yet I would be very puzzled—so puzzled, I was upset —when, coming into the kitchen, I would find my mother pouring water from one of those dull plastic bottles of Lourdes water, the blue label now frayed, onto my father's head, she standing over him as he sat in his rocking chair. He remained still as she rubbed the water into his thin gray hair and prayed. I was puzzled because I did not know what this little ceremony meant, and I was upset because of the meaning that it might have had for them: for a miracle that would not, that could not, occur. I thought that my mother, defeated by it after all, had not only given in to my father's religion of primitive superstition but had taken it over and was acting on it in a way that she had always resisted. They appeared to me to be preparing to die, and that that alone would unite them filled me with horror.

One hot summer, Donald and I were sitting in the kitchen. My father, motionless in the rocking chair he had been sitting in all afternoon, seemed to be unaware of us. All at once he stood and said that he was going to see his mother. His mother had been dead for more than thirty years.

My brother suggested that it was too hot to go now, that they should wait until the evening, when it was cooler.

My father sat back in his rocking chair.

When my mother, walking about the house restlessly, came into the kitchen and saw my brother still standing over my father and looking at him carefully, she asked what was wrong.

My brother didn't answer her. Like my father, he was dark, with black eyes and black hair.

My mother said about my father, who was sitting still, his eyes closed, "I never know what he's thinking."

"He's thinking about his mother," my brother said.

"I never knew what she was thinking either."

On leaving to return to London, I leaned down towards him to say good-bye, and, unexpectedly, he put his hand on my head and said hoarsely, *"Sois sage, tsi gars."*

This sudden blessing and admonition shocked me, for it inspired in me, all at once, a depth of devotion to him that I had never before felt as I did then, a devotion that I longed to give myself up to but that frightened me.

He died of heart failure while I was away.

After his death, my mother became more and more withdrawn, and, unable any longer to walk about the house restlessly and wrapped in a blanket in a chair in the dim living room, she became as silent as he had been.

The last time I saw her—Donald was no longer able to cope, though he visited her every day—she was in a home. She simply stared at me. I left her feeling, with utter starkness, that nothing, absolutely nothing, was possible that might give meaning to this world, and that any longing I had for such a meaning led only to a false devotion to what did not exist.

She died in a hospital bed during the night.

After her death, I remained for a week back in the house in the parish I was born and brought up in, back in the house that long before had been cut from the forest, back in that wooden clapboard bungalow the attic roof beams of which exuded, hot summer after summer for years and years, hot tears of resin.

In bed in my former room, I lay as if waiting for something to happen, and it occurred to me that all my childhood I had, night after night, woken in that room in the wonder and terror of a face appearing at the dark window.

Now, the face would be one of the many, of the millions, who stood outside in a vast forest outside my window. Out there, massed among the trees, one of them might appear at my window and look in, or even appear at the foot of my bed and stare down at me, and the appearance would confirm all my feelings that, though I did not believe in this, the dead were among us.

I prayed for my mother to please not to appear to me, but if she did appear that she confine my vision to the world and help me with the demands of this world she so insisted I fulfill, not punish me for not fulfilling, even failing in, such demands. I prayed, in her, to stand in the light, which is temporal and illuminates the things of the world. I prayed for her to put the world right.

I prayed for my father not to appear, but if he should appear that he open to me all the darkness beyond the world, in which I knew was my greatest fulfillment. In him, I prayed to give in to the darkness, which is eternal and makes insignificant the things of the world, all those things that can never, ever be put right.

I thought of how, as I had grown into my manhood, I had always believed I was closer to my mother than to my father, loved her as I didn't love my father, felt not only that she understood me but that I understood her more than my father did. But now I felt I was closer to my father, loved him as I had never loved my mother, felt not only that he understood me but that I had understood him more than my mother did. I felt that if the parent who I felt defined my life was the father, then my mother was my father, for my mother always tried to strengthen my resolve to stand away from her, independent of her. And if the parent who I felt most gave me life in all its undefined possibilities was the mother, then my father was my mother. My father weakened me and made me long to be accepted into his arms.

22

MY BROTHERS LEFT ME ALONE IN OUR FAMILY HOUSE
to go through our parents' belongings.

As a break from sorting out household goods—the
clothes to be given to charity, the furniture also, as the house
was to be sold—I visited Matante Cora. She was eighty-six,
younger than I had thought. She had always seemed very old
to me. She still wore the green visor against the light that
hurt her now-almost-blind eyes intolerably, and I watched
her bathe them with water she collected from a little pond on
the flats below the parish on a certain day when God blessed
all the waters of the earth and rendered them especially
curative.

I asked, "That prayer he got from his mother to cure
burns—was that an Indian prayer?"

"*Je n'sais pas,*" Matante Cora said, no longer interested in
prayer that had not been passed on to her.

My father's prayer died with him.

Matante Cora recited her own prayers, with what appeared to be a vibrating chin, while she bathed her eyes.

Back in my parents' home, I found, in my mother's bureau, all the pretty nightgowns that I had bought her over
the years and which she had never worn. Again, I looked
through my father's wardrobe, knowing now what was in it,
except for a hernia truss I had not seen before. The drawers
smelled musky. I took the folder of his papers to keep.

I had been through the Chippendale desk a number of

times when my mother was still alive, taking from it records of the family life before she threw them out, as I knew she was in the process of doing. I thought there could not be anything left of any interest to me. In the bottom drawer, among newspaper articles about people she had admired, recipes from magazines she had never used, and old Christmas cards, I found a manila envelope on which she had written, in her perfect handwriting: "Plante Genealogy." My mother, the keeper of the official records, had saved it.

Typed on an old typewriter on gray sheets of paper I read:

Lignée d'ascendance Plante

Première Génération:

Nicolas Plante, mort le 21 Mai 1647, et Elisabeth Chauvin, morte le 19 février 1649, de Laleu, faubourg de la Rochelle, Aunis en France.

Deuxième Génération:

Jean Plante. Marié à Françoise Boucher. Le 1 septembre 1650 à Notre-Dame de Québec.

Troisième Génération:

François Plante. Marié à Louise Bérard. Le 26 octobre 1694 Château Richer à Québec.

Quatrième Génération:

Jean-Baptiste Plante. Marié à Jeanne Millet. Le 28 avril 1721 à Ile Dupas à Québec.

Cinquième Génération:

Jean-Baptiste Plante. Marié à Marie Louise Coutu. Le 7 février 1752 à Lanoraie.

Sixième Génération:

Antoine Plante. Marié à Geneviève Gouin. Le 29 août 1791. Rémarié à Louise Cheverette. Le 18 août 1800 à St. Cuthbert.

Septième Génération:

Louis Plante. Marié à Josephte Soulières. Le 30 juin 1824 à St. Cuthbert à Québec.

Huitième Génération:

Cyriac Plante. Marié à Claire Francoeur. Le 11 juillet 1864 à St. Barthélémy à Québec.

Neuvième Génération:

Anaclet Plante. Marié à Modeste Lajoie. Le 2 juillet 1895 à St. Barthélémy.

Dixième Génération:

Anaclet Plante. Marié à Albina Bisson. Le 12 juillet, 1922 à Providence, Rhode Island.[1]

---

1. Ancestral lineage Plante

First Generation:

Nicolas Plante, died 21 May 1647, and Elisabeth Chauvin, died 19 February 1649, of Laleu, suburb of la Rochelle, Aunis in France.

Second Generation:

Jean Plante. Married to Françoise Boucher. 1 September 1650 at Notre-Dame de Québec.

Third Generation:

François Plante. Married to Louise Bérard. 26 October 1694 at Château Richer in Québec.

Fourth Generation:

Jean-Baptiste Plante. Married to Jeanne Millet. 28 April 1721 at Ile Dupas in Québec.

Fifth Generation:

Jean-Baptiste Plante. Married to Marie Louise Coutu. 7 February 1752 at Lanoraie.

If I was, through my father, a first-generation United Statesian, I found I was, through him, an eleventh-generation North American.

But, reading quickly all the names from 1647 down to my parents' names on their marriage in 1922, I felt come over me a great tiredness, and more than tiredness, and without studying it I put the genealogy along with the other papers back into the envelope and closed it with the little metal clip through the hole in the flap.

And yet, as tired as I was and not that interested, I took the list to Matante Cora, who had me read it, her hands over her eyes, which apparently gave her great pain. When she lowered her hands, she said nothing, and she seemed to be as little interested as I, our knowing about our ancestry perhaps not mattering after all.

I asked her who had given the list to my grandmother.

"A relative in Canada, no doubt," she answered.

"We have relatives in Canada?"

Sixth Generation:

Antoine Plante. Married to Geneviève Gouin. 29 August 1791. Remarried to Louise Cheverette. 18 August 1800 at St. Cuthbert.

Seventh Generation:

Louis Plante. Married to Josephte Soulières. 30 June 1824 at St. Cuthbert in Québec.

Eighth Generation:

Cyriac Plante. Married to Claire Francoeur. 11 July 1864 at St. Barthélémy in Québec.

Ninth Generation:

Anaclet Plante. Married to Modeste Lajoie. 2 July 1895 at St. Barthélémy.

Tenth Generation:

Anaclet Plante. Married to Albina Bisson. 12 July 1922 in Providence, Rhode Island.

"Oh, yes."

"Who?"

She shrugged her large, round shoulders.

"My grandma wasn't in touch with any of them?"

"She was in touch with a sister who stayed in Canada, but she died."

"She had a sister?"

"She had a lot of stepsisters and stepbrothers, I can't remember how many. She was the only daughter of her mother, Rosalie Cliche, who died some time after she was born, and her father remarried."

"Another Indian?"

"A French woman."

It occurred to me that the genealogy did not trace my grandmother's ancestry, and I wondered if that was because, on her mother's side, it was untraceable.

I went back to London thinking I would never, ever return to my parish.

I put the manila envelope with my father's papers, including the genealogy, into a bottom drawer in the desk in my study.

All that I really felt about my revealed ancestry was that I must protect myself from it, perhaps by forgetting about it.

23

IN LONDON I LED A LIFE WITH NIKOS THAT WAS SECURE in his love for me. In his love, he made me aware of the world socially, politically, historically, and even, as a force that could ground a floating life, religiously, for I went with him every Greek Easter to the midnight Resurrection service, sometimes with friends whom we invited later to our flat for a meal of dyed red eggs, a soup called *magertiza,* and a brioche called *tsourekhi* and flavored with a spice I had never heard of called *machlepi.* His world became my world for the particulars of it.

But, together, we both lived in the larger world of England, which had its politics, its own history, its own religion, its own particulars.

We were friendly with the historian Steven Runciman, who, every time he came to us for dinner, brought us eggs from his hens and whom we visited in his haunted castle in Scotland.

As an entertaining gesture of recognition of my history, he always set at my place at the dining table a plate printed with a scene of a French Jesuit and Indians paddling through rapids. Surprising me, he told me that North America *should* be French. I said that of course it should be, but I was unable to explain to him, on his examining me, why, and he, "deploring" my ignorance of my history, gave me a tutorial on the machinations of the founder of the British Empire, William Pitt, whom he disliked intensely. I did not tell Steven how little I knew about William Pitt, whose monumental marble statue I vaguely recalled having seen in Westminster Abbey. I did not even know that the American city of Pittsburgh was named after him. So I was taught by Runciman how Pitt, a stubborn, gouty man in London, organized the British to take over North America from the

French in order to command the lucrative trade in cod and beaver pelts.

The revelation to me was how important the city of Quebec was in determining the history of the entire continent, for I had thought the conquest of Quebec by Wolfe had to do only with Canadian history, not that of the United States; and, in any case, Canada had not really existed for me as a country with a history, but only as an ahistorical country of miracles. The conquest of Quebec on the Plains of Abraham, where the French Montcalm was surprised by Wolfe's troops, who during the night had climbed up the cliff side to the plateau of the plains and by dawn were in formation for battle, opened up the whole of North America to the English, opened it up, in effect, to the expansion of the colonies of New England. Canada took on a history relevant to the United States, even though this was for me a negative history, because I saw for the first time that the French, my ancestors, had been dispossessed of La Nouvelle France— dispossessed, I suppose, of territories they considered theirs simply because they had dominated them with their forts. With an ironical laugh and yet a slight but familiar sense of having to accept defeat, I said, "I wouldn't have had to feel inferior to the Yankees."

"You've been to Canada?" Steven asked.

"I haven't."

"Shame on you."

He and Nikos then discussed Nikos's history, which was that of a Constantinopolitan Greek dispossessed of *his* history by the Ottoman Empire.

24

FOR LIFE, FOR A WEEKEND WITH NIKOS IN THE
Wiltshire countryside with friends, for a walk with them
through valleys and streams to the overgrown arboretum,
for drinks with them in the smoky village pub, for dinner
and gossip with them about other friends, I had to reject
my country, which was not really the United States of America
but some other country of darkness that antedated the
United States of America. Nikos helped me.

I had a letter from Gloria, with whom I remained in
touch, but as if in touch with a former life that was at the very
tip of my index finger. Having been escorted by the police to
the Spanish border by the police and warned not to return,
she'd lived in Berlin for some years, singing in a dive. But
Berlin was a dump, and she was coming to London, where
she had a job singing in a dive. I went to see her there. Her
eyes always appeared wide open and the irises spinning, and
her voice cracked on even the low notes of her blues songs.
She asked me if I had a girlfriend yet. No, I said, I was with
a guy. As my European mother, she wanted to meet Nikos
to approve or not. I didn't want her to meet him, but she insisted.
When she came to our flat, she talked about Spain as
if to exclude Nikos from it, a Fascist country he, in any case,
would not go to. She would go back, she didn't care if she was
arrested, but she'd go back to Spain. Harold and Debbie had
already returned. London was a dump. She hardly said goodbye
to Nikos, and at the street door with her she told me she

didn't like him. Nikos didn't say anything about her, but she had revealed herself to me in his eyes as a woman who, if I had tried to live according to her prejudiced approvals and disapprovals, could have destroyed me. She left for Spain.

I counted on Nikos to make me see what I hadn't seen before, in people, in politics, in history, and what I saw opened dimensions upon dimensions in my life. But there was always the moment, especially on a winter Sunday evening, when everything about me became dimensionless, and I would find myself thinking, starkly, of my parish and, secreted within the tabernacle of the church of my parish, my Canuck God, the God of that country of darkness.

At those moments, which always occurred while I was at my desk writing, the window before me misted and dark, I would feel, with a sense of panic that made the need acute, that what I most had to do in life was to protect myself against my God, to whom I was fatally drawn. He was the God of death.

I had no reason to want to die, had every reason to live my life with a richness that I, growing up in my parish, had fantasized might be possible outside the parish, the life I had with Nikos.

Immediately, I would assure myself: No, I don't want to die.

That these moments always occurred while I was writing meant they would perhaps not occur if I stopped writing; but I went on writing obsessively, so much so that Nikos would come into the room where I was alone and tell me writing too much was not good for me and I must come away and listen to music with him. If I insisted on going on, he would leave me to it, but resentfully, as if I were defying him. He called me stubborn, willful, even, at times of my having given into an obsession that would last the entire weekend when we might otherwise have gone to a gallery or a concert or out for a meal, selfish.

One Sunday he warned me that if I didn't stop writing, we would be late for a dinner party given by Sonia Orwell, the widow of George Orwell, with whom we had become friendly.

That Sonia and I were both lapsed Catholics was, she had said to me when we'd found this out about each other, "our secret."

She rejected God, any God, with a force that would have destroyed God had God existed. A cigarette in one hand and a glass of wine in the other, her ash-blond and gray hair shaking as she, frowning deeply, shook her head from side to side, she would rage, rage, not only against any belief in God, which she found totally uninteresting, but against God himself for ever having supposed he existed, for ever having supposed he was of any interest to anyone. He had *never* existed, and he was of no, but absolutely *no,* interest.

As a beautiful girl and athletic and blond, Sonia was born in India and then educated in the convent school of the Sacred Heart nuns in Roehampton, England. She hated, then and forever, the nuns, and if you were with her out in the street when a nun appeared, even one in an abbreviated veil and dark blue pleated skirt and white blouse and plain cardigan and black pumps (not unlike the skirt, blouse, cardigan, and pumps Sonia herself usually wore), her face would contract into a scowl of hatred, and sometimes she would spit.

The nuns, she said, had made her bathe in a long white shift so she wouldn't see her body, had denied her a mirror to brush her hair, had insisted she lie in bed with her arms crossed over her girl's bosom as if she were a corpse so that she would be in the position to receive God if he came during the night to take her away into the hereafter, that hereafter for which she must sacrifice everything *here*. She left the convent determined to reject everything promised in the hereafter for everything here.

Sonia's house in South Kensington had polished parquet floors, bright rugs, and small, round tables with long, delicately curved legs and, always, vases of flowers on the tables, and books. There were, around the sitting room, shelves and shelves of books, for Sonia was a great reader. The fire in the fireplace might be lit. The air in her house appeared filled with reflected light from polished surfaces, from crystal, from mirrors, even on grim, gray days. There would be drinks in the sitting room, then dinner in her basement dining room, where the table was set with a starched white cloth and starched white napkins and gleaming china and glasses and silver, at the center a small bunch of pretty flowers. She wanted everything to be pretty. The meals she prepared were mostly French, as were the wines she had opened and put on the buffet to breathe. A Francophile, she said the French enjoyed life more than the English did, and, at the end of a meal, instead of asking everyone to go upstairs to the sitting room for coffee, she would keep her friends around the table for the coffee and more wine and talk, as she said was done in France. This was a France I did not know.

Her dinner parties required of her a great effort, a duty

even, and after having made the effort, performed the duty, as if to confirm that the things of this life matter because there is no other life, she would hardly eat what she had prepared but would sit a little removed from the table and drink and smoke as her friends ate, and she would, as the evening deepened, take a more and more commanding view of her friends, all of whom she devoted herself to. And it usually happened, when everyone was sitting about the table long past coffee but with smudged glasses of wine, that there would occur in Sonia's devotion, which was like a great cloud that enveloped everyone, a sudden shock of thunder and lightning. She would attack a friend for something he— always, as far as I knew, he—said.

At a dinner party, she suddenly attacked a friend, in the context of a conversation about the German Nazi concentration camps, for expressing horror at them. There was, she would insist, no expression of the horror of the camps that was equal to what they had been. She recounted having been to, I think, Belsen with her friend Marguerite Duras and her rage when Duras expressed horror, Sonia answering Duras' horror with, "*What* did you imagine it would have been like? *What?*" To Sonia, the extermination camps were so indicative of the fact of human baseness, she took them as a given: of course people would exterminate other people, for whatever reason, *of course*. She even became angry at her Jewish friends for any bewilderment they might have had about the baseness of humans towards humans, for they, above all, should know just how base humans could be. When Sonia read the unpublished memoir of a former inmate of a detention, not an extermination, camp which he was trying to get published, she said, "He was in a very minor concentration camp." Friends took this as a parody of Sonia's snobbery —and she was, she herself admitted, an intellectual snob, perhaps instilled in her by the Sacred Heart nuns, also intellectual snobs: if you read about the French philosopher Jacques Lacan in the review section of newspapers, you soon met him at Sonia's house—but her denouncing the former inmate of what Sonia called a minor camp for presuming to use his experiences there to promote the publication of his memoirs, which Sonia found badly written, showed the depth of her basic conviction that everyone really *is* vain, that vanity really *is* everything. Beyond stating the starkest facts, you could not express any feelings about horror that were not expressions of your basic vanity, and the more emotional your expressed feelings the more you were filled with vanity.

She would have reacted with the same outrage to your saying that humans can be more than human, that when they are touched by God's grace they transcend themselves, cease to be selfish, and become selfless and devoted and helpful to others, that a person has a soul and that after death the soul is meant to be united with God in eternity. She would have denounced you: humans cannot be more than human, are motivated only by utter selfishness, which is totally destructive, and are incapable of selflessness. Humans have no souls and no other fate but to die, and to die means to cease to exist and nothing more.

I admired her, I admired her even when, drunk, her denunciations became relentless. "How could you say that? How could you? How?" You drew back into silence, and the other guests tried to change the subject, but Sonia kept after you: "How *could* you have said that?"

I never minded Sonia denouncing me at one of her dinner parties, not only because I knew she would telephone the next morning to apologize and to invite me again, but because I believed that she had the right to, believed that in her rejecting a faith that tried to destroy her in the name of trying to save her she had earned the right to denounce hypocrisies, had learned that all expressions of feeling are in an essential way hypocritical. It reassured me to be denounced by Sonia.

Though Nikos more and more refused to go because he saw her as a destructive person and would not submit to being denounced by her, I, against his warnings, went alone to Sonia's dinner parties and was denounced. When I said, drunk on wine, that I wondered if, even for an irreligious writer, it was possible to write a book that was religious, she said, "You can't be a *deep* writer if you say that. No one who says what you've said can be a *deep* writer." Religion in a novel, in any work of art, she said, made the work obvious, made the work banal and pretentious. "I know you're right," I said, "I know," and I had that curious, slightly thrilling sense of having said what I'd said just to get Sonia to react as she did. Maybe I risked bringing up religion with Sonia so she would reproach me for bringing it up. I was drawn to Sonia partly because she reassured me in my being lapsed, and I sometimes made provocative statements about religion that I knew she'd condemn me for, because her reaction, which I could count on, reassured me all the more about my being lapsed, and, more, the very attention she gave me by condemning me reassured me. I almost felt rejected by her when she desisted.

She said, "Hrumph," and, as if to make up for turning her attention away from me, asked me to open more bottles of wine, which were on the buffet. I did, with pleasure. Wine was essential. Food was essential. Dinner parties were *essential.*

Why, I wondered, didn't Sonia kill herself? I then thought, Sonia might wake up every morning filled with remorse for having attacked a friend the evening before at a dinner party and wanting to die, but she wouldn't kill herself because the desire to die was an expression of a religious longing to be elsewhere, which she had absolutely denied herself, and she had denied it because all such longings were false, and they were false because *there was no elsewhere.*

She invited me to tea, maybe to reassure me after having attacked me at her dinner party. I found that when I was alone with her, she would get onto a subject—almost always a friend—and talk and talk about that friend as if the talk itself would sort out that person, who badly needed to be sorted out. Most often when I tried to add to the sorting out, she would say, "You *don't* understand." That afternoon, a grim winter afternoon, her sitting room warm with a fire and bright with all the lamps lit, the person was the writer Rosamund Lehmann, whom I told Sonia I had met at a dinner party. I described Rosamund Lehmann, tall and big-boned with a very white face and long, white hair, as looking like a moon goddess, which made Sonia frown severely at me. I should have known by that frown not to continue to talk about Rosamund Lehmann, whom Sonia evidently disapproved of but whom she nevertheless felt compelled to sort out. I said I wondered if what explained Rosamund Lehmann —whom I didn't know at all well—was her belief in the ghost of her dead daughter appearing to her, which she'd written about in her book *The Swan in the Evening*. Sonia frowned even more severely.

"You *read* that book?"

"Yes, I did," I answered.

"How could you have? You don't believe in ghosts, a stupid, childish, self-indulgent belief, so why should you indulge someone else's belief in ghosts? I don't understand."

"I wanted to find out about what she had to say."

"About a ghost appearing to her?"

"Yes."

"That interests you?"

"Well, yes, it interests me, in a way."

"How *could* it? How *could* you be interested in anything so stupid, childish, self-indulgent?"

"I guess it is stupid, childish, self-indulgent."

Sonia lit a cigarette, shook her hair back and stared at me with narrowed, bloodshot, angry eyes and said in a low, hard voice, "It *is*."

While she talked, the smoke of her many cigarettes making the air dull, I had one of those moments of wanting to die. I told myself I must not indulge myself in it any more than Sonia would indulge me in it. But I wasn't able to concentrate on what Sonia said. I wanted to be as hard on myself for the longings that occurred to me as I thought Sonia would have been had she known about them. She would have considered any expression of my longing to be in a world where I would no longer have to endure the agony of the longings as nothing more than an expression of my vanity, because, again and yet again, *there was no other world.*

Sonia stopped talking and looked at me, and I suddenly imagined that her most driving desire was to push her non-belief down and down—or, better, up and up—until it blanked out all possibility of belief, everywhere, in any form of transcendence, until the space all around the earth became totally dark and, instead of drawing people's attention farther and farther outward, deflected it back to the world. The real horror for Sonia, I realized, was not so much in the world as in the God she had once been made to believe created the world.

As soon as I was out in the street, I saw through the windows, over which she hadn't drawn the curtains, the lights in the sitting room go off abruptly.

At the end of her life, she lived in London in a hotel because she had, through litigation with the lawyers of the Orwell estate who were, she thought, criminally mismanaging the revenues, lost her beautiful house. I visited her for the last time in her room in the hotel. She was in bed, in a long white nightgown with pretty white ribbons at the throat. When I asked her how she was, she said, "Well, I'm dying," and this was said as the starkest fact. All I could do was nod my head.

Suddenly, as if in a moment of grace that distracted her from her constant disposition to be enraged about something, Sonia's face changed totally from the haggard, puffy, and wrinkled, frowning face of an aging, resentful woman to the smooth and clear and bright face of an innocent and vulnerable girl.

"I'm dying," she said again.

25

I CONTINUED TO GO TO ORTHODOX EASTER WITH Nikos, because, though I did not believe in God, Nikos did, and his was a God of life.

One Easter, I went with him to the midnight Resurrection service, not in a Greek church, as Nikos stayed away from Greeks in London, but the Russian one in Ennismore Gardens. In the dark church, people seemed to move about in a thickness of incense, their thin candles, stuck in circles cut from cardboard, held ready for the moment at midnight when Metropolitan Bloom, a Jew who had converted to Russian Orthodoxy, called out that Christ was risen and all the candles would be lit from one central candle to illuminate the church. Nikos and I stood next to a young woman, a beautiful young woman with a smooth white face and black hair, who, I noted, kept staring up into the semidomed apse behind and above the iconostasis. The service was approaching the moment of the Resurrection, when the doors of the iconostasis would open and Metropolitan Bloom would emerge. I kept shifting from one foot to the other, restless in body and soul with that restlessness that comes from anxiety that seems to have no cause, and to be all the more overwhelming for having no known cause. I glanced from time to time at the young woman at my side, whose eyes, wide open, were fixed upward, and suddenly, as if my glancing at her were the reason, she began to scream, to scream so the chorus stopped and the entire church went still. I stepped away from the young woman, and as I did an older woman from the congregation stepped towards her, put her arms about her, and held her, and the young woman became quiet.

Nikos said, "Let's go," and we left the church before the Resurrection.

Whatever sense of celebration Nikos had intended for us both was gone, and, back home, we spiritlessly ate the soup, *mageritsa,* he had prepared and the brioche, *tsoureki,* he had bought from a special bakery near the Greek Cathedral in Moscow Road. Nikos turned on the radio so we could listen to the service, as if to give it, from a distance, another chance, but over the radio we heard the screaming again. The announcer asked us to pray for the young woman. Soon after, we heard, beyond the insistently driven chanting, the siren of an ambulance, and Nikos shut off the radio.

"Why do you think she was screaming?" I asked.

"She was mad," Nikos said.

I began to weep, and, unable to control myself, I went to a wall and stood facing it and sobbed, tears and saliva running down my face.

When he asked, "Why can't my love for you be enough?" I turned around to him and held him to me, and this physical contact with him calmed me.

The next day, Easter Sunday, I, as on every other day, sat down to write, against Nikos's admonition that I stop writing for a while. I couldn't stop.

A terrible anxiety would overwhelm me whenever I stopped even for a meal.

I would ask myself, Do I really, really *need* to write?

This question would impel me to write more and more. The more I wrote the more possessed by my writing I became, and the more possessed the more anxious to relieve myself of my possession. I wrote out of anxiety, and the anxiety was never eased, but always heightened, by the writing.

Unable to make a narrative cohere, this requiring more *intention* than I was capable of, I concentrated on making images exist so much in themselves that what they revealed would have to do with *them* and not with me. What happened was that they became detached from the text and appeared unrelated to it—and in their detachment they drew so much attention to themselves that the only effect they'd have would be to make the reader wonder what their meaning was.

Reading something I'd written, Nikos, whom I trusted totally, would ask, "I don't understand—why the glass of water in the dark room?"

I had hoped the glass of water in the dark room would *in itself* infuse the story with so positive a sense of *some* meaning, however incomprehensible, that the very positiveness of the sense would negate any question of incomprehension, and, more, would resound with the deepest, because the most mysterious, meaning of the story. The story, Nikos pointed out, became incidental to its images.

I couldn't sleep.

The more I wrote, the more I tried to account for everything, everything, everything, everything I saw, heard, touched, smelled, tasted. Though I wrote fiction, the fiction was incidental to the diary that I'd started when I first came to Europe as a student and that I continued, more and more obsessively, to keep. Over the years, it swelled and swelled into millions of words, millions of images in words, in my attempt to get everything in. This possession—by what? by the world? by something all around but beyond the world? —dated back to my early years in my parish and became more and more demanding; and the more demanding it became the more I knew I would never be able to possess the possession, never.

I asked myself what would happen if, as an experiment, I stopped writing. Would I die? I thought I would. Was writing that necessary to me? I thought it was. I would lose everything and I would die.

On a quiet, still Saturday afternoon in London this happened:

I heard a church bell ring, and it suddenly sounded to me like the church bell of my parish ringing for evening vespers. The ringing was both distant and near, and, hearing it, I felt what I had always felt about my parish when the bell for vespers rang: that there was no one to hear it, that all around was deserted, abandoned, like an abandoned fortress. The bell, both far and near, sounded both feeble and loud, as if it were, in the empty space about it, echoing itself, and it sounded as infinitely sad as a tolling bell.

I felt what I had felt as a teenager when I lived in the parish and went to vespers, which itself appeared, on a starkly quiet and still Saturday afternoon, an isolated ritual of a tired priest and a few tired parishioners. I felt that the parish was dead, and that this deadness circled me in ever-deepening and enclosing circles, so that I, too, died inside, and, as though I could sense the very moment of my death in everything about me becoming flat and colorless, I knew that I would never, ever come back to life, that I was eternally dead.

And yet, against that eternal death, I began to write a novel about my early life in the parish. But the writing was completely incoherent in my need to account for *all* my early life in the parish, as if to get it all in would in some way bring it and me back to life. Image followed image as they occurred to me without order, and I was unable to relate them to one another. The recollection of the drawer in my bureau in which I kept my treasures as a boy—a squirrel's skull, a crystal prism from a chandelier, a rusty key—would impel me to give those things their full context, which was the context of the entire parish, of the only authentic reality I had ever known. And when I tried to write about the relationships between my mother and father and the relationships among all my brothers and my relationships with them all, I was lost.

One night I woke and for a moment thought I was back in my bedroom in the house in the parish, hearing, from behind the headboard, the voices of my parents in their bed.

I thought more deeply than ever about being a Canuck, which at my most authentic I was, though being a Canuck meant, at the deepest, being a failure.

Nikos did everything possible to reassure me that I was not a failure.

But I felt humiliated in all my ambitions, and I was sure

that everyone I knew and had ever known, apart from Nikos, was aware that I was and would always be a failure in my ambitions.

Even when I was a boy, in the foyer of my parish church after early morning Mass, *les bonnes femmes de la paroisse* had gathered, and, *chuchotants,* talked about my expectations and my failings. Who was I to think that I could leave the parish and become something other than a parochial Canuck?

Why should I feel anything but failure? Why should I feel a success in anything, when, as a Canuck, it was foregone that I would not succeed? Expect nothing, I told myself, expect nothing.

We were the white niggers, the Canucks, the people for whom this very term was thought up. We came down from Canada, from the forests of Canada, to the States to do the jobs the blacks wouldn't do. And we did the jobs well; we performed our duties; we never complained, and there was no bitterness in us against injustices. We were invisible.

We were invisible, and it was better for us that we were invisible, better for us that we should become more and more invisible and disappear.

I didn't want to know anything about my Canuck ancestry, but at the same time I didn't want to be anything but a Canuck, because, in my own ignorance and in the even greater ignorance of the world about Canucks, that meant disappearing, and that was what I wanted to do. I was different from the American Yankees, the American Irish, the American Jews, the American blacks. I was different for being a lowly part Indian Canuck Catholic American, and I insisted on being this because I sensed in my own deeply se-

rious, deeply unironical, deeply clear religious purity everything I wanted to be, which was to be altogether invisible. At
moments I would find myself thinking:

Purifiez nos coeurs.
Purify our hearts.

And this meant: Purify our hearts with great space, in
which we expect nothing, in which our awareness is the
awareness of the great darkness, nothing but darkness.

We Canucks prayed for this. We prayed to be ghosts.

On a crowded London bus in the rain at night, an inexplicable panic came over me at the sound of the donging bell
that the conductor rang to let the driver know the passengers
boarding were now on and he could continue, and the only
way I could cope with the panic was not by willing myself to
sit still but by believing that I was asleep and dreaming.

Then, off the bus and crossing a street, the headlights of
the stopped cars shining on me and illuminating the falling
rain in vague, bright circles, I felt I couldn't walk any farther,
exactly as in a dream, and I wanted to lie on the street and sleep.

Nikos insisted I see a doctor.

Physically healthy—if I didn't know anything more
about my ancestry than names and places, I did know that
I came from a strong stock of *habitants,* the farmers and
woodsmen of French Canada—I was reluctant to go to my
GP, whom I hardly ever did go to. The doctor recommended
psychiatry, but I said no. I didn't want to go into myself in
that way, refused to go into myself, and however much that
refusal to go into myself might have been the beginning of a

psychiatric treatment of therapeutic revelations to me, I wouldn't do it. I knew that no revelations made within myself would save me. As psychologically unhealthy as this might have been, I felt a sense of purity come to me as if from some vast outside when, seeing keys on a key chain on a desk, a notebook and a ballpoint pen, a pair of shoes in the corner of the bedroom, tears welled into my eyes. Objects, banal, man-made objects, could be, for me, the points of focus of an otherwise unfocused tenderness and love for everything and everyone in the world. This grief in the awareness of objects —which I knew, choking up at the sight of a suitcase being carried by an old person crossing a street, could so easily become an embarrassment, not only if expressed to others but to myself—nevertheless meant everything to me. Maybe, I thought, it was only the age a person lived in that determined what was embarrassing or not, and the age I lived in found everything that did not have to do with success embarrassing. I thought this age I was living in should look for and find its greatest and most sincere expression in its feeling for a bouquet of white and yellow daisies, or in a broken baby's rattle, or in a blue enameled tin cup of steaming tea on a wooden table.

I didn't sleep and day after day sat at my desk and wrote, knowing that everything I wrote was formless beyond the details I concentrated on. I concentrated on more and more refined details—not the glass but the rim of the glass, not the egg but the bit of straw stuck to the shell, not the shoe but the frayed lace. I couldn't stop myself.

At night, I lay with my eyes open. Unable to sleep, I often woke Nikos, who put an arm around me to try again to reassure me, but even then I lay still, my eyes open.

26

I FOUND IT IMPOSSIBLE TO MAKE CONNECTIONS.

I tried to make an act of faith that in some way, out beyond my rational understanding, *things* connected themselves. But this led to an infinite anonymous chaos of *things*.

I tried this: in my reading, which was itself chaotic, I would write down in a commonplace book whatever passages struck me, imagining that if one passage struck me and not another, it would be for a reason that I needn't be conscious of, but that it must have some relevance, though relevance to what, I left vague about.

Here are entries from my commonplace book:

O if I am to have so much, let me have more!
Walt Whitman

The meal in the firkin; the milk in the pail; the ballad in the street; the news of the boat; the glance of the eye; the form and gait of the body.
Ralph Waldo Emerson

The more I get into my drama itself, the more magnificent, upon my word, I seem to see it and feel it; with such a tremendous lot of possibilities in it that I positively quake in dread of the muchness with which they threaten me.
Henry James, *Notes to "The Sense of the Past"*

There are innumerable consciousnesses of *want,* no one of which taken in itself has a name, but all different from each other. Such a feeling of want is *toto coelo* other than a want of feeling: it is an intense feeling. The rhythm of a lost word may be there without a sound to clothe it; or the evanescent sense of something which is the initial vowel or consonant may mock us fitfully, without growing more distinct.... What is that first instantaneous glimpse of someone's meaning which we have, when in a vulgar phrase we say we "twig" it? Surely an altogether specific affection of the mind. And has the reader never asked himself what kind of a mental fact is his *intention of saying a thing* before he has said it? It is an entirely definite intention, distinct from all other intentions, an absolutely distinct state of consciousness, therefore; and yet how much of it consists of definite sensorial images, either of words or of things? Hardly anything!...One may admit that a good third of our psychic life consists in these rapid premonitory perspective views not yet articulate.... It is, the reader will see, the reinstatement of the vague and the inarticulate to its proper place in our mental life which I am so anxious to press on the attention.

William James, *The Principles of Psychology*

"The word is on the tip of my tongue."... James, in writing of this subject, is really trying to say: "What a remarkable experience!" The word is not there yet, and yet in a certain sense it is there,—or something is there, which *cannot* grow into anything but this word. But this is not experience at all. *Interpreted* as experience it does indeed look odd.

Ludwig Wittgenstein, *Philosophical Investigations*

Can anything appear in a vivid image that has no image?

Fyodor Dostoyevsky, *The Idiot*

God alone is man's true good, and since man abandoned him it is a strange fact that nothing in nature has been found to take his place: stars, sky, earth, elements, plants, cabbages, leeks, animals, insects, calves, serpents, fever, plague, war, famine, vice, adultery, incest.

Blaise Pascal, *Pensées*

These are the imaginary forms that appear before the final vision of Brahman: a mist, a smoke, and a sun; a wind, fire-flies, and a fir; lightnings, a clear crystal, and a moon.

Svetasvatara Upanishad

Are we, perhaps, *here* just for saying: House,
Bridge, Fountain, Gate, Jug, Fruit Tree, Window,—
Possibly: Pillar, Tower?
Rainer Maria Rilke, *The Duino Elegies*

Whatever else is certain, this at least is certain—that the world of our present natural knowledge *is* enveloped in a larger world of *some* sort whose residual properties we at present can frame no positive idea.

William James, *Is Life Worth Living?*

A pitcher, a harrow abandoned in a field, a dog in the sun, a neglected cemetery, a cripple, a peasant's hut—all these can become the vessel of my revelation. Each of these objects and a thousand others similar, can suddenly, at any moment (which I am utterly powerless to invoke), assume for me a character so exalted and moving that words seem too poor to describe them.

Hugo von Hofmannsthal

He said "tree" out loud and it was a word. He saw branches with vague substance blocked round them, he saw lawn, all green, and he built up a picture of lawn and tree, but through were gaps, and his brain reeled from the effort of filling them. . . .

Flashes came back to him of things seen and remembered, but they were not clear-cut. Little bits in a wood, a pool in a hedge with red flowers somewhere, a red-coated man in the distance on a white horse galloping, the sea with violet patches over grey where the seaweed stained it, silver where the sun rays met it. A gull coming up from beneath a cliff.

Henry Green, *Blindness*

These images vanished altogether from the broad dark background which every man sees when he closes his eyes.

Anton Chekhov, "The Kiss"

"I was going to say..."—You remember various details. But not even all of them together show your intention. It is as if a snapshot of a scene had been taken, but only a few scattered details of it were to be seen: here a hand, there a bit of a face, or a hat—the rest is dark. And

now it is as if we knew quite certainly what the whole picture represented. As if we could read the darkness.

Ludwig Wittgenstein, *Philosophical Investigations*

One who is learning further details concerning any
office or art proceeds in darkness, and receives no guid-
ance from his early knowledge, for if he left not that behind he would get no further nor make any progress; and
in the same way, when the soul is making most progress,
it is traveling in darkness, knowing nothing....

For the nearer the soul approaches to God, the blacker
is the darkness which it feels.... So immense is the spiritual light of God, and so greatly does it transcend over
natural understanding, that the nearer we approach it, the
more it blinds and darkens us.

Saint John of the Cross, *The Ascent of Mount Carmel*

I experienced an inexplicable distaste for so much as
uttering the words *spirit, soul* or *body*.

Hugo von Hofmannsthal

All religions will pass, but his will remain: simply sitting in a chair and looking into space.

Vasily Rozanov, *Solitaria*

27

I WASN'T ABLE TO READ ANYTHING AND WOULD STARE
at my collection of Henry James books, as if even to take one

down and read here and there required making connections that were beyond me to make.

One day, a friend telephoned me to say that I might be interested in a letter from the writer she had found among boxes of papers she had just been given by her mother relating to her great-grandfather, the high-Victorian painter William Blake Richmond, to whom James wrote on the death of Richmond's wife. She asked if I'd like to come round with Nikos to have supper and then read the letter. Nikos always encouraged me to go out, however much I didn't want to. He also said I must in some way revive my interest in Henry James, who had been such an inspiration to me, and the letter would be a way of doing that.

Our friend had some of her great-grandfather's paintings, of classical figures and landscapes, hanging in her sitting room.

Sir William Blake Richmond, R.A., was the son of George Richmond, R.A., a painter who in his youth had been a visionary disciple of William Blake and had named his son after him. Sir William Blake Richmond stayed for a while in a villa outside Florence. He was a friend of Sargent. Given the world Richmond lived in, Henry James would naturally have known him. In 1915, Richmond's wife died after being hit by a motorcar in London.

After supper, in the sitting room, I read the letter, written in vermilion on creamy paper, with the address across the top:

21 CARLYLE MANSIONS

CHEYNE WALK

S.W.

At an angle in the top-left corner, also in red, was

TELEPHONE 2417 KENSINGTON

The handwriting was a scrawl, with blots and scratchings-out, in brownish ink that must originally have been black. It started on one side, went to the other side, and, with not enough space there, went back to the first side and up the margin and across the top, where it was signed.

MY DEAR OLD FRIEND,

How can I "write" to you under this cruellest & most unspeakable of calamities, & yet how can I be silent? ... To have been what she was, with that flawless distinction, all the years, with this black atrocity *waiting*, makes one ask what is the sense of life? The only thing that glimmers out to me is this light of measureless human pity (just) in which I think of you—poor for you as is the value of *that*! Please believe at any rate how embracingly I reach out to you, and that I am more than I can say your old, old friend

Henry James

P.S. I am badly unwell—so please excuse the poor troubled blots of this wretched page.

November 23rd 1915

This was one of Henry James's last letters. He died on February 28, 1916.

I was struck by his having thought of the accident, "the black atrocity," as *waiting*, which was what James had done, I imagined, all his life, and I imagined that this waiting for the black atrocity had given his life its deepest meaning. If death had a secret, I prayed that it had been revealed to him in the end, as I prayed that it would be revealed to me in the end.

But there was *nothing* to be revealed in the end.

I was aware that Nikos watched me closely. He rang often from his office in the publishing house, and if I didn't answer, he became worried; not to worry him, I would ring him to let him know I was going out, even if this was simply to go shopping for our supper.

His mother died in Athens, and he went for the funeral.

For the week without him, I didn't sleep and longed, with a physical longing, for his return.

When he did come back, he said about death, "It's a part of life."

I had never heard this. I realized that I had always assumed death was altogether other than life, the commencement of another state of being that divided itself off from being as I knew it. I didn't understand how death could be a part of life.

In bed with Nikos asleep beside me, I would look at the very faint light that showed around the closed curtains of the bedroom, just enough light for me to see the geranium plant on the bureau, a book on the floor, a shirt hanging on the silent butler.

28

WHENEVER I WAS ALONE, I WOULD SUDDENLY FIND myself staring at the wooden acorn pull of a window blind, a light switch, a leaf fallen to the floor from one of the many plants Nikos kept and tended.

Out of details recalled from my early life, all seen against the vast, dark space that seemed to make them vivid, I managed to assemble some novels, and these novels—to which I gave the simple titles *The Family, The Woods, The Country* —were published in the 1970s.

One was reviewed by the writer Mary Gordon, who subsequently became my closest friend.

Nikos encouraged me in my friendship with her, believing that on some level Mary and I shared what he and I didn't, perhaps because she accepted, in her highly personal but principled terms, Catholicism, and I had rejected the religion on any terms.

When I was on a visit to New York, Mary invited me to stay with her and her family in their home in New Paltz. We visited her mother, who lived in a house nearby, in a neighborhood with maple trees along the sidewalks not unlike the neighborhood I was brought up in. Mary's mother, crippled, was in a wheelchair, a rosary hanging from one of the arms, and while Mary prepared lunch for her, I talked with her about the prayers she said, and, a woman who seemed to have withdrawn almost entirely into herself, she became outgoing.

After, Mary asked me, laughing, "How did you know what to ask my mother?"

"I asked her what I used to ask my mother," I answered.

On the counter in Mary's kitchen, among scrunched-up cellophane wrappings, envelopes and open letters, half-eaten apples, orange peels, and a dog's leash were rosaries and yarmulkes. Mary, her mother Irish Catholic and her father a Jew who converted to Catholicism, said she was trying to bring up her children with a sense of both religions, Judaism and Catholicism. Her husband, Arthur, was Protestant.

It was October, and Mary asked if I'd like to go to a Kol Nidre service with her and her children at the synagogue in New Paltz. I didn't know what Kol Nidre was, and Mary explained: when Jews asked forgiveness for their sins.

"Jews asking forgiveness for their sins?" I asked.

"You think Jews don't sin?" Raising her chin, Mary said, "Let me tell you, Jews sin."

The wooden clapboard synagogue was down a side street, dimly lit with streetlights on poles that leaned slightly in different directions, with wooden clapboard houses that reminded me of streets I had seen in Russia. The synagogue was dark when we entered. We got into a pew with Mary's children, who immediately began to wave to children in other pews, all of whom left to go downstairs to the synagogue hall to play together. A cello was droning, and, intermittently, a cantor chanted mournfully.

I wanted to stay with Mary in that dark synagogue until what I felt from the mourning of the cello and the rabbi became much greater than what I felt when I had come in. Whatever it was I felt, I suddenly wanted it to overwhelm me.

I couldn't recall when I had last been to confession. Was it when I was still living in my parish and the pastor in the dark confessional box heard me tell him, *"J'ai dit des mensonges cinque fois"*? I had committed sins of more than lying in all the years since then, and my biggest sin, I knew more and more, was my possessiveness. My biggest sin, which was to want everything, had become grotesque in me, and my envy of anyone I thought had anything I didn't have was commensurate with my possessiveness. My possessiveness was such that I felt if I couldn't have everything, then everything should be destroyed, and everything others had in terms of success and money and good looks and sex should be taken away from them and they left overwhelmed by failure. What could my desire to be pure mean to me, whose possessiveness and envy made me so impure? Purity could come to me only by my being overwhelmed by some force greater than myself. And the only overwhelming feeling I could find in myself that made me think it was possible to be pure was the feeling of grief. But grief for what?

The lights were switched on, and the cellist, a beautiful young man wearing a white satin yarmulke like the pope's, left the room, carrying his cello. I noted the different-colored yarmulkes and the prayer shawls the men wore. The interior looked somewhat Protestant American: a large, simple, white room with severe wooden pews but red velvet curtains over the tall windows along each side. The rabbi took over the service and gave a sermon. There was a red velvet curtain before the arc at the front, which, during the service, was opened and shut by a drawstring that got caught. Mary talked with people in pews before and behind and introduced me.

I was sorry that the lights had come on, that the cello had stopped playing, that the cantor had stopped chanting.

After, Mary and I went for dinner to the house of friends she had introduced me to at the synagogue. They broke the fast they had or had not been keeping with slices of apples dipped in honey and crushed berries, and we ate gefilte fish, lox and cream cheese and bagels, herrings and chopped chicken livers and coleslaw, and we drank wine.

The next morning, Mary drove me to the Mohawk Reserve to walk along the Mohawk Trail, over paths through the forest of huge, autumn-brown and -yellow trees with thick roots that crossed the paths, and with heavy branches sometimes so low we had to crouch to pass under them.

Even early on in our friendship, Mary had a way of knowing what I was thinking. She asked earnestly, "Do you think grief is the strongest feeling a person can have?"

I thought, How, *how* did she know what I was thinking?

I said, trying to draw back a little from her earnestness, "Yes."

Mary looked at me with her large, sad, hazel eyes, which became sadder and darker the more they stared. Her sympathy made me feel a little foolish. And yet Mary allowed me, as if *she* were not embarrassed, to say what I had never said to anyone else, and with Mary I felt I could risk embarrassment.

"Do you think the worst thing that's ever happened to you is the loss of your religion?" she asked.

"Yes," I said.

Mary said she wanted me to meet her close friend Gary Seibert, a Jesuit priest who worked in a parish, with whom she was taking tango lessons. We met in her apartment in New York, near Barnard College, where she was teaching. Mary's closeness to him made me a little jealous of him, a good-looking man with a serious face and a bright laugh. He had Mary and me laughing with his descriptions of preparing the children of the parish—a very poor parish—for their First Communion.

"You wouldn't receive Communion?" Mary asked me.

"I can't. I haven't been to confession in thirty years and am in a state of sin," I joked. "I'm not a pure boy."

Gary said, "The Church has changed since a penitent had to go to confession before receiving. You can receive now just after asking forgiveness of your sins privately. Really, the Church is very different in many, many ways from when you were young. The Church has become much more aware of social problems, the essential and unfair differences between the rich and the poor, the exploiting and the exploited, the powerful and the helpless. In some deep way, the Church has become Marxist after Marxism has everywhere failed as a state institution. That's what the Church is about now."

"What happened to the Church Militant?" I asked.

"I'd like to think it has been replaced by the Church Compassionate," he answered.

"I see," I said.

Mary saw that I was, as she knew I could often be, just being polite, that I wasn't convinced.

Gary said he had to get back to his parish.

After he left us, Mary said, "Gary has hope. He leaves things to God but works enormously for people. He's with people, all kinds of people, in so many different ways. He's with people who are drug addicts, who are dying of AIDS, who are homeless. Gary is in a place I want to be in, a place he's made me aware of as never before, a place unlike any other I've ever been in. It's a place no one has to earn, a place that's open to everyone—the poor, the mad, the filthy, the stupid, the boring, the wicked. I'm in the Church because I see that it's a place that has nothing to do with distinction, that does away with the whole idea of distinction, and I want to be in that place. I want to be in a place where words like 'grace' and 'hope' and 'mercy' are used naturally, without self-consciousness, as practical things, ordinary things, like the names of food or tools that are for everyone, absolutely everyone."

All at once very tired, I sat on the sofa in Mary's living room.

She stood above me. She said, "I realized that nothing—not art, sex, friendship, nothing—evokes the feeling in me that is evoked by prayer. Nothing means more to me than the power of certain New Testament stories: the Prodigal Son, Jesus spitting on clay and touching the eyes of the blind man with the spittle-soaked clay so the man saw, Jesus writing on the ground a mysterious message to the adulterous woman, Jesus' agony in the garden. And Jesus' words: 'Weep not for me but for yourself and your children.' What is in any way better that can replace the idea that selfless love is without end, that pity is without end?"

I wondered what Sonia would have made of this, Sonia who was, in her denial of religion, heroic, as I would have liked to be but was not.

But Sonia's God was different from my God, and Mary's God, too, was different from my God, who, as a Father, appeared in all his darkness to have little, if anything, to do with a Son.

Mary sat beside me. She said to me, "You feel despair."

I said, "Oh, if I gave in—"

"What would happen?"

"You don't know what a Canuck could do by giving in to his feelings, a totally humorless, unironical Canuck like me."

"What?"

"When a Canuck gives in to his feelings, it's not enough for him to cry and hit his head, tear at his hair, roll naked in thorns."

"I hope you won't do that."

"I'd try not to, but I can't be sure I wouldn't, so I'd better not give in."

"Give in."

"I'd only embarrass myself."

"Embarrass yourself."

"A Canuck has to protect himself from being made to feel embarrassed by non-Canucks."

"Not with me."

"No, not with you."

"Give in."

"You want to hear my lament?"

"I do."

I grabbed Mary and hugged her.

29

IN NEW YORK, I STAYED WITH A FRIEND FROM THOSE five neurotic years in New York who had remained a friend, and going to sleep one night in his guest room I thought of a dream I had had often when I lived in the house in the parish: that of being inside the house, terrified that the door was locked, and I, pulling at the knob, couldn't get away from what was inside and, simultaneously, that the door couldn't be locked, and I, pressing my body against it, wasn't able to stop what was outside from coming in. Now that I was in New York, my parish was just a few hours' ride along the southern New England coast.

Mary invited me to dinner at her apartment with her family and friends, among them Gary, in an open-neck collar and a pullover.

His church was Holy Cross on West Forty-second Street, and his congregation consisted in large part of theater people and the homeless. He would, the next day, Ash Wednesday, hold morning, afternoon, and evening services for those who wanted to receive ashes.

Mary said to me, "Why don't you come with me?"

If it were for Communion, I said, I couldn't, because I'd be presuming on my immortality and committing a sacrilege. But I wouldn't feel that by receiving ashes and being reminded of my mortality I'd be committing a sacrilege.

"So you'll come?"

"Tell me once more where the church is," I said.

Before I left, Mary said, "Look, I don't want to force you to come, though I think I *should* force you. I'll be in the church at three o'clock, and if you come, fine, and if not, fine."

The next morning, out in the streets of the city going from one appointment to another—because, as I was in New York, I thought I must *try* to be professional as a writer— I often saw on the foreheads of people I passed along the crowded sidewalks the crude cross of black ash. People who, from the point of view of their native identities, were so different that their differences implied separate worlds, were, for this one day, visibly marked as all belonging to the same world. I passed a small, wrinkled Oriental woman with a great black cross from the bridge of her nose to her hairline, from one side of her forehead to the other, and as I looked at her she glanced at me, and then quickly away. I knew something essential about her, which she didn't know about me.

I returned to my friend's apartment. When the time came for me to go to Holy Cross Church to meet Mary, I thought I wouldn't go, and yet I thought I would go. The contradictory feelings I had were just like the feelings roused in me by that recurring dream of simultaneously being in a house unable to open the door to get away from what threatened me inside and unable to lock the door against what threatened me from outside. In my friend's apartment, I delayed my departure without directly intending to, delayed until I'd be too late, but, at the same time, whatever I did to delay I did so quickly—telephone calls, lunch on my own from the refrigerator, notes in my diary—I found I had plenty of time.

I had enough time to walk across town to the West Side along Forty-second Street, past the shops that had been porn shops but now were closed up with corrugated metal sheets painted pink, green, and blue and locked with shining steel locks, to the Port Authority Building, where out-of-state buses were entering and leaving and where the homeless gathered. Holy Cross Church was just across from the side of the Port Authority.

I was in fact early. A few people were in the pews—each one of them, again, of a different identity, or so it seemed to me—but Mary wasn't among them. Without genuflecting or making the sign of the cross or kneeling first to pray, I sat in a pew halfway down. I was among people who, kneeling or sitting, were deeply silent and still, so there was a great silence and stillness in the church, and I, in that silence and stillness, went into what I can only call a state of grace.

I was deep in that state when Mary sat beside me. She didn't appear surprised to see me, though I was surprised to see her only because everything surprised me. And yet Mary's presence beside me was exactly as expected.

Gary and another priest, the actual pastor, came out from the vestry, both in green chasubles with yellow crosses, and while Gary sat, the pastor, a large man who looked as though he had at one time been a heavyweight boxer, talked to the congregation. He talked about why people should come to church: if for nothing else, to be near one another bodily, to be aware of one another, and, during Mass, to wish one another peace. I listened with an attention I had never before in my life had given to a sermon. What the pastor said sounded so reasonable to me, but, then, my state made everything seem both reasonable and at the same time surprising—made, maybe, reason itself surprising. It was entirely reasonable, enlightened even, that people should gather together and wish one another peace, and yet it was an extraordinary idea that I seemed never to have heard expressed before.

The two priests stood side by side before the altar, and people formed lines in the main aisle to receive ash on their foreheads. I followed Mary out of the pew and with her joined the line leading to Gary. As we advanced towards him, I felt both very far from and very near to everything that was happening, and the closer I got to Gary the farther away I felt I became and also the nearer, so I was seeing the whole interior of the church from a vast distance and seeing the stitching of the hem of the chasuble Gary wore, seeing his hands, seeing the little silver boat of ashes in his hands. I felt totally detached and at the same time totally attached, felt that nothing was happening to me and that everything was happening. Mary received ashes before me and turned away, and Gary, smiling, embraced me before marking my forehead with the cross of black ash. I followed Mary down a side aisle and directly out of the church into the street.

I couldn't speak. I told myself that of course I could speak, of course, but what stopped me was that I had nothing to say. Mary didn't speak but took my arm, and we walked towards Eighth Avenue.

She asked me, "Why don't you give in?"

I told myself I could have answered if I had had an answer.

"Why don't you?"

I couldn't answer, and I couldn't because, my mouth open, I couldn't get my breath. Mary held my arm more tightly in hers. As we crossed Eighth Avenue, a car sped close to her, and Mary shouted at the driver, "Fucker," then, turning back to me, said, "It's just that Canuck stubbornness that won't let you give in."

On the other side of the avenue, trying to catch my breath, all I could say was, "Why does this happen when I'm with you?"

"What I'm saying means something to you that you insist on denying but that won't be denied."

I stopped her, and suddenly a little angry because she was

pressing me and I had had enough of being pressed, I said in as assertive a voice as I could manage, "Mary, I *do not* believe in God. All I believe is this: *There is no salvation for us, there is no life after death for us, there is no eternity for us. God does not exist.*"

Mary reacted to my anger with argumentative insistence. "This world exists," she said, "and we've got to have a reason for going on living in it all together without destroying it."

I didn't answer, but we resumed walking to Seventh Avenue, where we waited on the corner for the light to change.

I said, with my own argumentative insistence, "It's impossible to give into something that doesn't exist."

But Mary insisted even more on her argument. "No," she said. "What you long for exists in the very longing for it."

"Any longing I have that remains with me from the time when I did believe I find silly, just silly, and I won't tolerate the silliness in me."

"Go ahead, risk your silliness."

I said, "I can't believe we're having this conversation here in New York City."

She said, "It's just because we are here in New York City that we're having this conversation."

We crossed, and she left me to go down into the subway station; I continued to walk across town, now marked with the cross of my religion, which, however, was not my religion, but which everyone passing would have assumed to be mine. When I passed someone marked as I was, our eyes very briefly met in recognition of one another, though what the passerby recognized on me had really nothing to do with me, because, though marked as a believer, I would have had to say, if approached by someone who spoke to me as one, that I wasn't.

Maybe because so many people saw me as an introspective person, a person who was impelled to act much more in terms of feelings that made him look inwardly than made him look outwardly, a person who was altogether more subjective than objective, I had assumed the same about myself. But, more than ever before, I realized that this wasn't at all true of me. I wasn't a person to find faith, love, or even the inspiration to write from a depth within my subjective self, which I wanted in fact to leave behind me by dying to myself, but was instead a person who needed confirmation of faith and love and the inspiration to write from outside me, from a depth as objective as all the space that surrounds the world. No belief, ever, that came from within myself would convince me of the existence of God. To believe in God, I would have to be convinced by a force as positively outside me as a bright light flashing through the darkness of all that space. Mary didn't understand this about me, and I only now really understood: I expected to be made to believe not by giving in to my feelings but by being taken out of my feelings into something entirely other than my feelings.

And I rejected, right away, any imputation that I was committing only the sin of pride in such an expectation. It wasn't pride that made me think that if I were to be a believer, God, as I expected God to do, would have to come down and overwhelm me totally, so that I would be knocked to the ground, unable to rise unless God helped me. It wasn't pride, because I knew God would not do it. God had never, even in my youthful years of great devotion when I went to early Mass every morning before going to school, come down, and all I could honestly say I believed was that God would never come down.

Mary woke me the next morning by telephone to say she'd decided we were going to drive up to Providence to visit my parish. I may not have wanted to see it, but she did.

I said, "I'm sure my parish doesn't exist anymore."

"Then you should see that," she answered.

I realized how much Mary tolerated in me, which I, when I was aware of it, found intolerable in myself: not that Canuck stubbornness but, on the contrary, that Canuck will-lessness, that deepest Canuck longing to give in to what was beyond will. What Mary was trying to do was to make me use my will, and she was right to do this, as right as my mother had been, and to the degree that I saw that my mother was right I wanted to act on what Mary said; but I was, to a greater degree, like my father.

I met Mary at her apartment early in the morning a few days later, and she drove us out of Manhattan along the West Side Highway, past great, craggy ledges of stone on the side of the highway, from the cracks of which winter-bare trees grew. Those ledges gave me a disorienting sense of suddenly being far from the city. There was little traffic on the highway, seemingly abandoned, littered with broken branches.

Mary drove along the Connecticut coast, from where the Atlantic Ocean was dark gray, and into southern Rhode Island and through low scrub woods, where a war between a native tribe and colonists had been fought which the colonists won. We crossed overpasses into the city of Providence.

I got lost guiding Mary out of downtown Providence onto Atwells Avenue, which led up a hill called Federal Hill, where there was so large an Italian parish that the traffic line down the middle of the avenue was red, white, and green. We rose up the hill through the Irish parish, through the Polish parish, all with brick churches with rosette windows, which I told Mary I used to visit during Holy Week when, on a certain day I couldn't remember, you received a plenary indulgence—meaning you were completely cleared of sin and any punishment in purgatory due to sin—if you said a certain prayer in seven different churches. Mary knew the day—Good Friday—and was able to recite the prayer. We drove up past bare maple trees along either side of the highway, clapboard tenement houses with snowdrifts still not melted in the yards between them, bars on corners with wide but blackened windows in which a little neon sign flashed: BUD. And we came to the French parish, Notre Dame de Lourdes, red brick with a rosette window as opaque as if covered by a huge cataract.

Mary wanted to see, first, the house where I was born and brought up. Again, I lost my way, now among the narrow streets that were so familiar and so strange, and impatient to go on and also frightened and wanting to pull back, I told her to turn at corners without knowing where they would lead to. It was exactly as though I were dreaming. We rose over the crest of a hill and started down the other side, and I, still disoriented, saw the white clapboard bungalow on a corner and I shouted, "There it is." Mary parked the car in front of the house. If it hadn't been for Mary, I would not have got out of the car. If it hadn't been for Mary, I wouldn't have been there. I looked at the front porch, the glass storm door and the wooden door behind it, the porch lamp of a hanging lantern with yellow glass, the black numbers 128 over the door. I began to shake. Mary was the first to get out of the car. I got out.

The house looked dilapidated, as it had looked, I recalled, when it had been sold, after the deaths of my parents, to a Franco couple. The floorboards of the porch were rotting, the shingles of the roof were curling about the edges, and the maple trees that had spread their branches over it had been cut down to stumps.

Looking around at the other houses of the neighborhood, Mary said that she'd been brought up in a very similar place.

Suddenly, I felt that I no longer had anything to do with this house; I never had. I couldn't imagine living in it, couldn't imagine my parents living in it. It was not a haunted house.

As Mary and I left, I thought, I'll never come back here again.

We stopped at the church, which was locked. Mary suggested we come back in the morning for Mass, and I wanted to say, Never mind, it doesn't matter, but I said yes. And we went downtown again to book into a Holiday Inn—a hotel, Mary said, suitable to our class. We had dinner in an Italian restaurant on Federal Hill.

"For all my fantasies when I was growing up in Providence," I said, "never, never would I have fantasized about having dinner here with a fellow writer. My fantasies about being a writer were all based somewhere far, far outside Providence."

Before we went to our rooms for the night, Mary and I

went to the pool, and there, floating about each other in the illuminated lapping water, talked quietly and intimately about our childhood. And as we talked I became aware in the closeness of Mary's full body of a sadness I always felt with her. It was not, I thought, the sadness of our sexual incompatibility but, instead, of our suprasexual compatibility.

Mary woke me at six o'clock to go to my parish church for early Mass. She had found out about the hour. The parish seemed deserted, and we parked on a side street where there were no other cars. As we approached the church, I noticed a hole in a stained glass window at the side, made as if by a stone thrown through it. I expected the door to be still locked when Mary pulled at the handle, but it did open and we went into the foyer, where the linoleum tiles on the floor, brown and green, struck me with the force of years and years of fear. I was terrified of entering that church. There was the rounded marble holy water font, and the glass in the double doors, each door with a translucent purple cross, and, beyond the doors, the main aisle of brown and green tiles into the nave.

Mass had started. A priest I didn't recognize was at the altar, facing the congregation of about five people. Mary went right up to the first pew, and I followed her in.

I remembered the long kneeler along the pew on which I knelt with Mary. She went to receive Communion while I remained kneeling, my face in my hands. I went on kneeling, my face in my hands, when Mary returned, and I went on in that position until the end of the Mass.

I wanted to leave, but Mary said, "We're going into the vestry." I had never been into the vestry. As devout as I'd been, I'd never been an altar boy and had never viewed Monsieur le Curé as a man I could have visited in the vestry after Mass. I had never spoken to him outside of confession. I would have been as incapable of opening the door to the vestry—as Mary did matter-of-factly—as I would have the tabernacle on the altar. Mary went in first. The priest, already divested, was putting on a yellow baseball jacket over his black shirt with a clerical collar. He seemed to have expected us and said, "Come on in." Father, who was gray-haired, almost immediately said he was going to retire soon.

I didn't remember him, but when I gave him my name he said he'd buried my father and mother, and that was all he had to say about them.

Mary, who talked to him familiarly, asked him more about his retirement.

"Did you also bury my aunt Cora?" I asked.

"I did, yes," he answered.

"I wasn't able to come to the funeral. I live far away." Smiling a little, I asked, "Did she go on saying her prayers?"

Father frowned. "Her prayers were everything to her."

"I know, I know," I said, trying to correct the impression I'd given that I'd made fun of them, which I had done.

Father said, "You know, just before she died she requested that she be buried in the habit of that order of nuns she'd wanted to belong to when she was a girl. I asked for permission from the bishop, and he said go ahead. The problem, I thought, was finding a habit from those old days. But she had one, Cora did, had it hanging in her closet for decades. So she was laid out and buried in it."

I said to him, *"Ses prières sont exaucées,"* but he said he didn't understand French. Most of the parishioners, as few as they were, were now Mexican.

Then he said he had to go; a baseball team of kids he coached was expecting him. "Stay and look around the church," he said. And when Mary asked him where she could get a couple of candles, he said, pointing to a brown cardboard box on a counter, "Help yourself." He left.

I watched Mary take two large votive candles from the box. She said, "Let's go light these." We went, she carrying the candles, into the nave of the church again. Dim gray light was showing through the windows on the left side, and the church was chilly. We went up that side and up a little flight of circular wooden stairs into the organ loft where the organ was very dusty, then down and into the foyer and into the little space to the side of the foyer where the baptismal font was, by the font a pile of cardboard boxes as in a storeroom. Back in the nave, we went down the side aisle on the right side, the side where there was a window with a hole in it, reading, below each window, the names of the French parishioners in black Gothic script who had donated money for them. The brown and green floor tiles were cracked, and some had come unglued. Mary still carried the candles, looking for a place to light them.

Mary said, "This church looks like the butt end of something."

"It is," I said.

In a niche was a life-size statue of the Virgin Mother with large, sad eyes, before which, I told Mary, I had, as a boy coming into puberty, fervently prayed for purity, and sometimes I'd been sure the Virgin Mother's eyes filled with tears.

"We'll light our candles here," Mary said.

"No, no," I said, "not here."

"Why?" Mary asked.

"Because I'm not pure."

Mary held the candles out.

I looked around at both side altars and said, "In front of the crucified Christ."

Mary lit her candle from the only one burning in the stand, and I lit mine from hers. She knelt to pray and I stood behind her, looking at Christ's white body hanging on the black cross, blood running from his thorn-entangled head, from his nailed hands and feet, from the lance wound in his side, from his scourged flesh.

I looked away, and I thought: my ancestors had, from generation to generation, lived through the stark facts that the doctor would not arrive in the snowstorm in time to save the dying mother, the crop would fail, the bank would foreclose. The son of this God, who had come down to earth to help them, had failed them. This greatest failure to help us was also his greatest grief. All he could do for us was to purify us in his grief. In his grief we were forgiven. In his grief was our tenderness, our gentleness. In his grief was our love for him, and in our love for him was our love for one another. He was, in his suffering and in his death, the personification of a longing that would never, ever be realized. He was the Canuck son.

30

ON MY RETURN TO LONDON, NIKOS FOUND ME BETTER than when I had left.

One afternoon at my desk I took out the old manila envelope I had found in my father's wardrobe and held it in my hands without opening it. In the same way I had wanted and hadn't wanted to go to my parish with Mary, I wanted and didn't want to open the manila envelope, closed only by a metal clip through a hole in the unsealed flap. I put it on my desk, and over the next days I would pick it up and tell myself to go ahead and open it, then I'd tell myself it wasn't really interesting and I'd put it down. There were moments when I thought of throwing the envelope away unopened, and I'd hear, simultaneously, *Go ahead and throw it away* and *Open it*. There was an almost playful lightness, a delight even, about this contrariness in me.

The winter passed, and, almost laughing to myself, one spring day I opened the envelope as if incidentally, to extract the genealogical list of my ancestors. Their fates were not, I thought, my fate. I spread it out on the desk before me and studied it.

It started in France, with the burial of Nicolas Plante in Laleu, a suburb of La Rochelle, in 1647, and then crossed over to the forests of the New World with Jean and Françoise Plante, who were married in Quebec in 1650 and ended, after ten generations, with the marriage of my father and mother.

As I studied the names, I invented histories for them, histories for which, in my somewhat frivolous attitude towards the genealogy, I wouldn't do any research at all but which I would let come to me just by allowing my fantasy to invent out of the air. The more my fantasy invented, the more surprised I was by who came out of the air and stood about me in slouch hats, boots, bonnets, feathers, wooden clogs, and moccasins, carrying halberds, lace fans, knives and axes, bows and arrows, and shifting about in different clothes and carrying different things with each successive generation.

I hadn't written anything in months, but I began to write down these histories.

NICOLAS (DIED 1647) AND ELISABETH (DIED 1649) PLANTE, BURIED AT LALEU, OUTSIDE LA ROCHELLE, FRANCE

I could not imagine their lives.

JEAN AND LOUISE PLANTE, MARRIED IN QUEBEC, 1650

I imagined Jean Plante as an indentured servant, which meant that his duty was to be a laborer; this duty was owed not only to his temporal seigneur but to his Eternal Seigneur. The bond could no more be broken than a religious vow, and Jean did not try to break it.

FRANÇOIS AND LOUISE PLANTE, MARRIED AT CHATEAU RICHER, QUEBEC, 1694

I tried to imagine François, the first to be born in the forest. I imagined him and his wife, Louise, sometime after their wedding, the 26th of October 1694, at Château Richer, Quebec, walking through the autumn-bare forest after Mass on a Sunday morning. I imagined them standing together for a moment in a clearing to listen, their sense of hearing and sight, all of their senses, different from those of their parents, and altogether different from the senses of hearing and sight, from all the senses, of their grandparents in France. François' aged parents, born in France, don't understand him and his wife, Louise, as François and Louise won't understand their children, each generation different from the last, each hearing and seeing what the last couldn't hear, couldn't see.

François and Louise first heard, then saw a red and black bird perch on a bare branch above their heads, just to the edge of the clearing. They had never seen a bird like that or heard its cry. It flew to a branch of another autumn-bare tree in the forest and, perched, cried out, then flew to another tree deeper into the forest.

"Allons le suivre," Louise whispered to François.

For a week they were lost in the forest. When it rained, they splashed through water until they found a wide, black fir tree, and they crawled under the low, dripping branches. Shivering, they sat close together on the ground. They were awake all night in the rain falling through the branches. At dawn, the rain stopped, but the air was damp and cold, and their clothes were wet. François couldn't kindle a fire. All day, the couple wandered, trying to get their bearings by a glimpse of the sun, but the sky was covered. The path they found had been made not by humans but by animals. They followed an animal path to a pond, and by the pond François began to make a shelter by bending together into a dome spindly saplings that grew near one another and securing them with vines, but the trees kept springing back. Louise, straining to reach, wound vines around and around the bent saplings, but the moment François released his hold, the saplings whipped back upright and the vines tore apart. Both panting and sweating, the couple had to lie still on a pile of leaves and pine needles, holding one another. Snow fell.

From deep within the forest, a low voice called, "Louise, François." Dazed, the couple got up and walked towards the voice, and as they walked they saw a light, like that of a small sun, shining brightly deeper among the trees, and they turned away from it. The voice called, "François, Louise, come here," and, unable to look into the light except in glances, they saw as they approached a woman, dark against the light, and behind her a larger, darker woman, and behind her a still larger, darker woman, each going farther and farther back into the light. The couple knelt, their heads bowed low. And the voice said, "Repeat this prayer after me."

A wild woodsman, *un coureur de bois*,[1] and his Indian companion found them.

Once, when François was on his way back with a group of men from an expedition to trade kettles, knives, and buttons for rolls of pelts with savages, he saw, on the bank of the

---

1. *Un coureur de bois* has no equivalent in English; it is purely French Canadian. It means a man who lives in the forest, makes his living from the forest, and dies in the forest.

river down which he and his companions were paddling their loaded canoes, a white man among the trees. He, dressed in hides and his legs wrapped in bands, simply looked at the canoe pass. His hair and beard were dark, his eyes clear. He must have been younger then François. Unlike François, he knew how to live in the forest, and, unlike François, he did live in the forest.

"*C'est un coureur,*" the man paddling in the prow of the canoe said.

François, at the rear, paddled as if to get away quickly, and the canoe swerved.

At the ends of their lives, François and Louise talked about the prayer they had been given, wondering if it really came from their God and if they should pass it on to any of their children or die with it.

JEAN-BAPTISTE AND JEANNE PLANTE, MARRIED
ILE DUPAS, QUEBEC, 1721

At Mass, during the sermon, Jean-Baptiste was aware that behind the high altar, walled in with nothing but the clothes she stood in, was a girl who had begged to be walled into a cell, where she would see no one and speak to no one for the rest of her natural life. Food was passed to her through a slit in the stone, through which she passed out the pot she peed and shat in. Now, as sometimes happened when the priest was giving a sermon, the girl was heard singing.

The priest stopped speaking and returned to the altar. Tears fell from the priest's face onto the altar cloth.

Long after vespers one evening, Jean-Baptiste went into

the church when he knew it would be empty. The small vigil lamp hanging before the tabernacle was the only light in the dimness, the remaining outside light illuminating nothing but the glass figures in the windows. Jean-Baptiste went to the front of the church and by the door at the end of a side aisle into the vestry, where he saw, behind a half-pulled curtain, a small door. He opened it into darkness except for a narrow beam of gray light from a high window, and he saw enough to realize he was in a passageway, and along the wall of this passageway, at the level of his shoulder, was a solid wooden shutter. He was about to open this but heard the door at the end of the passage from where he had come open, and he rushed to the opposite end and pressed himself into an angle. He saw the *curé* of the church come in and feel his way along the wall to the shutter with his fingers as though he were blind and open it; then the *curé* leaned with his forehead against the wall and spoke in a murmur. There was silence, then Jean-Baptiste heard the voice of the girl, who was confessing her sins. The *curé* kept his forehead pressed against the stone wall as he listened.

Then Jean-Baptiste heard the *curé* plead with the girl to be reasonable and leave her cell. There was no answer from the girl, and the old *curé*, sighing deeply, closed the shutter and left.

Jean-Baptiste, able to see only shapes, went to the shutter and opened it. He heard from within the cell a faint cry. He waited. No other cry came. There was the smell of a cooped-up animal.

"Listen," he said, his face at the opening. He repeated, "Listen."

The girl's voice, when she suddenly spoke, sounded very near, and Jean-Baptiste, frightened to be so near her, drew back. "What do you want?" the girl asked.

"I want a prayer," he whispered.

TI' JEAN-BAPTISTE AND MARIE LOUISE PLANTE,
MARRIED AT LANORIE, 1752

Their wedding celebration was held in a long, low-ceilinged log cabin. The guests, the other farmers in the parish, sat on benches about the walls, and food was served from pottery dishes. A violinist played and there was dancing. Many of the men wore fringed chamois coats and leggings that were usually worn by the natives, and their hair was as long as that of the natives. Some of the young men wore feathers dangling from knots in their hair. They went out to talk with the natives sitting on the ground and give them brandy. One of the dances consisted of passing around a broom, faster and faster, until it was thrown and caught, thrown and caught as the dancers sped round one another.

The dancing didn't stop when the *curé* came in for food and brandy, which quickly made him as drunk as most of the men. He was old, and some of his fingers were stumps, burned to the last joints by the natives he as a missionary had gone out to baptize and had succeeded in baptizing to save them for eternity, overcoming even worse tortures, the scars of which were hidden by his soutane. His missionary garrison had become a parish when people from up the river came to populate the island, and not many natives went to church now, whereas once there had been only natives at his Masses and he had given his sermons in their language. Now, they often went to his presbytery for brandy, and he gave it to them.

The *curé* laughed when drunken Indians, for no reason, set fire to his presbytery.

Ti' Jean-Baptiste's second child, a boy of six, came down with a fever. His small skull showed. The *curé* gave him extreme unction, which might cure him, omitting the confession because the boy had not yet attained the age of reason. After, Ti' Jean-Baptiste gave the priest some brandy, and the *curé* said, "Oh, he's a bad boy. He told me, his voice feeble, to get lost. *[Il m'a dit, sa voix faible, de m'en ficher le champ.]* He may not be culpable yet, but even so, I'm not sure he will go to heaven." When he laughed, the gaps where his teeth were missing showed, and the teeth that remained were rotted.

As he left the church, Ti' Jean-Baptiste remarked on the old Indian woman sitting motionless in a back pew, her blanket wrapped completely about her.

His father, Le Grand Jean-Baptiste, sent word that he was dying in Quebec, and Ti' Jean-Baptiste went to him. His father was skeletal, as though he had starved himself. Ti' Jean-Baptiste sat by him, and Le Grand Jean-Baptiste raised his head just enough for Ti' Jean-Baptiste to lean closer, and Le Grand Jean-Baptiste let his head fall to his pillow. He said, "I have a prayer for you, for you alone, to pass on to your eldest when you are leaving this world." Ti' Jean-Baptiste leaned even closer to hear the prayer.

Back in his parish, alone in the church, Ti' Jean-Baptiste said the prayer for the life of his son. His son died.

He did not pass on to anyone the prayer his father had told him.

ANTOINE AND GENEVIÈVE PLANTE, MARRIED AT
SAINT CUTHBERT, 1791

Ti' Jean-Baptiste's son Antoine went hunting in the forest with Indians, a group of them. Some of them were half-breeds or quarter-breeds. The French never minded much about interbreeding with the Indians. When he'd been young, Antoine had thought of going to live in an Indian camp to escape the life of the parish. But those camps had been different when he'd been a boy. Now, they were more than half decimated by disease, and of the rest a lot of the men were wasted by drink. Antoine knew it was only a left-over idea from his childhood he had of going to live in an Indian encampment, one that seemed, however, to make him nostalgic, as if he had once lived in a camp and wanted to return.

In their bivouac in the forest, they sat around the fire and drank. The Indians fell asleep, and Antoine was left to put wood on the fire. One of the Indians, full blooded, woke up, reached for the bottle, drank, and with Antoine looked silently into the fire. He drank more and stood; then, staggering a little, he danced around the fire, jumping over the bodies of his companions lying on the ground. He had become, Antoine knew by the way he danced, a wolf.

At dawn, the hunting party had to go farther into the forest than they'd ever been before for game, as overhunting had killed off the wildlife near the farms.

When he married Geneviève, Antoine moved where the forests were still solid and filled with deer, wild swans and turkeys, and walnut, chestnut, and wild plum trees, and where the oaks were hung with grapevines.

At the First Communion of his son, Antoine, seeing from his seat the priest raise the host over the boy's head before he lowered it to the boy's outstretched tongue, thought not of the body and blood that the host had miraculously become but of how the Indians called on their namesakes, called on the powers of a black crow, a running deer, a lean wolf when they went out to hunt or fight, so they were no longer Indians, they were a black crow, a running deer, a lean wolf; crows, they flew, deer, they were swift, wolves, they were cunning; their black feathers were wings, antlers grew out of their heads, hooves cleaved their feet, and their necklaces of wolves' teeth extended their jaws, so they were no longer what they had been, they were no longer men. And if they prayed, their prayers were not the prayers of men.

One morning Antoine woke to find that Geneviève had let the fire go out. Rolls of beaver pelts he had traded rifles for with the Indians lay on the floor before a bench. Geneviève was not in the house. Antoine went out, calling her. Snow was falling. He saw no tracks. It happened that French women went to live with the Indians, and he wondered for a moment if his wife had gone off with one of the Indians he traded with. He knew the one. But, no, she couldn't have, because she would know he'd find her. He woke his children and told the oldest to light a fire, and he, in snowshoes, went out to the Indian winter camp. The dogs barked as he approached. He entered the main lodge, made his salutations to a circle of men crouched about a fire, and sat at a distance from them until one asked him to come nearer. The man he thought his wife might have gone off with was there. When he said his wife had disappeared, the man grunted but said nothing. She wasn't found that winter. In the spring, with the thaws, her body was found in a clearing in the forest not far from the house where the snow had drifted over it.

Because she might have committed suicide, a mortal sin, no prayers were said for her, and she was buried in unconsecrated ground.

LOUIS AND JOSEPHTE PLANTE, MARRIED AT SAIN CUTHBERT, 1824

Nine years later, Antoine married again, to a woman born in the parish.

His son from his first marriage, Louis, stayed in the parish when he married. His wife's name was Josephte. They had so few belongings in their house, Josephte, laughing, said their lives were as basic as those of the Indians: no curtains, no rugs, no candlesticks, no mirror, no comb or brush, and only a *chudron*, a big iron pot, to cook in over the fire. Josephte said often, "We can do without."

She was always pregnant. Their children slept in the same room as she and her husband, some in the same bed with them.

In the midst of a field of corn rotted by too much rain and no sunlight, Louis's wife and children, their bare feet up to the ankles in mud, were trying to find young ears of corn that could be saved and boiled. As they ate the boiled corn with lard, Josephte said, "It doesn't matter," and when Louis asked, "Well, what matters?" she laughed.

The oldest son was killed in a brawl among French, mixed breeds, and Indians, all of them drunk.

Josephte, who never prayed, died saying, "It doesn't matter."

Their second son, Cyriac, attended the death of his father, Louis. Louis seemed to want to tell something to Cyriac before he died, but, opening and closing his mouth over and over, he seemed not to be able to remember what it was.

Cyriac moved to the parish of his wife, Claire, to get away from his parish. He took over the farm of Claire's father and by hard work made the farm pay; years later he bought a carriage to go to church in on Sunday. He fulfilled the obligations towards his religion, but nothing more. He never thought about God, as if there was no way to think about him. When Claire, at moments of crisis such as when a child was ill, told him they must pray and got him to kneel with her on the floor and say the rosary, he was a little embarrassed because he didn't feel that praying was going to do any good, and his wife's insistence seemed an affectation. All religion embarrassed him a little, and even when, at Easter, he received Communion because he was obliged to once a year, he went to the altar in a stiff way and returned in a stiffer way. He gave the minimum amount of money at the collection and never offered to pass the basket himself. The *curé* stayed away from his house. Cyriac didn't drink.

His children were closer to their mother than to him. The one son he loved, though he would never have used the word, was a weak, thin boy, whom everyone expected to die soon. Cyriac refused to believe the boy would die. He sat by René's bed and listened to him talk, his head and shoulders propped on a pillow. René talked a lot, his voice high, and he made delicate, feminine gestures with his long-fingered hands. He talked about being in the kingdom of heaven, where the men and women were beautiful, and as he described meeting each one he made flourishes of salutation in the air. The nuns at the parish school had told him about people in heaven, but he saw them as he wanted to see them.

"What do you talk about there?" his father asked.

"Oh, what we talk about is marvelous. We say pleasant things to one another, and compliment one another on our beautiful clothes. And we talk about the Good Lord."

"And what do you say about him?"

"How he loves us and how we love him."

When René became delirious, the nuns came to write down what he said, as incoherent as it was. While they were with the boy, Cyriac stayed away. He didn't like the nuns interpreting what René said. But they, not he, were present when René died. Cyriac didn't want to hear from them what his last words were as he approached God, the remembrance of which made their faces shine.

"A prayer," a nun said. "What he said was a prayer."

"That should be his secret," Cyriac said.

René appeared, shortly after his death, to two of Cyriac's daughters, who became nuns, and a son, who became a priest. René never appeared to his father, not even in his sleep. Cyriac, in any case, said he never dreamed.

Cyriac became lazy and left the working of the farm to hired labor, as the sons who remained at home were too young. He sat in the shade. Every Sunday, however, he went to Mass in his carriage, his wife beside him. She had learned never to ask him to pray, never to cause him any embarrassment with her religious affectations. Eventually, Cyriac had to sell the farm before his sons could take it over from him.

ANACLET AND MODESTE, MARRIED AT SAINT-
BARTHELEMY, 1895

One of his sons, Anaclet, a carpenter by trade, married a half-caste French Indian woman named Modeste.

The *curé* understood that his parishioners were drawn to leaving for the States for better lives, and he admonished those who stayed behind not to be severe with those leaving, but he regretted the breakup of the homes, the beds dismantled, chairs and tables overturned, cooking pots and pails and dishes piled on old mattresses, exposed for the auctioneer to come and access their meager worth. All the farming equipment was for sale, and the cows too. The farmers stood aside, silent, as the goods were auctioned off, and after the sale the windows and door of the house were boarded over, and the farmers and their families spent their last night with relatives to leave early the next day. From his pulpit, the *curé* announced each year the names of the dead, which, with each successive year, outnumbered more and more the births.

As Canada had not belonged to them, the French, for generations, they didn't feel they were really leaving their country.

Anaclet and Modeste, a year after the birth of their first son, who was called Anaclet after his father, decided they would move to the United States and sold their household goods and house. The train fare was paid for by the sale of a cow.

In making up their cases and bundles to move to the United States, Modeste inserted among the clothes various holy images, the largest one of the Holy Virgin showing her heart stabbed with seven daggers and envelopes containing dried herbs and seeds.

In Providence, Rhode Island, in their tenement apartment, Modeste would sit on the floor for as long as there was nothing to do, and when her husband asked her, "What are you thinking?" she answered, "Nothing." They lived in the parish of Notre Dame de Lourdes, close to the church, which was being built.

Her husband died, and years later she, on her deathbed, called her son Anaclet to come. She said she had a prayer for him.

ANACLET AND ALBINA, MARRIED, PROVIDENCE,
RHODE ISLAND, 1922

My father and mother.

3 I

WHEN I DID GO TO CANADA—TO MONTREAL IN 1990 TO teach for some weeks at L'Université du Québec à Montréal, though I realized, standing before the class, that my French was barely adequate—religion had gone from the language. That religion, for which *le Canada* had been, when I was growing up, the mystical country of miracles, had vanished as much from Canada as it had from my parish in *la révolution tranquille* of the 1960s, when, overnight it seemed, Catholic French Canadians stopped going to church. Boys no longer had vocations to be priests or girls to be nuns, and the seminaries and convents were left to the old religious who could no longer function, or they were sold. The parochial schools became secular. Walking about Montreal, along narrow paths made on sidewalks through the banks of snow—paths that made me think of paths through a snow-bound forest—I saw churches abandoned and boarded up. A large section of an old church had been incorporated into the recently built university. My students were writing in a language that had nothing to do with God.

It was in secular French Canada that I realized something about my parish that I had never before thought of, especially not while living there: because I grew up in the parish, a fortress that had held for at least during my childhood against the Yankee Puritan world, I was not a Puritan.

My students and people I met told me stories:

Of having been lost, he and two school friends of about ten, from morning until sunset in the forest, where they'd gone looking for autumn leaves to bring to school.

Of never having left their villages to go to the capital, Montreal, before starting their studies at the university.

Of having known an old woman in the village who frightened away little boys from throwing snowballs at her house by coming out onto her porch with a bearskin raised over her shoulders, the bear's jaw on her head, so heavy she staggered under the weight.

Of having had a full-blooded Indian grandmother who,

however, never talked of being an Indian—nor did her son
—but who asked not her son but her grandson to promise
to make sure she would be buried in the Indian clothes she
had made herself and put away (a chamois dress embroidered
with beads), and that she would have Indian burial rites. She
was given a Catholic burial, but in her Indian clothes.

Of being born in Magog, a village close to the border
with the United States, but of never crossing the border, and
of everyone coming out of houses because *un anglais*—an
American—was walking along the main street.

Of being convinced by a priest of having a vocation,
of having all the signs of disinterest in the world, a sense of
wanting to devote oneself to what was larger and more important than this world, a sense that there was meaning only
in transcendence, and of having spent two years in a seminary; and of having left the seminary—just by walking out
still wearing a soutane—and going home and taking off the
soutane and dressing in old clothes and swearing never again
to enter a church.

Of a brother who, twenty-eight years old, decided to live
dans le bois and went to the Laurentides, bought a piece of
land, built a log cabin (without electricity), dug a well, which
was twenty feet deep and took him a year, and became a
trapper.

Of having as a boy been given the job, at the time of
slaughtering the animals, of holding the basin to catch the
flow of blood when a pig, hung up alive, had its throat slit;
of having to stir the hot blood with a wooden spoon so it
wouldn't coagulate; of the boy's father, in his old age, insist-
ing on slaughtering the pig as he had always done, but who,

while squeezing the wound to regulate the flow of blood, died of a heart attack because "he couldn't bear the emotion of killing."

Of having an uncle who knew a prayer for curing burns, who didn't have to be present for the prayer to work its cure but who, when telephoned by a neighbor whose husband had burned himself badly at the kitchen stove, told her to wrap the burned arm in a wet towel while he said the prayer; which she did, and the next day the burn was gone.

I became friendly with Yves Lacroix, the director of the department, and his wife, Louise, who, when I mentioned Sainte Anne de Beaupré as a center of parochial mystery to me, offered to take me. I did see the chapel in which crutches, leg and arm braces, even false arms and legs were hung after miraculous cures. But the reality of it all made me want to leave quickly.

Yves and Louise also offered to drive me to Saint-Barthélemy.

I both wanted and didn't want to go, as I had both wanted and not wanted to find out about my ancestry. I expected the village to be run down, even something of a slum, but with the sun shining brightly on the smooth, clear-surfaced snow as we drove into the village, I was surprised to see big, well-kept white clapboard houses with porches supported by pillars. The village square—*la place*—before the church was large, and the church itself grand, built of gray stone with a bell tower on either side of its broad facade. The interior was of white and gold, almost rococo.

And yet, as I walked down the main aisle, I again felt that I wanted and didn't want to be there. And when I got to the baptismal font, neogothic and of dark wood, by the side of the altar, I felt such a split in me, as if I were in fact split inside and the two sides were pulling against each other, that I put my hands to my chest. Here, where my father was baptized, I was at a center that had everything to do with my father in his most powerful past. Here, my mother didn't exist. And yet, at this center, my mother, it seemed to me, existed everywhere outside the center in the equally powerful future.

I was more aware than I had ever been of the split in me (which is the split in this book): the split and the pull between the secular and the religious, between the definite and the vague, between what can be said and what cannot be said, between law and freedom, state and self, politics and poetry, between light and darkness, between life and death, between my mother and my father.

Wasn't there anything meaningful to me that my mother and father shared that made them one? that united them in an eternal marriage?

I found being there was unbearable, and all I wanted was to leave. But Yves had gone for the pastor, *le curé*, who was not, I saw as he approached me, an old man but of my own age. He had a broken nose and wore not a soutane but a pullover and a gold chain about his neck, from which hung a large gold cross on his broad chest. He started out by saying he was too busy to let me see the old registry in which the birth of my father was inscribed—he had a baptism to officiate at in the afternoon—but, as I simply stared at him, he agreed, and I followed him out of the church, Yves and Louise behind me, over the snow to the presbytery. Even so, he said, as he showed me into his office with dark wainscoting, that many Americans came to look up their ancestry, therefore taking up a lot of his time, which he resented. I said nothing. As I knew the date of my father's birth, he took from a large iron safe the registry of the year 1897, found the date of November 8, and placed the large book on his desk and turned it towards me. The registration of the birth, written with a nib pen, was signed by my father's father, also named Anaclet, but not by his mother, beside whose name, written perhaps by the priest, was noted *qui n'a pas su signer.* My grandmother didn't know how to sign her name. I saw, over and over on the page, the same statement: *qui n'a pas su signer.*

A sudden sob broke from me. My ancestors had not been able to sign their names, had not been able to read or write. That I wrote my novels without any precedent made writing for me a pretension, but I accepted this, as I had learned to accept all the pretensions of my life (that is, all my life outside the parish) as the condition that most allowed me to live. For them, for generation upon generation of the fact of life, the unlettered and dumb fact of life, just life, did I feel rise in me on the sob such a need for their lives to have meaning; because those lives, one engendering another over and over, must mean something beyond reading and writing, beyond, even, articulation; must, by the engendering impulse of generation upon generation that was greater than any split between life and death, between hope and despair, between faith and no faith, between God and no God in any individual's beliefs or nonbeliefs, attest to some universal, some drive to survive; must, given that survival in this world was defeated generation after generation, finally break the bounds of this world into the eternal world, where those lives, generation after generation, had their fulfillment, had their meaning, all together. I wanted this, I *longed* for this, for all my ancestors. And at the same time I knew, with the same starkness of fact that came to me when I saw how many in my ancestral world could not sign their names, that what I wanted, what I longed for, was impossible for them, or for anyone, because there was no world beyond this world.

Oh, but there was. There had to be.

Outside, we encountered an old man, smartly dressed in a brown fedora hat and brown overcoat and fawn scarf, who, curious to see people in the village he didn't know, spoke with us. I asked him if there were any Plantes living in Saint-Barthélemy. He said he remembered a certain Cyriac Plante, but he had died, and as far as he knew—and he knew everyone in the village—there were no Plantes.

I asked him where the cemetery was, as I hoped to find stones with the names of my great-grandfather and great-grandmother carved on them—separate stones, perhaps, as my great-grandfather had remarried after her death.[1] However, the old cemetery, the man said, no longer existed. The

---

1. I asked a professor of anthropology if, his expertise being Indian history, there was any way I could go back from my great-grandmother to her mother, and, even further back, to her mother's mother. He frowned—annoyed, I thought, that I should bother him with such a banal request, for almost all French Canadians, he said, had Indian blood, so I must not think I was special, and he said no, I wouldn't be able to find out anything about my great-grandmother's past before she married my great-grandfather unless a census had been taken, which, as she was a Blackfoot and he a woodsman and they'd met in a lumber camp in North Dakota, was highly unlikely. And it wasn't likely that they were married or that her taking the Christian name of her husband's mother meant that she had been baptized. She was probably not Christian.

remains of the dead had been reburied in a new cemetery, outside the village. It would now be deep in snow, the stones themselves buried.

Yves drove on to Quebec City, and along the way I saw signs for Ile du Pars, for Lanoraie, and for Saint Cuthbert, where my ancestors had lived.

And, as if in a state that vivified everything I saw, I noted, as objects of awareness, fishing cabins on a frozen river, lumberyards with stacks of newly sawn wood under snow, an old barn collapsing under snow, a black skidoo racing across a snow-covered lake. We passed through woods, mostly birch, that were coated with white ice, all in a whitish mist. Large black birds sat on the banks of snow on either side of the highway.

We spent the night with friends of Yves and Louise in Quebec.

My fiftieth birthday occurred when I was in Canada. I was invited to spend the weekend in the country, with Yves and Louise, by another professor and her husband. On the day of my birthday, I went out into the snowbound forest on snowshoes.

I went with the nine-year-old son of my hosts, Alexandre. We passed through sparse woods on a knoll of thin trees, almost bushes, covered with dry, pale, tawny leaves through which the sun shone and the wind blew. From the knoll was a view of valleys and mountains and forests. We descended the other side of the knoll into the forest. Alexandre kept falling off his snowshoes. He said often, *"J'espère qu'on ne se perde pas."*

Deeper in the forest, snow swirled among the trees and, in sudden gusts of wind, formed into almost invisible beings, sometimes one, sometimes a group that, whirling, passed by us.

I imagined going in the direction they went in after they passed us. They made low *whishing* sounds. I felt on my face the sting of the flashing flakes they were constituted of. I imagined more and more of them, whirling around us silently except for that faint *whish*.

A strong wind blew through the forest, raising still more beings from the snowdrifts, so a congregation of them whirled up and combined and, all together, streamed in a cold draft that the boy and I huddled against, our backs turned towards it. And after this gust a deep stillness filled the air, and snow fell slowly through it.

32

BUT I HAD A DEEPER ANCESTRY. IF, WITH HIS COMING to La Nouvelle France, I looked forward from Jean Plante's arrival to my own presence in North America, didn't I have as much reason, having lived in Europe now for longer than half my life, to look back from his parents, Nicolas and Elisabeth, who had remained in France, to a past in Europe?

Jack Kerouac, a Franco-American whose novels, including *On the Road*, in which he identifies himself as entirely American, are deeply Franco-American, wrote a short, messy book called *Satori in Paris,* about his attempt to find his French ancestry in France.[1] He failed.

Like Jack Kerouac, I decided to go to France to trace my ancestry there. But, torn as I was between the sincerity and the vanity of every desire, I in fact wanted much more *not* to go than to go, as if to go were only to satisfy a vain curiosity. I had for many years had as one of my mottoes to counter just such overwhelming curiosity about everything —the curiosity to see, hear, touch, taste, smell everything— this corrective by Blaise Pascal, whom I had read in college and been deeply impressed by: *Curiosité n'est que vanité. On ne voyage sur la mer que pour en parler.* Really, I had no more pressing longing to go than the longing to write about what-

---

1. When he went to France in 1965 in search of his ancestry, Jack Kerouac was far gone in alcoholism. As he recorded in *Satori in Paris,* he believed his full name to be Jean Lebris de Kérouack and to be of noble descent. At the National Archives, obviously drunk, he had a great deal of trouble finding records of "les affaires Colonielles," yelling at a librarian in a rage because she didn't understand. "Don't you have a list of the officers in Montcalm's Army in 1756?" he demanded, presumably in English. "My ancestor was an officer of the Crown, he came from Brittany, he was a Baron they tell me, I'm the first of the family to return to France to look for the records." Unable to make himself understood, he went to Brittany, to Brest, on his own to make contact with his French past, which would be his moment of illumination—or satori—but, more and more drunk, he gave it all up and returned to his mother in Florida, where he died.

He wrote in that same book that he came "from Medieval French Quebec-via-Brittany stock" and spoke "old French," from the days when "you said not 'toi' or 'moi' but like 'twe' or 'mwe.'" His Quebecois French comes across as authentic: "J'n'ai rien à jeter en dehors du chaussi, ainque ma tête." He uses expressions that I heard in my parish: "la maille" for the mail; "weyondonc"; "je m'en va" for "je m'en vais"; and, as the worst possible curse because it was sacrilegious, "Ciboire!" meaning chalice! But his claim to speak what my aunt Cora called French French is hardly borne out by the examples in his book, which at best have a phonetic accuracy: "Le roi n'est pas amusez."

ever discovery I might make to connect me to an even greater ancestry than that of my North American ancestry, and to do anything to write about it after seemed to me to do it out of real vanity. And yet I did go.

I knew just where my French ancestors had come from—from the region of Aunis, outside the city of La Rochelle, in a suburb, at their time a separate village called Laleu. I knew that Nicolas died at the age of sixty-seven, in 1647; she at the age of seventy-four, in 1649. As little as I could imagine their private lives, except to assume that they were peasants, I could imagine something of the world around them, informed as I was, however haphazardly, of the history of that world. If they were peasants, *their* ancestors would have been serfs—but serfs who, because the Hundred Years' War left the nobility bereft of help, were able to make demands that eventually led to their liberation from serfdom. When young, they would have known of the discovery of La Terre Neuve and the huge profit made from importing dried and smoked cod, then also furs, and the consequent expansion of the city walls. They would have been told by their parents of the building of the towers on either side of the port of La Rochelle, with a great chain between them lowered during the day for the traffic of ships importing and exporting and raised at night for safety. Catholics, as I was sure they were, they would have known, without giving the cult a name, of the growing numbers of Huguenots in La Rochelle, and though they would not have called the movement the Reformation, they would have heard of Calvin and his followers. They would, I think, have been shocked and frightened by stories of Huguenots, now a majority, murdering Catholic priests, the Catholic churches stripped of their sacred objects and demolished, the stones used for stronger fortifications. Perhaps not quite understanding, they would have heard of the Massacre of Saint Bartholomew in Paris and cities throughout France when tens of thousands of Huguenots were massacred and of the Edict of Nantes, which finally gave civil rights to the Huguenots—rights that some thirty years later Cardinal Richelieu began, with royal approval, to destroy by destroying the Huguenot cities. In their fifties at the time, they would have known of the 1627 siege of La Rochelle by Richelieu, commanding the action in a red cardinal's skullcap and robes over full body armor, which ended with the total capitulation of the Protestants and the demolition of the city walls. They would have heard the bombardment of the walls by cannon.

Staying in a hotel in the center of La Rochelle, before going to Laleu to find the graves of Nicolas and Elisabeth, I at first wanted to see whatever there was in the city that they might have seen, if they ever did come into the city from the village. It pleased me that the long arcades, extending over the pavements and sustained by arch after arch, would have been in place, and Nicolas and Elisabeth would have walked under them as I was now walking under them. Any church they might have gone to Mass in within La Rochelle had been destroyed by the Huguenots, but the towers were left, in particular the gothic tower of the Church of Saint-Barthélemy, itself from the twelfth century, named after one of the twelve apostles. I walked around the narrow streets at the base of the tower, telling myself that I was seeing, against the blue sky, exactly what my ancestors saw. I studied a short flight of worn stone steps that they could have walked up, minutely wearing down the stone. From a little courtyard below the tower, I entered the cathedral of La Rochelle, Saint Louis, which was begun with the Catholic Counter-Reformation, the building suspended during the French Revolution, and finished, finally, in 1862, a long time after the deaths of Nicolas and Elisabeth. I wandered along the *déambulatoire*, rather disengaged until, in a transept, I noted a large painting, inserted into the wall above a side altar, of an aged man with white hair and white beard, lying back on an outside stairway, half naked and surrounded by men in, apparently, Arab dress, one of whom, with pincers, was tearing off a nipple of the man, another holding out a curved dagger, and another unsheathing a sword while others looked on. A woman, clearly not an Arab, was running up the flight of stairs above the man, her arms raised, her hair undone, in hysterics. The painting, executed by Omer Charlet in 1863, depicted the martyrdom of Saint Bartholomew. He was flayed alive by Armenians, his emblem a butcher's knife. My immediate connection with the picture was more suggestive to me than the gothic tower of Saint-Barthélemy, and it was because it was more personal: my father was born in the village of Saint-Barthélemy in Canada. Also, the painting was as gruesome as any of the holy images Matante Cora was devoted to. And yet, this connection, as personal as it was in its suggestion, suggested more, much more than the personal; it was only one of too many connections for me or anyone to separate out and diagram. I felt suddenly engaged in some vast interconnectedness, this vast interconnectedness centered in this one bad painting.

The same feeling occurred when, walking down the Rue de L'Escale, I was, as I had read, walking on paving stones that had been brought back from Canada as ballast, the weight of fish and furs not great enough to keep the ship steady.

And the same occurred when I visited Le Musée du Nouveau Monde, in a mansion of the eighteenth century, where, all alone in the entire building, I studied, from behind a glass partition, a room filled with eighteenth-century Chippendale and Duncan Phyfe furniture from America and was able to see myself reflected in a Chippendale mirror. And of course I thought of the desk my mother called Chippendale, but, as centered in the personal as that thought was, it expanded outwardly into the impersonal narrative of Chippendale furniture around the world that superseded the personal.

In that museum, I saw early maps of the Monde Nouveau, one of La Nuova Francia by an Italian, Giovanni Battista Ramusio, 1485–1557. I saw prints of seventeenth-century fantasies of the New World, in which the natives looked very much like Europeans, one depicting the ease with which native Canadian men and women (Indians) married and then divorced, another depicting these natives in a long row, dancing joyfully in a ceremony following a death. With small, tight crowns of upright feathers, these natives wore, loosely speaking, antique Roman or Greek dress.[2] I saw an 1878 painting by Raynaud Auguste, *L'Indien Chactas sur la*

2. I had for some time wondered about the neoclassical names of my parents, Anaclet and Albina, which I assumed derived from the Neoclassical movement, which movement they themselves would have been unaware of. They were surprised to find, scratched on the wall of a catacomb in Rome, where they went on a visit with my brother Donald, the graffito *Albina*.

tombe d'Atala, with Chactas almost naked and prostrate on the tomb, a cross seeming to float above his head. And in a glass case below this painting was a copy of the original 1801 edition of Chateaubriand's novel.

On higher floors, up elaborately balustraded marble stairways, I saw arrowheads, peace-pipe tomahawks, and the tiny model of a birch-bark canoe. I saw a frame made of branches in which a baby was carried as a papoose on its mother's back, as I imagined my grandmother was carried on her mother's back.

There was an engraving based on a painting of the death of the marquis de Montcalm alongside another engraving based on Benjamin West's painting of the death of General Wolfe after his defeat of Montcalm.

There were more realistic, nineteenth-century images of life among the natives and the colonists: trappers repairing a canoe; a canoe being pulled along a river by a swimming deer tethered to it; the interior of a cabin with fish being kippered over a fire or dried on walls and pelts stretched on frames, the small panes of the window edged with snow.

And on the top floor was an entire room hung with the brownish photographs of Indians by Edward Curtis.

I was drawn to all that I saw for personal reasons, but, as if my personal interest were nothing but a narrow slit window in a narrow tower of stone onto a view that extended farther than I could see, it was everything that was impersonal about these images and objects that drew me more impulsively, because everything, everything all together, could only ever be impersonal.

In La Rochelle, nothing had more personal interest to me

than the ancestors whose names I knew, and nothing extended more into the impersonal than those names.

I might have thought, as Henry James might have thought, that I had lost myself in the vast connections.[3]

The taxi driver who had driven me from the small airport near La Rochelle into the city had suggested, when I'd told him why I had come, that he drive me to Laleu, and we made a date to meet. On the way, he had a call on his cell phone, which he answered by saying, laughing lightly, that he was on a job: *à la recherche d'une tombe*. This amused me. The village of Laleu consisted of small, blank houses along narrow streets. The driver first brought me to a cemetery, Saint Maurice, near a modern building that looked like a school, except that it had grilles on the windows. Within the wooden gates, we separated to look for the gravestones of Nicolas and Elisabeth, but all the stones, white and soft so the names and dates were almost effaced, were from the nineteenth century. The driver said there was an older cemetery, Saint Pierre,

---

3. I didn't think then, but I do now, of a quotation from my commonplace book taken from William James's *Varieties of Religious Experience*, which quotation, it seems to me, indicates a similar and deep sensibility he and his brother Henry shared:

> We count and name whatever lies upon the special lines we trace, whilst the other things and the untraced lines are neither named nor counted. There are in reality infinitely more things "unadapted" to each other in this world than there are things "adapted"; infinitely more things with irregular relations than with regular relations between them. But we look for the regular kind of thing exclusively, and ingeniously discover and preserve it in our memory. It accumulates with other regular kinds, until the collection of them fills our encyclopedias. Yet all the while between and around them is an infinite anonymous chaos of objects that no one ever thought of together, of relations that never yet attracted our attention.

and we went there, with no great anticipation on my part, as if, suddenly, it was not important that I should find the grave-stones—not important, in fact, that I should have any inter-est at all in my ancestry. The gothic church was in ruins, with a well-tended lawn for a floor and flowering plants among the ruins, and the main door boarded up with thick, gray-weathered planks that appeared to have been there for many years. And in the small, well-kept cemetery with gravel paths among the graves, I noted, as soon as we entered, that most of the tombstones were new, horizontal slabs of shiny pol-ished stone in rose or pale gray flecked with white on which were bunches of plastic flowers. Here and there, as if pushed to the side, were stones blackened by age, rough, some bro-ken, and with nothing decipherable on them. The keeper was a young man, perhaps a little dim-witted and carrying a handful of dry grass, who told us—the driver hadn't known —that the church and the cemetery were bombed during the Second World War, after which the bodies had been ex-humed and buried in a communal grave; the cemetery was now used for the recently deceased.

Were there any records, I asked, of those who had been buried centuries past? The young man didn't know, but the driver was sure there would be records in Les Archives Départementales.

The archives were outside the city in a new building. I had to register and was given a card with my name sealed in clear plastic and a little box with a microfiche of the church registry of Laleu from the years 1600 to 1650, and I was shown how to insert the microfiche into a machine for view-ing. My first view, of white letters shining through black, was in English: "Microfilmed by the Genealogical Society, Salt

Lake City, Utah, date filmed 2 Oct 1993." The Mormons had filmed all the records, from as far back as records were kept, presumably to take copies and keep them in their deep, bomb-proof caves—a considerate act, no doubt, to ensure the salvation of all those whose names were collected. And so, my search for my ancestors was now within the context of the Mormon Church, a context that gave a dimension to the search that *really* had nothing to do with me personally. Ruined pages had been filmed, pages damaged by damp had been filmed, and many of the pages had been filmed upside down, making it impossible to read them unless I stood and tried to turn my head upside down. The originals were kept in the archives, but these, I was told, I was not allowed to see. I went through the microfiche again and again and was unable to find Nicolas and Elisabeth Plante.

I spotted, suddenly, "Marie plante," the family name in lower case, and read the white, luminous writing against the darkness in which it appeared.

Le Dernier jour d'aoust mil six cent quatre ving quartoze a esté inhumeé dans Le Cimmetière de ce lieu Marie plante aageé de soixcent dix ans eut assisté à son enterrement plusieurs personnes qui ont declare ne savoir signer de ce ducment requir [?] a lexeption du soubsigné J. Vescian Minet ptre curé de H [?] Maurice.[4]

---

4. The spelling and accents appear as in original document. "The last day of August sixteen hundred and ninety four was buried in this cemetery of this place Marie plante aged seventy years assisted at her burial were several people who declared they did not know how to sign [?] with the exception of the undersigned J. Vescian Minet priest pastor of Saint [?] Maurice."

It was almost enough for me that I had found Marie Plante, though she died almost half a century after Nicolas and Elisabeth; it was enough because her name was a point of contact from which spread out relationships that could easily, even from such a small village, have extended everywhere in the world through emigration and marriage and even friendship, so that the generations and generations of descendants of Marie Plante, who, like Nicolas and Elisabeth, stayed behind, connected through her without knowing that they did. She was important not in herself, as Nicolas and Elisabeth were not important in themselves, but in being a connection, as were Nicolas and Elisabeth. That I was separated from them by twelve generations meant that I was one among a multiplying multitude who most likely had no knowledge of them at all.

I asked for a microfiche of an earlier date and inserted it in the machine for viewing. Time was passing, and I knew that there was no question of my staying on. I couldn't find any other Plantes, and I left before I was told to leave.

That evening, in a small restaurant, my table was next to one where an attractive couple ate. We began to talk. Her parents were from La Rochelle; his mother was Rochelaise and his father Spanish, a Spanish Republican who had escaped the Spanish Fascists and come to live in La Rochelle. My spirited mind vibrating with associations, while talking with the young couple it occurred to me that I had traveled around Fascist Spain with Öçi, and he entered into my thinking. I thought about how Öçi had finally gone to America and become an American citizen; about how he had, in New York, lived a life of marvelous sensual pleasure that led to a virus his immune system could not cope with; about his death. And, thinking about Öçi, I thought, too, about Gloria, about how she had returned to Spain, where soon after, she died of a heart attack. All the while, I continued to talk to the couple, both *avocats*, who wanted very much to go to New York, where they had never been and where I had been just five days earlier. They asked me why I was in La Rochelle, and I told them about my Rochelais ancestry, which went more deeply into the past than the young woman knew of her Rochelais ancestry. They insisted I share their bottle of wine, and we raised our glasses to one another.

After, I walked under the deserted, dimly lit arcades along streets that were empty except, from time to time, for a bicycle bumping along the cobbles from Canada. I did not so much think about anything—if thinking implies intention —as have thoughts occur to me without my intending them, thoughts inspired, perhaps, by my simply being alone in the architecturally intimate but empty streets (so essentially different from the streets of New York), though the thoughts that came to me had nothing to do with La Rochelle. The thought came to me of Öçi once telling me he had been to a male brothel in Aleppo, in Syria, where most of the boy prostitutes were pale, limp-limbed Americans. I did ask myself why this thought had occurred to me but had no idea why.

To the degree that I was able to think with any intention, my mind more and more flashing with its own associations beyond my understanding why, I told myself that as close as I had been and now was to certain people, it was the incidental details of their lives that at moments had more significance to me than the people themselves did. So, for example, I remembered vividly an English friend—one of my closest friends in London—showing me photographs of a trip to India, among which was one of a circle of jagged stones, which were the gods of tribal Indians, and the significance of her having seen those stones and photographed them struck me for the moment as greater than her significance to me as a close friend. And because Nikos was always in my thoughts, I remembered being with him in Athens in his mother's apartment and his showing me a diploma from Robert College in Istanbul, where his mother had graduated from: the diploma was inscribed on papyrus.

It came to me that, really, I didn't care about finding the names of Nicolas and Elisabeth Plante in the archives, wasn't interested, tunneling through twelve generations and even deeper into unrecorded history, to identify myself as their descendant, David Plante, in terms of them. Perhaps I had come to La Rochelle, an enchanting city, not to center myself in my Rochelais ancestry but to free myself from it.

I thought of all my brothers, who had exactly the same ancestry as I did but who were not at all interested in it, who had, perhaps without ever intending to, freed themselves from it. My brothers had left the parish. In the army, Robert met an Irish American girl, Grace, and married her and moved to western Massachusetts, where he worked in a company as an inventor of precision gauges, with a number of patents to his name. After the deaths of our parents, and long after his retirement from the Marine Corps, Donald married a Japanese woman, Michiko, and with her moved to Hawaii.

After his military service, Raymond went to live in Kentucky with an army buddy, and though he returned home shortly after, never explaining what had happened, he so often said he was going to leave to make a life of his own somewhere else, it was as if he was more away than not. He had a modest job in a printing shop, where he printed funeral cards for the funeral parlor, flyers for the local liquor store, and calendars. Roland, while in the air force, married a German American, Nancy-Lee, from Texas, where her father had a cotton plantation. They married and moved to a town outside Boston, and he worked for a company that was contracted by the American government for classified projects in defense. René married an Iraqi woman, Cécile, born and brought up in Baghdad, and rose to the rank of captain in the navy. Lenard married a Yankee, Jean, the daughter of a Presbyterian minister, whose church was north of Boston in Newburyport, where she grew up in the Old Manse on High Street. Both with jobs in investment banks in Boston, they settled in Quincy. Not one brother married a Franco.

This made me suddenly think of how I was, all my life, drawn to differences as much as I was to the concurrence of all differences. That I should be so attentive not only to the differences in details between myself and people close to me but to the differences in details between their lives and the seemingly incidental events in their lives came to me as a thought I had never had before. And the thought had never come to me before that in close friendships it was the meetings of differences, however small, that made the friendships so exciting to me. Nikos's world dated back to the use of papyrus and mine to the use of sheepskin, and it was just the differences in our worlds that made our love for each other, in which all the differences met, amazing. I understood something about myself I had never understood as I did now. I longed for unity in everything because I longed for diversity in everything.

The next day, I went again to the Achives Départementales, presented my card, and asked for the microfiche of an earlier date. Many people at different machines were already studying the negative images of microfiched pages, and I wondered if any among them were, as I was, searching for ancestors, and of those if any were Americans.

Soon enough, I came to the year 1647, and in a column to the left, where all the names were inscribed in delicate cursive, I spotted the underlined name "Nicolas plante," the first person of the parish to have died in, as was written, May 1647. I read with difficulty the faint entry, too faint to see any accents, if there were any: "Le 21 a ete inhume le corps de Nicolas plante aage denuiron soixante ans."

I scrolled down farther, to the year 1649, my eyes focused to see another Plante but stopped at the name Chauvin, which I knew to be the maiden name of Elisabeth, and under the date Janvier 1649 read, again in lettering too faint to see any accents, if there were any, "Isabelle Chauvin Le 19 a ete inhume le corps de Isabelle Chauvin femme de Nicolas plante aagee denuiron 49 ans."

So there they were. I was puzzled that Elisabeth, as I had known her, was registered as Isabelle, and in her maiden name, but she had to be my great-great-great-great-great-great-great-great-great-great-grandmother because she was the wife of my great-great-great-great-great-great-great-

great-great-great-grandfather. That she died in 1649 at about the age of forty-nine meant that she was born in 1600. That he died at the age of about sixty in 1647 meant he was born around 1587.

I found them in the registry, and I might have stopped there, thinking I had what I had come looking for; but finding their names wasn't enough because, though I had been brought back far into the past, I didn't want to stop there. The dates of the deaths of my distant ancestors were, in terms of my history, arbitrary despite their being registered, because there was a still deeper past, that of *their* ancestors. I had come so far, but I wanted to go further, wanted to go back from Nicolas and Elisabeth, as I still thought of her, through their ancestors into an always more diversified—because deeper—past, and yet a past that was, however diversified, however contradictory in its diversification, connected, a past that included everything, *everything*, if not all of world history, then all of the history of the Western world. I wasn't interested in finding out anything about my most distant ancestors that would help me to define myself in terms of any beliefs in any God. On the contrary, I wanted to find, in whatever information was available to me, evidence of the syncretism that so attracted me, the sense that everything does, within everything that is divided and contradictory, and especially within one's own inability to make connections, connect. And I wanted to find such evidence not in history that generalizes, such as the history of all the wars my ancestors had lived through, as far back as Roman times, but in details, details that extended with references that were too complex for any generalization to be made from them, such as a fragment of carved stone, a pottery jug, an old shoe, the names of people.

But I had gone as far back into the past as the archives registered, for no earlier parish records were kept.

That afternoon, I went to meet the owner of a bookshop recommended to me by my French publisher, and when I told her that I had in the Achives Départementales found the names of the ancestors who were the parents of a son who had left La Rochelle for his future in Le Nouveau Monde, but that I wanted to find out more about the ancestors of those parents whose past was all in Le Vieux Monde, she suggested I ring a friend of hers who worked as an expert in the archives, a young Canadian woman who had moved to La Rochelle some years earlier. I went to her office. On her computer, she typed my family name into a slot on some Web site, and there appeared on the screen:

PLANTE, JEAN NO 411857

Né vers 1626 La Rochelle (Charente-Maritime:17300), marié, fils de Nicolas et Isabelle Chauvin

ARRIVÉE OU PREMIÈRE MENTION AU PAYS

1650. Migrant

ANNOTATIONS(S)

Catholique. Son père a été inhumé le 21-05-1647 à Laleu (St-Pierre). Sa mère, decedée le 14-02-1646 a été inhumée à Laleu (St-Pierre), qui fait parti de La Rochelle.

RÉFÉRENCE
DGFQ, p. 926
SOURCE DE L'INFORMATION
Archange Godbout, AG-LAR, p. 193; DGO t.1.[5]

Well, there were inconsistencies between the information I had from the archives and the information on the Web site. I had the name of Nicolas's wife as Elisabeth, and I had her dying after him. The young Canadian woman said that Isabelle was in fact a nickname—*un surnom*—for Elisabeth. Why was her death registered under her maiden name? That was the practice. As for the discrepancy in dates, a mistake had clearly been made somewhere, but not, I hastened to say against her defense of the Web site, with the original archive. But this confirmed that they had been buried in the cemetery of Saint Pierre. And I understood, from the genealogical list I had, that Jean married only after he arrived in Quebec. Did the information on the Web site suggest he was married in La Rochelle, and then, on his arrival in Canada and a long way away from his first wife, married again? The inconsistencies didn't matter to me, because I wasn't—it was clearer than ever to me—after a fixed point.

I asked if there were any references to the ancestors of Nicolas and Elisabeth on the Web, but beyond them, all was unknown, and I left thinking that it was as well that the

5. He was born around 1626, was married, the son of Nicolas and Isabelle Chauvin. His arrival or first mention in the country (meaning Canada) was 1650. He was a migrant. He was Catholic. His father was buried 21-05-1647 at Laleu (St. Pierre). His mother, who died 14-02-1646, was buried at Laleu (St. Pierre), which forms part of La Rochelle.

connections they made, those all-inclusive connections as I imagined them going back and back even beyond Roman times, remained invisible.

I lay on the bed in my hotel room and tried to concentrate, though concentration was, as always, difficult for me. Thoughts that had never before occurred to me before occurred there in La Rochelle, and there were, I sensed (sensed in the way William James wrote of *sensing* an idea before being able to articulate it), more thoughts on their way to occurring. I wanted to help them, but flashing recollections of many different people from many places—why should I now think of Nikos, a Greek, holding up to his face an African mask from the collection of African masks of a friend in London?—made me helpless. *Perhaps*, I began to think, *I was so drawn to diversity—and simultaneously to unity—because of those divisions in my life that...* Why should there flash in my mind the sight of a little black girl assembling a tiny log cabin on a brick sidewalk on Beacon Hill? ... *because of those divisions in my life that most likely predated my birth...* Why should there come into my mind the image of a little red plaster Buddha on a shelf in the dry cleaner's in the French Catholic parish? ... *because of those divisions in my life that most likely predated my birth and that were widened by the division between my father and mother.* The moment this thought emerged, with our without my help, fully formed, I thought, as if the thought were no longer relevant at the very moment it emerged, *You are exaggerating, and always have exaggerated, the divisions.*

And yet, exaggerated or not, seeing in La Rochelle the name of Jean Plante, who had left Europe for North America, I became aware of a division in my life to a heightened degree I'd never before been aware of: that is, I'd spent some forty years of my life in Europe, and in the recent five years or so I'd been spending half of every year in America, as a professor at Columbia University in New York. I was an American citizen, and I was now also a British citizen, which made me, by extension of the European Union, a citizen of Europe.[6]

By a shift in perspective that occurred of itself, as so much was occurring of itself, I began to wonder about the brothers and sisters of Jean Plante who had remained in France. I had no idea about them, and it did not help me to try to personalize them, however fictitiously, by placing them within the history of the years of, say, 1600 to the present, not only in terms of their reactions to historical events but in terms of their reactions to the historical personalities of the successive generations. (Would any of them of the seventeenth century have been affected in any way by the burning of Giordano Bruno for heresy in Rome in 1600? by the publication of part 1 of *Don Quixote* by Cervantes in 1605 or Francis Bacon's *Advancement of Learning* in the same year? Would it have made any difference to them that Galileo Galilei in 1632 declared that the earth was not the center of the universe? that in 1632 Descartes published his *Discourse on Method*? And even to

6. I became British, but, in the same way my father in the United States never became a Yankee, I would never be English. That I was a *citizen* of the United Kingdom, as designated on my passport, and not a *subject*, had to do, I imagined, with the United Kingdom aligning herself with the republics of Europe. I should add that I had the verbal approval of the American embassy in London before I became both British and American.

what extent would they have felt their lives changed by Louis XIV becoming king of France in 1643? or, more remotely, Charles I of England being beheaded in 1649? And would the writings of Blaise Pascal of 1656 have meant anything to them? or Isaac Newton's Law of Gravitation of 1672?) Unlike the French Canadian descendants of Nicolas and Elisabeth, I could not personalize—as Matante Cora might have said—French French descendants of Nicolas and Elisabeth, for I could not even be sure of the evolution of their religion. And this, surprisingly, made me feel not so distant from them that they meant nothing to me but that they were meaningful to me for being as depersonalized as they were. Though I asked at the hotel for a telephone directory, curious to find out if there were any Plantes living in La Rochelle, and though I found two Plantes listed, I didn't ring them, partly out of shyness and mostly because I did not want to know about their European ancestry. I did feel some deep association with them for having a shared family name that went back centuries, into a past as remote as the past of my Indian great-grandmother, but, more than any desire to contact them and, if they were willing, presume on that association, I felt expansively free in *not* contacting them—felt that not knowing about the European collateral cousins of Jean Plante, among whom I might have counted myself but for the displacement of Jean, gave me a greater sense of freedom than the chronological list of the French Canadian descendants of Jean Plante that I had, since I was a boy, been so eager to find out about.

If I had, as a student, first come to Europe filled with the American romance of Europe (as Jean might have gone to

North America filled with the European romance of that continent!), I had, living for so long in Europe, seen through the romance to the reality (as, no doubt, Jean had done after some time in North America). Vaguely, I had seen Old Europe become New Europe, more and more loosened of received ideas of what defined Europe, and I had also seen New America become Old America, solidifying into received ideas of what defined America. Also, America was a religious country, and Europe was secular.

And yet, was I really divided in myself by leading a life in both worlds? Certainly, I would never want to have to make a choice between the two worlds, in large part because I was as constitutionally incapable of making choices as of having opinions, and in small part because I felt that it was possible to belong to both worlds. *The fact was,* I found myself thinking as I lay on the bed in my hotel room, *I had lost a sense of division, wide or narrow, in my life, and I had lost it because...*

There flashed in my mind the image of my parents' gravestone, in the cemetery of Saint Anne, in Providence, Rhode Island: a pinkish, highly polished stone with their names engraved in it and the dates of their births and deaths:

ANACLET PLANTE NOVEMBER 8, 1897– JANUARY 14, 1980

ALBINA PLANTE MARCH 8, 1901–DECEMBER 7, 1982

I had lost the sense of division, not through any resolution of the opposing sides, if, really, there had been opposing sides, but in the massive confusion of everything I thought and felt, so mas-

sive that there could be no fixed center in it all. And this, instead of filling me with the anxiety of being nowhere, expanded my impulse to be free and, with the freedom, my light-spiritedness. I was nowhere and everywhere.

My longing for unifying transcendence was now not deeply serious to me, even a source of amusement, and, as amused as I was by it, I could now, I realized, have it—I could have it in the complexity of connections radiating out not from a fixed center but from any object as arbitrarily made the object of awareness as a shoe, a sickle, a bowl of boiled potatoes. Amusing as it was, the longing for the awareness of everything, everything all together, remained forceful enough that it made it impossible for me to make choices, to have opinions. But all I needed was any object, any image, *any name,* to focus my attention, more than on it itself, on the vast, always shifting and expanding interconnections that ultimately include everything in the universe.

I left La Rochelle with less of a sense of definition of myself than when I had arrived, and in the plane back to London and Nikos I thought—as always in the midst of many other thoughts—that going to Saint-Barthélemey in Canada to see where my father was born, to see the record of his birth and baptism, had also left me with less of a definition of myself than before. After years and years of trying to find out about my ancestry, starting with my childhood eagerness to investigate it through to my discovery of the genealogical list, I was, by finding out about it, undoing myself. This was a great relief, a great pleasure, a joy.

And in London, looking at the photographs I had taken of the ruined church of Saint Pierre, it came to me—never

having allowed myself to recognize the deepest impulse—
that I had gone to La Rochelle for what I could only call a religious revelation, as if there, among the ruins of the church
where Nicolas and (as I continued to name her) Elisabeth
had probably been baptized and married, and where their son
Jean was probably baptized, something would have occurred
to me that would have confirmed me in a faith that had survived—that had more than survived, that had sustained generation upon generation—through hundreds and hundreds
of years, the mere survival and moral and spiritual sustaining of it enough for me to be moved to accept that there is
a divine force that *does* help us survive, that *does* sustain us
morally and spiritually. But instead of being convinced by
the very need for this force, strong enough to break through
the confines of time and space into infinity and eternity, in
which God dwells, the only sense of a divinity I left La
Rochelle with was the divinity of awareness.

33

EVEN IN BED WITH NIKOS, ONE OF MY ARMS OVER HIM
as he slept, I wasn't able to fall asleep for hours.

Lying awake, I devised a way of helping me give up what
I considered irrelevant but persistent thinking and allow my
mind to become free to detach itself and float away into the
darkness. I would try to fix an image in my mind that had no
personal associations and that was as vivid, as luminous, as
possible—say, a shining blue ball against a red background
—and focus all my attention on that. It was difficult, and

very often I would find myself thinking again, the thoughts, always as stupid as they were persistent, breaking my concentration. But I kept refocusing, and eventually the shining blue ball against a red background would appear to clarify and shine brightly, though that red background was always vague about the edges. A moment later, however, the ball would begin to take on other shapes and colors, so that even as I stared at it with my mind's eye, it might become a hand, or a foot, or a head. And the red background would fade into darkness, so that the hand, the foot, the head, the hat, the umbrella, the automobile tire, the chicken coop, the tweed jacket splattered with mud appeared in that darkness but remained for only an instant before they too changed into images that could not have come from any experience because they were beyond anything I could have experienced, even beyond descriptions of them. It was at the point that my thinking would give way to the protean images, evolving in more and more complicated ways in the darkness, and those images would seem to evolve me into sleep, which was to enter into that darkness.

Against all evidence to the contrary, I believed that these images came not from some subjective, inner self but from the objective outside.

Saint Thomas Aquinas, as far as I knew, had no concept of the unconscious self, but only of the conscious self. For him, the objects of consciousness all came into consciousness by way of outside stimulation of the senses. As we were born *tabula rasa*—empty slates—everything that made us what we are had to come from outside to be inscribed on that slate. I tended to think this was true. I had no interest in an unconscious self, but only in the conscious self, the self that was aware. Confronted with the problem of the integration of all the chaos of information that the senses inscribed on the empty slate, Aquinas did suggest a sense beyond the five senses that integrated and gave coherence to all that chaos of information, a—perhaps—transcending sense of awareness.

I began to do this:

In bed at night, while Nikos slept beside me, I would write down, in a large book dummy, images that occurred to me even before I closed my eyes, one image a page, one image a night. I did this for two years and ended up with a book of more than six hundred fifty images. How, on the whole, they cohered I didn't know, nor did I think that that coherence on the whole had anything to do with me, but with something whole all around me that I, myself, had no direct experience of. I made the images as simple but as vivid as possible.

A skull on an unfolded white napkin—

A glove hanging over the edge of a lamp shade—

A lit bulb at the back of a closed shop—

A tennis ball on an empty beach—

On the stoop of a closed doorway, an open valise with a sheet of paper in it—

A blue shirt, its sleeves rolled up, hanging off the corner of
the back of a wooden chair—

Lying among weeds in a vacant lot, a rusted car fender—

The images that had occurred to me in my mind were now images in words and now entirely outside me, for, the dummy filled and put aside, whenever I picked it up to look through it, I couldn't connect myself with them even enough to imagine that they had occurred to me and that I had in fact written them down. But now that they were on the page in words and outside me, I found myself studying them with more fixed concentration than I had been able to when I had tried to fix them in my mind. The phenomenon was this: I was not able, however much I tried, to see the image, even as reduced to details as it was, wholly. As much as I tried to "see" the skull entirely, I couldn't but, perhaps, the thin septum dividing the narrow triangle of the nasal cavity, or a ridge at a temple, or a cheekbone. These details were not fixable and kept disappearing. And then, strangely, I began to "see" other details that were not in my image in words, details that appeared as others disappeared: the grain of the wood of the table the skull was on, the fragments of a shell of a peeled egg, a saucer of salt, a toothpick, and, with amazing incongruity, a frayed length of golden cord, a flower in wallpaper, an apple on a windowsill.

Mental images kept changing, and they never appeared fully, but in disconnected details that, themselves, kept changing. And yet, however protean the image in its fragmentation, I always had, say, a *Thomistic sense of something whole, something whole outside and around me,* which in some way seemed to make the image steady and entire.

Oddly, this *sense* became all the more pronounced the less I was able to see, in my mind, the image. I began to think of images that could be depicted only in words and in no other depicting medium, images that made writing miraculous for writing's ability to depict them. They were luminous images inseparable from the darkness in which they occurred.

Light invisible.

This image, which emerged as a very definite mental image but one that could not be depicted and could exist only in words, gave me a *sense* of all-encompassing wholeness. And yet, this image, which could not be depicted, kept appearing and disappearing in the vast darkness that surrounded it, much in the same way that thought emerged from a state deeper than thought; darkness that, itself, appeared to go on and on and on in all directions into infinity. It was this vast, infinite darkness, I believed, that, like Aquinas's sixth sense, made the image possible, much in the same way that thought is made possible because of some state deeper than thought. That darkness made visible an invisible image; that darkness, I believed, gave meaning to the image. It was, after all, the darkness that was read.

I began to see everything about me more and more in terms of the sixth sense, which was of infinite darkness, and there came with it, as if the one sense came simultaneously from the other, a greater and greater sense of freedom.

With Nikos, in London as we sat together in Wigmore Hall listening to a piano recital, or with him in the Tuscan town of Lucca, where we walked around the walls on a bright winter afternoon, or with him on the terrace of the little house on the island of Páros watching the moon rise over the Aegean Sea, I would, if only for a moment, think: I *am* free.

Later, I would record those moments in my diary, for, even though they passed, I had documented them, and I could, looking back at my diary, read an account that verified them.

It was in those moments of freedom with Nikos that I was most acutely alive to that sixth sense. In the village on Páros, I would suddenly see a book open on a marble-topped table with red bougainvillea blossoms fallen on it, see a pair of leather sandals on a stone step, see a glass of water in the Greek sunlight, and I would be made aware more startlingly than ever before, would be made aware of the wonder of awareness, would be made aware of the wonder of awareness that emanated, like pointed brightness, from the darkness of that sixth sense. And I never felt that that pointed brightness had anything to do with me, but felt, instead, that it was somewhere behind me and I simply stood in its light, in which anyone and everyone could stand, and what it illuminated was a lemon, a pot of basil, a key. Nikos made me aware, Nikos himself made me more and more aware, because Nikos, in his love for me, freed me.

I was free of imagining that Yankee America dominated me as a Franco-American, because I knew that Yankee America no longer existed. I was free of the old fantasy of Louisburg Square being the hub of the hub of the universe, or even of Boston and Faneuil Hall and Cobbs Hill being where American history originated. My history was too complicated to be just American history, or to be any recordable history.

I was free of the laws of sexual, familial, social, political, and even religious duty that I had been commanded to abide by in ways that would have subjugated me to an authority that was as imposed as Roman law on that village in remote Gaul. And I had never been part of the Puritan ethic. With Nikos, I felt free of all the received ideas that once dominated my life; and if I was, with him, socially, politically, and even religiously engaged in ways that I had learned from him, I accepted this engagement on trust, because I believed he was more intelligent and cultured, more politically informed, and more religiously observant than I, while I, in myself, remained socially, politically, and religiously disengaged, which he, in his love for me, allowed me, as if he, knowing me now as no one else had ever known me, saw in this disengagement my necessary freedom, as a writer, from all ideas. He understood that I wrote not to understand but to negate understanding; that I wrote not for discursive thinking but, by describing a wet pebble, to stop thinking, to be purely aware. He understood that not only did I have no opinions of my own but I wanted no opinions of my own. The sexual, familial, social, political, and civic duties I abided by became, in my detachment from them, as spontaneous to me as they had always been to Nikos, with whom I was happy in a responsible relationship that was anything but Puritan.

With him, I felt free of the obsession to possess—in a constant state of panic that this was always and ever impossible to me—everything, everything. With him, that obsession would go, and, waking up beside him at night, rain falling against the bedroom window and he asleep, it would seem to me that there was nowhere else in the world that I could possibly want to be but where I was. I would try to fix in my mind the images in the dim room of the geranium plant on the bureau, the book on the floor, the shirt hanging on the silent butler, and these images, which I would later record in my ever-expanding diary, would seem to me to center all my feelings. The feelings were not of security, because I didn't feel there was any threatening outside world against which I needed to be protected from, nor did I feel there was anything threatening inside I must escape from; they were not of peace either, because I was unaware of anything troubling that that peace would be in contrast to. All I could think, finally, was that being with Nikos made me feel totally *present,* a feeling that became absolute before I fell back to sleep.

And the greater this freedom I felt with Nikos, the greater that sense of awareness, the greater the wonder of this amazing awareness.

As much as I told myself that with Nikos I was free of my parish, that with him I was free of my Canuck God, it would, however, happen, with or without Nikos, that I would suddenly become aware of my grandmother sitting next to me on the top of a bus going along Oxford Street, of my aunt Cora, in her nun's habit, at a table next to Nikos and me in a restaurant, of aunts and uncles on park benches as I alone or with Nikos walked through Kensington Gardens.

However incongruous, I would become aware of the nuns from my parochial school, Mère Sainte Flore, Mère Sainte Epiphane, Mère Saint Felix de Valois, Mère Supérieure, not only at moments in London but in Lucca, in Athens, in New York, even in Moscow, usually when I was out in a crowded street and I sensed they were among the crowd. And our pastor, Monsieur le Curé, would be there, in his black soutane and biretta with a black pom-pom, in the crowd.

Sonia was very often there, was always there in a shop near her house in South Kensington, in the presence of a woman glimpsed buying a pack of cigarettes or a bottle of wine, or in a greengrocer, choosing a ripe melon.

Gloria would be there, in the presence of a black woman in a shop choosing a silk dressing gown.

And Öçi would be there, in the presence of someone in a Greek shop buying *kaseri* cheese, in a Turkish shop buying *lokum*, in a Hungarian shop buying a pastry, speaking the language of each shop.

Nikos's mother would be there, for him more than for me, in the presence, unbearable to him, of an old woman carrying a suitcase in a crowded train station.

My beloved brothers Robert and Raymond would be there, raking leaves fallen in a backyard, mowing a lawn.

Friends, acquaintances, people met at parties and then forgotten would be there, at the openings of gallery shows, at the crush bar of the opera, in the foyer of a theater.

All those ancestors would be there, from Nicolas and Elisabeth back into a France that deepened and deepened into its most remote past and forward from Jean into the future, on the decks of crowded ferries, in packed underground trains, in milling street markets.

And my parents would be there, my mother and father, among the thousands, the hundreds of thousands, the millions, too many for me to see them except at moments so brief I could not be sure I did see them before they disappeared among the countless dead.

I was with Nikos on the island of Páros in the small house, white inside and outside, in a white village. Every afternoon, we walked to the sea along a rough path delineated by dry stonewalls though tawny fields. On the way, we stopped in a restaurant for soda water at an hour when we were the only people there.

We sat at the table on the terrace, below which were olive trees, the silver-green leaves shaking in a breeze; and beyond them was the sea, darker and darker blue until blue-black towards Naxos, that island so clear the houses were vivid white against slightly vaporous lavender, the rough mountains above brown, and above them the sky, flat but luminously blue. Nikos and I were silent.

Then I said to him, "If I were to fix one of the moments in my life which I would like to last forever, it would be this one."

He seemed not very interested—he had his own thoughts, and I mine—and asked, "Why fix any moment?"

I thought, Yes, why? I shouldn't want to. But I said, "Because it's so pleasant—because I feel it's so *whole*."

He didn't ask what I meant by this, and after our cold drinks we walked on, down the dirt road bordered by red oleander bushes to a beach and among sunbathers lying naked on towels (an elderly man with a white beard, emerging naked and smiling out of the sea) and up onto rocks and along the narrow seaside path to our small beach, where we were almost always alone. On the way, I asked myself, Why did you feel the moment *whole*? I answered myself, because his love *is* enough.

The enchantment I felt with this realization continued on our beach, where, while I, naked, sat on a heap of dry seaweed and simply looked at the delicate surf; Nikos, also naked, wandered about, picking up bits of rubbish to put later in a rubbish bin. This thought suddenly came to me: In his love for you, go as far outside of yourself as is possible, far, far outside, and look at everything from that far distance, without thinking or feeling.

With this thought, everything seemed to open up and, simultaneously, come together, as if just this had for some time been on the point of occurring. And an image came to me, an image so ancient it was traceable back to ancient Greece and sustained through the centuries no doubt even up to the present time in the minds of some people; an image that, for all the atavistic ignorance needed to continue to sustain it, filled out graphically the sense I had of everything being so suddenly *whole*—the universe was a sphere, a vast, transparent sphere, on which the sun and the moon and the stars rotated about the earth, which was at the center of the sphere.

Then this happened—as if this image occurring to me and drawing me to it gave the dead the impulse they needed to be drawn to it themselves, I sensed them, the known and unknown dead whom I had glimpsed at moments in the streets, in shops, in theaters, in parks, on boats and trains and buses, begin to rise up from the earth towards that sphere. The dead did not remain on the world but after a while left it. All the dead were leaving the world, to rise up to that spherical extremity of the universe. From there they were aware inwardly of the small, revolving earth. Their eyes were stars.

And what gave them their star-bright awareness? They were as aware of what was outside the sphere as what was within it, and what was outside the sphere was the infinite darkness of God. I thought: Their awareness is illuminated by that infinite darkness behind them, which makes their awareness so acute, so dazzling, so utterly without personal thought or feeling, so utterly without commentary, utterly without opinion, utterly without judgment, but radiant with attention to everything all together, with impersonal compassion for everyone, with all-inclusive love, which the living themselves are incapable of.

34

NOT I, BUT SOMEONE ELSE NEAR ENOUGH FOR ME TO hear him, someone I didn't know and didn't want to know, prayed to God. I doubted that he himself believed in God any more than I did, but he did pray to God, as if he could pray only to a God he didn't believe in. Whenever I heard him, he was, very quietly, praying in French.

> Dans votre noir, Dieu,
> Aidez-moi voir
> Le carafe d'eau, le verre,
> Les lunettes posées sur le livre ouvert,
> Et l'orellier sur le lit défait.

> In your darkness, God,
> Help me to see
> The carafe of water, the glass,
> The spectacles left on the open book,
> And the pillow on the unmade bed.